POLICIES FOR HIGHER EDUCATION IN THE 1980s

Intergovernmental Conference
OECD 12/14 OCTOBER 1981

ORGANISATION FOR ECONOMIC CO-OPERATION AND DEVELOPMENT

Pursuant to article 1 of the Convention signed in Paris on 14th December, 1960, and which came into force on 30th September, 1961, the Organisation for Economic Co-operation and Development (OECD) shall promote policies designed:

- to achieve the highest sustainable economic growth and employment and a rising standard of living in Member countries, while maintaining financial stability, and thus to contribute to the development of the world economy;
- to contribute to sound economic expansion in Member as well as non-member countries in the process of economic development; and
- to contribute to the expansion of world trade on a multilateral, non-discriminatory basis in accordance with international obligations.

The Signatories of the Convention on the OECD are Austria, Belgium, Canada, Denmark, France, the Federal Republic of Germany, Greece, Iceland, Ireland, Italy, Luxembourg, the Netherlands, Norway, Portugal, Spain, Sweden, Switzerland, Turkey, the United Kingdom and the United States. The following countries acceded subsequently to this Convention (the dates are those on which the instruments of accession were deposited): Japan (28th April, 1964), Finland (28th January, 1969), Australia (7th June, 1971) and New Zealand (29th May, 1973).

The Socialist Federal Republic of Yugoslavia takes part in certain work of the OECD (agreement of 28th October, 1961).

Publié en français sous le titre:

LES POLITIQUES
D'ENSEIGNEMENT SUPÉRIEUR
DES ANNÉES 80

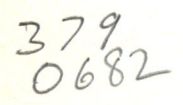

© OECD, 1983
Application for permission to reproduce or translate
all or part of this publication should be made to:
Director of Information, OECD
2, rue André-Pascal, 75775 PARIS CEDEX 16, France.

Higher education, whose rapid growth was one of the most remarkable social phenomena in the post-war history of OECD countries, faces an uncertain future as it moves into the eighties. There are many causes behind this change and much public debate about how future policies in this area need to be developed. The main concern in this debate is how to sustain the vitality of higher education systems under prevailing conditions of financial constraints, growing employment difficulties for graduates, diminishing enrolments (which result both from the demographic downturn and changes in the demand for higher education) and waning morale among teaching and research staff.

The first part of the book reviews the main issues and questions confronting higher education in the years ahead. It was prepared by the Secretariat for discussion at the Intergovernmental Conference on Policies for Higher Education in the 1980s convened by OECD in October 1981. Policy responses to these issues as they emerged from the discussion at the Conference are also included.

The second part contains a more detailed analysis of trends in the development of higher education, with particular emphasis on changes in patterns of provision and in admission policies. This report was also prepared under the responsibility of the Secretariat, with Dorotea Furth as the main author.

Also available

THE UNIVERSITY AND THE COMMUNITY. The Problems of Changing Relationships (forthcoming)

THE FUTURE OF UNIVERSITY RESEARCH (March 1981)
(92 81 03 1) ISBN 92-64-12160-9   78 pages   £3.00   US$7.50   F30

SELECTION AND CERTIFICATION IN EDUCATION AND EMPLOYMENT (August 1977)
(91 77 01 1) ISBN 92-64-11611-7   146 pages   £3.60   US$7.50   F30

Prices charged at the OECD Publications Office.

THE OECD CATALOGUE OF PUBLICATIONS *and supplements will be sent free of charge on request addressed either to OECD Publications Office,*
2, *rue André-Pascal, 75775 PARIS CEDEX 16, or to the OECD Sales Agent in your country.*

CONTENTS

The Message of the Conference 7

Part One

ISSUES IN HIGHER EDUCATION
IN THE 1980s

Overview of Issues 13

Notes for discussion

Theme 1. Access to Higher Education 23

Theme 2. Changing Relationship between Higher Education and Working Life 32

Theme 3. New Patterns of Authority 40

Theme 4. Financing and Redeployment of Resources 49

Concerns and Dilemmas in the Years Ahead 55

Statement by the General Rapporteur 61

Part Two

ACCESS TO HIGHER EDUCATION

I. Structure of Higher Education Provision: The Heritage of the 1970s 73

II. Admission Policies 101

III. Selection Methods and Criteria 144

5

| IV. | New Groups in Higher Education | 164 |
| V. | The Links between Finance and Admission Policies in Higher Education | 188 |

Statistical Annex 206

THE MESSAGE OF THE CONFERENCE

Chairman's Concluding Remarks
by
Professor Peter Karmel*

This Conference provided an opportunity for senior officials from Member countries to review recent trends in the development of their systems of higher education; to discuss the major problems confronting the development of these systems over the next decade; and to consider ways and approaches by which such problems might be tackled in the social and economic context likely to prevail during this period. The discussions covered overall policy directions in plenary sessions, and more detailed consideration, in working groups, of specific issues relating to access to higher education, the changing relationships between higher education and working life, new patterns of authority in higher education and problems of financing and redeployment of resources. We heard the detailed conclusions on these topics from the working groups.

Participants had available extensive documentation and analyses prepared by the OECD Secretariat which they found particularly helpful; written contributions submitted by Member countries; and general statements given at the opening session by Mr. Emile van Lennep, Secretary General of the OECD; Mr. A. Savary, Minister of Education in France; Mr. W. Clohan, Under Secretary in the Department of Education, United States; and Mr. E. Lämmert, Rector of the Free University of Berlin. BIAC and TUAC participated fully in the discussions.

Many of the issues under consideration did not differ from those discussed in the 1973 OECD Conference on Future Structures of Post-Secondary Education(1). This is not surprising in view of the pluralism of the purposes of higher education, their perennial nature and the long period of gestation needed to transform policy measures into changes in institutional attitudes and practice.

What was clear, however, from the Conference is the changed climate which now prevails in the discussion of these issues.

---

* Chairman, Tertiary Education Commission (Australia).
1. See: Policies for Higher Education: General Report, OECD, Paris, 1974.

In the early 1970s the central theme was how a vastly expanded provision for higher education, whose continued growth was taken for granted, could be made more relevant to the needs of students of all ages. This, in turn, raised questions of the structure of higher education and the manner in which governments should allocate and control resources so as to achieve a proper balance between academic freeoom and institutional autonomy on the one hand, and individual and social needs on the other. Moreover, there was an expectation that European systems would follow the American experience and, given time, participation in higher education would rise to American levels.

In contrast, at the beginning of the 1980s the overriding concern reflected in the Conference seems to be how to sustain public confidence in and support for a system, which, in most countries, is no longer growing in such a way as to ensure its continued dynamic evolution. It is also clear that participation in higher education in most OECD countries is unlikely to converge towards the levels of the United States, Canada and Japan; on the contrary, future patterns of development are likely to be distinctly different. In many countries there appears to be a crisis of confidence which is approaching alarming dimensions. Unless new policies are rapidly conceived and implemented there may be a real danger, over the longer term, that the potential of higher education for supporting countries' economic vitality and the welfare of their citizens through cultural, scientific and technological development, could be seriously and perhaps irretrievably compromised.

The main contextual pressures, against which this crisis has been developing, were examined during the Conference in some detail. These relate primarily to demographic factors, to the persisting slow economic growth, to high rates of inflation and unemployment, and to reduction in public spending. This is taking place in a situation in which higher education is being called upon to respond to new and more diverse needs: new types and changed quantities of qualified manpower; provision of services to the local community; educational, training and cultural opportunities for adults, ethnic minorities and the unemployed young. On the other hand, there is now a more realistic perception by the public, and indeed by students and graduates themselves, of the social and economic expectations which had been built into higher education in an exaggerated way during the heyday of its expansion.

The resulting changes in public attitudes towards higher education have coincided with the greater pressures which governments now face to constrain public expenditures and to establish priorities for the distribution of available resources. Higher education has to compete with the other sectors of education, as well as with other social policies - health, social security and youth employment programmes - and also with the functions of government such as defence and the provision of the public infra-structure. As a consequence, the allocation of resources to and within higher education has become increasingly associated with the elaboration of more or less explicit guidelines about its future development, in terms of its overall size, the relative weight of its various branches and their missions.

In allocating the available resources, those responsible for educational policy have to mediate between conflicting forces: the demands from individual students, from professional groups and from employers; the internal interests and claims for autonomy of the institutions themselves; and broader national priorities as defined by governments, including manpower requirements and the need to maintain a responsive system of higher education based on a diversity of institutions.

The reconciliation of those competing objectives is essentially a political matter; each country must seek its own solutions in the light of national circumstances and its relative priorities. However, there appears to be a general view that in all countries the central issues revolve around measures designed to ensure the vitality of higher education institutions. Such vitality is a necessary condition to enable them to respond to evolving social and economic needs, while at the same time maintaining the autonomy required for the achievement of high standards in the quality of their research and in the content of their teaching.

In the context of constrained resources, a reappraisal of some, perhaps all, institutions will be necessary. Some may have to shed activities which have a low priority, attract little student demand or involve unnecessary duplication. Such action, however difficult and unpalatable, will be preferable to a slow erosion of resources across the whole range of their activities. Institutions themselves must be prepared to respond to changing circumstances and, in this process, to accept the involvement of the wider community. On the other hand, the essential qualities of the university should not be sacrificed to short-term exigencies nor by an exaggerated responsiveness to outside needs.

For myself, the Conference provided a most useful focus on the problems that those of us who are responsible for policy on higher education face in the 1980s. The results of the Conference merit serious discussion and consideration in all OECD countries.

Part One

ISSUES IN HIGHER EDUCATION
IN THE 1980s

OVERVIEW OF ISSUES

I. INTRODUCTION

Most Member countries are currently reviewing their policies for higher education in depth; the reasons for so doing vary from country to country, according to national circumstances. Everywhere, however, the overriding concern is to sustain the dynamic evolution of the system, on the strength of past achievements, as a major factor in the cultural, scientific and technological development of highly industrialised societies and the welfare of their citizens. Many countries have difficulties in meeting this challenge because of the prevailing climate of uncertainty about demographic, social and economic prospects and such problems as persisting slow economic growth, high rates of inflation and unemployment, reductions in public spending as well as new and competing social objectives. While this situation affects the entire educational sector, the impact is most pronounced in the case of higher education, though it is perhaps the most difficult to pin down in precise terms.

The challenge is all the greater because so much more is expected of higher education, i.e. that it:

a) respond to new needs at local and community level;
b) contribute to revitalising the economy by producing the "right" kinds of highly qualified manpower and contribute to the further training of the labour force in the context of rapidly changing technologies;
c) sustain adequate levels of technological innovation through scientific research progress;
d) help to promote greater social equity, at a time when the more deprived sections of the population are hardest hit by the economic situation.

Given the inevitable plurality and long-term nature of higher education objectives, there is also the very real danger that responses to immediate pressures may not always be in line with longer-term needs and considerations. In discussing higher education policies it is, moreover, important to recognise the diversity which prevails among Member countries both in terms of the structure of the higher education provision and of the functions which are assigned to different institutions within this structure in the light of wider social and economic policies and priorities.

Admittedly a number of the problems in regard to higher education stem from its rapid expansion over the last two decades and the resultant changes in the traditional objectives, orientations and structure of the system. New roles and functions have developed, either as a result of grass root pressures - resulting from individual or local initiatives - or through policy action. Not all systems have been able to adjust to the inevitable confusion in the perception of roles and objectives which accompanied the transition from an elitist to a popular system of higher education. This transition was rendered all the more difficult by the fact that many of the radical reforms, formulated at a time of expansion and confidence in continuing growth, had to be implemented some years later in a quite different social context.

An attempt should therefore be made to clarify policy in regard to the role of higher education in the 1980s, both in terms of its internal dynamics as well as of the new challenges, pressures and constraints to which it must respond. This is all the more necessary in view of the growing concern on the part of both the policy-makers and the public, for accountability and relevance, which extends to the social services generally. As a key sector of social policy, higher education is confronted with a new challenge; how to maintain its rightful place in the political debate regarding priorities and claims on public resources.

II. FACTORS AFFECTING FUTURE TRENDS IN HIGHER EDUCATION

Given the wealth of purposes and functions of higher education in pluralist, advanced industrial societies, and the tensions and conflicting pressures that act on the system, any discussion of future policies in this area must start out by identifying and analysing the key factors which are likely to influence the development of higher education in the foreseeable future. An attempt is made below to outline the more significant among them.

i) Changes in social demand for higher education

After a period of steady growth in enrolments, a number of countries are now witnessing a serious slowdown in the growth of demand for higher education, and in some cases an actual decline in levels of participation, at least in certain sectors of the system[1]. Although this overall trend does not reflect the relative position of the various higher education programmes or institutions (some of which are experiencing increased competition for entry), there is growing concern among policy-makers and within the academic world about the significance of this change and its many implications.

---

1. See: "Development of Higher Education in OECD Countries since 1965", OECD, Paris, 1979 (mimeographed).

In addition to raising questions about some of the fundamental concepts on which the growth of higher education has been based, it also calls for a re-consideration of its role as an instrument of social progress, e.g. in promoting equal opportunities for all; the greater risk now involved in the pursuit of higher education, as well as its higher cost, may have a particularly adverse effect on low-income students.

The picture, of course, varies from country to country, but it is interesting to note that this levelling-off has occurred in countries with widely varying levels of participation, a surprising development in the eyes of many who, in the early 1970s, had thought that countries with relatively low full-time enrolment rates would follow the example of those which had achieved mass participation. Moreover, in many countries the decline in growth rates has taken place in spite of a steady growth in female enrolments. What some regard as disturbing is the fact that in a number of Member countries there is a marked levelling-off or even a decline in the transfer rates for upper secondary school leavers, particularly to universities; although partly explained by changes in admission policies, this is taken as further evidence of waning interest among youth in at least certain types of higher education. It is often argued on these grounds that if the viability of certain higher education institutions is to be maintained, the main source for new recruits might be from the non-traditional groups, particularly adults. This could in itself act as a catalyst for change, as the needs of such groups cannot be met through traditional programmes and institutions. In actual practice, many institutions have already found new and imaginative ways of tapping this new clientele, even though such initiatives tend to be institution-based rather than part of an overall policy strategy.

A second area of concern relates to demographic trends. The size of the traditional age group that will be entering higher education in the course of the next fifteen years can be gauged with a fair degree of accuracy. The majority of Member countries will witness a pronounced decline in this age group after 1985; in several of them this will represent an exacerbation of earlier trends; in others it will be in quite marked contrast to the expansion in this age group prevailing up to around 1985. The latter countries will therefore have to cope with a short period of further growth (depending to a large extent on trends in transfer rates), in the knowledge that it is likely to be followed by a sharp contraction. How to deal with this 'peak' in the context of present financial constraints remains an important policy concern in many countries.

Some countries have gone a long way towards evolving policies for providing higher education to non-traditional groups. However, on the whole, the potential demand represented by these groups is largely unknown and requires more thorough analysis. Wide differences may well be noted in national trends, reflecting different demographic patterns and such factors as the social or employment value of post-secondary education. A great deal will depend on broader changes that may occur in employment conditions, income policies and the redistribution of work and leisure time as well as on public policies to promote recurrent education through paid educational leave, etc. Two questions, however, remain: will this non-traditional demand compensate for the decline or slowdown in participation by young people? Will higher education be able to respond to the diversity of needs and interests that correspond to this potential new demand so as to attract and maintain this new clientele? This, to a large extent, will determine the priority accorded to higher education in the broader economic and social policy context.

ii) Employment prospects

Current discussions on the employment implications of the OECD growth scenario show that in most Member countries full employment will certainly not be attained in the near future; if anything, the pace of unemployment will grow, and young people will experience increasing difficulty in entering working life. What then will be the relative position of higher education graduates on the labour market and what will be young people's attitude to higher education, particularly over the long term?

In most Member countries, graduates have enjoyed a relatively privileged situation so far. They may, therefore, be expected to suffer less in the current employment crisis than other categories of workers: their risk of being unemployed is certainly lower and their range of options is wider than that of their less educated contemporaries. They may accept downgrading to less qualified occupations or take temporary jobs rather than face unemployment. Two major factors may have a severe impact on the employment prospects of young graduates, particularly women, in the years to come:

a) curbs on public expenditure are resulting in less job creation in the public sector (interpreted to cover all those areas which depend directly or indirectly on state or community financing), up to now the main employment outlet for graduates;
b) in most countries, stabilisation of school enrolment is progressively affecting the recruitment of teachers at all levels of the education system, also a major employment outlet for this category of young people.

At least during the 1980s, the employment prospects of young graduates will very much depend on their willingness to accept lower-level jobs in the public sector, and perhaps even more on the absorptive capacity and recruitment/promotion policies of the private sector. Up to now, however, the growth of qualified jobs in the private sector would seem not to have kept pace with the supply of highly educated people. Many young graduates will thus have to revise their career expectations and envisage new employment opportunities; this will result in a relative decline in the status of higher education graduates in society. Whereas many groups perceive this trend with concern, others, especially those who favour reducing the role of higher education in the social selection process, see it as a more positive development.

Views differ on the relative chances of higher education graduates entering intermediate level positions in the private sector.

Some argue that employers increasingly require higher levels of education for the same level of job and use education as a screening device. Others, however, take the view that young graduates may not always have received the most appropriate preparation for these jobs and that they might be handicapped in competing with adults and other categories of young people on the internal labour market; they also argue that recruiting the highly educated into these jobs may create social conflicts within companies. The latter view implies a high degree of differentiation among the various categories of graduates, some entering traditional graduate jobs, some being taken on at an intermediate level, others being forced into low-skilled clerical or manual work or unemployment.

It is difficult to assess the impact of these structural trends on the future of higher education. They will certainly affect social demand but, as recent experience has shown, not necessarily in a uniform way. A depressed labour market may stimulate demand for further education, even when private returns are poor, if the pursuit of studies is seen as a way of enhancing chances in the competition for better jobs or at least as a preferable alternative to unemployment. It may also have a dissuasive effect on young people who see no point in continuing higher education studies if their employment outlets fall short of their expectations, particularly if they succeed in getting a job upon completion of secondary education. Perhaps the more significant impact will be on patterns of attendance, with increased interest in part-time study. Also, attitudes are likely to vary according to social origin; for example, students from the lower social groups may be more hesitant to enrol in "high risk" options, i.e. those with low employment value or uncertain outlets, or less likely to apply for entry into strongly selective institutions.

Poor employment or career prospects may also foster a more consumption-oriented type of demand for higher education. Fewer work opportunities, longer periods of non-working time together with a decreased need for young people on the employment scene, may lead to increased participation by people who find they have more time for education or who enrol primarily for reasons of personal fulfilment.

Finally, rising rates of youth unemployment may and do effectively serve to justify both expansion and restrictive policies at the higher education level. Expansion may be favoured as a means of alleviating, at least temporarily, pressures on the labour market and be considered a less costly way of coping with unemployment than unemployment benefits or job creation. There would be some a priori justification for restrictive policies if, within an overall youth employment policy, priority were given to other categories of young people and/or other forms of education and training.

In the last instance, it could be argued that the main dilemma from an economic or employment standpoint is not expansion versus restriction but rather what qualitative changes should be introduced within higher education, in terms of the content and structure of studies, teaching methods and openness to the outside world, so as to contribute both to the technological development and structural adaptation of OECD Member countries. This, of course, is a fundamental issue which goes well beyond employment as such and on which the dynamic development of higher education ultimately depends. It is also an issue where new policies cannot be effectively implemented except with the willing and active support of the institutions themselves.

iii) Research and technology requirements

There seems little doubt that the economic crisis which OECD Members have been facing over the past few years will continue to rank high on the policy agenda for some years to come. Traditional methods of economic management are seemingly inadequate to combat the combination of inflation, unemployment, zero growth, energy and raw materials shortages which the industrialised world is currently experiencing. In many OECD countries traditional industries are now confronted with a challenge from newly industrialising countries which they will be unable to meet in terms of price alone. On the assumption that there as yet exists no acceptable alternative to the high technology/industrialisation model of development, there is growing agreement that what is needed is a new economic strategy which accords a major place to industrial innovation. Innovation would be particularly directed towards those industries where the advanced OECD countries could find a secure base for exports and production in the new economic order. The strategy involves embracing the most advanced micro-electronic techniques in production and other areas of the economy (whilst recognising, and taking steps to mitigate, the likely social repercussions). It also implies a major commitment to industrially-oriented, basic and strategic research carried out by industry itself. New technological opportunities must be sought, involving perhaps bio-technology and other technologies of general application (so-called 'generic technologies') for there is the possibility that these may give rise to entirely new job-producing industries.

This strategy will present a number of major challenges to higher education systems, not least to their capacities for research. A major problem for higher education policy will be that of steering a middle course between purely scientific research and research more relevant to short-term industrial development. New kinds of links between academic institutions and industry may be required to facilitate the transfer of know-how. Such links could entail innovative approaches to research training and a new kind of partnership at post-graduate level in which responsibility for advanced training is shared.

These considerations raise the more general question of the place of research in higher education. In the recent past, increased enrolment and a heterogeneous student population have led to more emphasis being placed on teaching rather than on research. At the same time, in quite a number of countries, universities are no longer the sole repositories of fundamental research, especially research involving very costly equipment. There has thus been a significant change in the role of many higher education institutions and in their internal climate as well as in the work and career development of academic staff. Given the place of research in the value system of the academic world, as well as in maintaining the vitality and relevance of the entire higher education system, a key question will be whether renewed emphasis on new forms of research to suit the interests of all higher education institutions will be feasible and necessary during this period of contraction or whether research will continue to be the prerogative of a limited number of institutions, primarily universities. In considering these issues, it must be borne in mind that the traditional function of universities is to provide a critique of social problems and objective analyses for their solution; moreover, the nature of the problems is changing, with increased concern for areas such as energy, the environment, relations with developing countries, etc., all of which call for a more interdisciplinary approach which is not always compatible with the traditional structure of disciplines in higher education institutions.

iv) <u>Financial considerations</u>

It is, of course, in terms of finance that the impact of the overall economic and social situation on higher education becomes most manifest. In most countries, a primary concern of governments in the prevailing economic conditions is to limit the level of public expenditure, particularly in policy sectors that are considered to be inflationary. In addition, within overall social policy, there is growing competition for scarce resources, such sectors as health or income maintenance, for example, receiving increased support at the expense of education. Other sectors of a pressing social nature, such as youth employment programmes and policies to facilitate the transition from school to work, may also be accorded more importance than higher education <u>per se</u>.

Inflation is often cited as an additional factor in the gradual decrease in the level of public financing of higher education, which has traditionally been the major source of funding in most OECD countries. Even where it is possible for governments to increase annual expenditure in proportion to inflation, to the extent that the cost structure of higher education is such that inflationary costs for higher education exceed those in the economy as a whole, the final result is an effective decrease in financing in real terms. A second important consideration derives from the fact that the level of financial support has been traditionally linked directly to enrolments. Whatever the merits of this practice (and there are many who would argue in favour of a change in order to avoid its adverse effects on research funding, for example), it is not unreasonable to expect that there will be pressure on public authorities to reduce spending proportionately, should enrolments decline. This is essentially a question of political priorities and how individual countries view the role of higher education in the pursuit of general social and economic objectives. It could well be argued that, in times of uncertainty about the future, education and culture remain a major resource which justifies 'over-investment'. The danger is that systematic cuts may have long-term consequences for the dynamism of the higher education system at a time when OECD countries are counting on their scientific and technological potential to maintain their position in the new world order. They may also force many institutions to look elsewhere for supplementary funding, such as entering the adult teaching market or turning to industry as clients for their research services. In many circumstances, this may be a desirable trend to be actively pursued so long as its possible detrimental effects on long-term academic objectives are obviated.

v) Internal dynamics of higher education institutions and changing power structures

The development of higher education will not be conditioned solely by societal pressures and externally determined requirements like those indicated above. The nature and impact of the internal forces at play within higher education itself will need to be more openly recognised. The particular history and traditions of higher education institutions, the problems resulting from rapid expansion, the interests of the different groups within the academic community are, in fact, key factors to be taken into account in any attempt to analyse the possible future development of this sector.

For the most part, these internal factors derive from the traditional value structures and functions of higher education institutions, in particular those of the most prestigious universities which set the pace and exert influence throughout the system. The emphasis on fundamental research, the wish to preserve academic freedom and the autonomy of institutions, to maintain a distance from political pressures or immediate social concerns are indeed generally accepted as legitimate requirements for guaranteeing quality and permanence. Often, however, they are seen as being used by certain members of the academic community and professional groups to resist necessary changes, adaptations and greater diversity of higher education. Also, like many bureaucratic organisations, higher education institutions struggle to preserve self-serving functions that are important for maintaining their internal power structure as well as functions that reflect their influence on society at large, such as the monopoly of certification or their role in social selection.

Most economic and political analyses of the links between education and society tend to view these internal forces as primarily conservative or defensive mechanisms in contrast to the progressive or innovative pressures stemming from different outside groups. While a substantial proportion of the academic staff admittedly tends to adopt a conservative stance on higher education issues, there is ample evidence not only of a diversity of viewpoints but also of changes and innovations initially opposed by large segments of society but which were successfully pushed through by higher education institutions. Furthermore, it is over-simplistic to assume that higher education institutions can and should adapt to all external requirements and expectations. There may be incompatibility or conflict among different external pressures; there may be difficulty in reconciling them and therefore in ensuring adequate and rapid responses; also, these pressures may reflect temporary or narrow interests which the educational sector must perhaps legitimately resist. It should not be forgotten that during the period of extraordinary educational expansion and rapid economic growth, these internal forces proved responsive by providing a framework for the accommodation of vast new numbers favouring innovation and structural adaptation. The key question today is whether these same forces will be able to react positively to the forthcoming period of contraction and make their contribution to the positive adjustments called for by the new social and economic context. Some rigidities, primarily stemming from the age structure and specialisation of the present teaching and research staff, may prove to be among the more difficult obstacles to overcome and will merit particular attention. Changes in the attitudes of higher education staff and in the criteria for recruitment are particularly sensitive in this respect.

III. MAIN POLICY CONCERNS AND DILEMMAS

Under the sharpened impact of the factors outlined above, particularly those related to the economic and employment situation of Member countries, there are clear signs that in the period ahead, governments will be led to adopt more active roles and explicit policies in the development of higher education. A major policy concern will be how to mediate between the pressures arising from these external factors (and also linked to the pursuit of broader social, economic and technological policy objectives) and those stemming from higher education institutions themselves, including the consequences of the rapid expansion of higher education in the past.

It is equally clear, however, that the way in which these policy concerns will be expressed will vary from country to country, so that generalisations are even more difficult now than they were in the past. Already during the Golden Age of education, when most pressures converged in fostering rapid growth, countries coped with the advent of mass higher education in quite different ways(2). On the basis of the experience of the late 1970s and of the different national forecasts and policy statements, it would be reasonable to argue that the coming decades will witness a far greater diversity among Member countries in the patterns of development of their higher education systems. The position taken will depend on: the stage of development of each system, particularly in terms of enrolment rates; the general image of higher education and its role in society; the politial weight of various types of criteria determining access policies in different countries; the degree of flexibility with which higher education systems themselves are endowed.

In order to illustrate and discuss these differences in patterns of development, four areas of higher education policy have been selected. These are:

---

2. "Towards New Structures of Post-Secondary Education", OECD document, Paris, 1971.

1. Access to Higher Education.
2. Changing Relationships between Higher Education and Working Life.
3. New Patterns of Authority in Higher Education.
4. Financing and Redeployment of Resources.

NOTES FOR DISCUSSION

Theme 1

ACCESS TO HIGHER EDUCATION(1)

THE CONTEXT

Two general trends stand out in relation to the discussion of specific issues covered by the general theme of "Access to higher education". The first concerns the changes which have been taking place in the demand for higher education in terms of numbers, composition of the student body, patterns of attendance, distribution by type of institution, field of study, etc. Whereas in some Member countries changes of this kind were already under way in the 1970s, many others are anticipating or planning for substantial change in the 1980s and beyond. The second trend is the move from a "demand" to a "supply" oriented approach in higher education policy. Governments are under pressure to monitor more closely the development of higher education and to formulate more precise and explicit guidelines for the future of the whole sector. In many cases this implies that educational policy-makers must assume a mediating role which endeavours to reconcile a number of often conflicting forces: the demand by individuals; the internal interests and claims for autonomy of higher education institutions; pressures stemming from different professional groups; broader national priorities as defined by governments.

Over the past years, governments have been increasingly led to exercise this mediating role through measures relating to access to higher education, a strategic area at the interface between supply and demand and one which is frequently more amenable to government action than other spheres of higher education.

While the situation varies from country to country, a number of factors can be identified behind the push for stronger government roles in the field of access. These factors also explain why decisions

---

1. For a more detailed review of trends and issues in this area see Part Two in this volume.

concerning the overall intake of higher education and the way students are distributed among the various options have acquired far greater political significance than formerly.

In the first place, it is clearly recognised that admission policies and practices in higher education influence not only the future development of this sector, but also other levels of education, particularly upper secondary, as well as strategies for lifelong or recurrent education. Second, there are new strains on the admission process as a result of the general trend to postpone selection in the education system and the need to allocate scarce resources at the higher levels in ways which are both equitable and cost efficient. Third, many countries are increasingly calling into question the policy of adapting the supply of places at the tertiary level solely to the needs and wishes of certain categories of school leavers(2). Finally, growing pressure on universities to justify their selection procedures, particularly in view of greater competition for places, has led to the requirement that admission policies and criteria be formulated in more explicit terms.

For a meaningful discussion of the policy questions involved, it is essential that access to higher education be viewed in a broad perspective, in particular:

a) as one stage in a much longer process involving the orientation, selection and distribution of students before entry, essentially during secondary schooling, as well as after entry, that is in the course of higher education studies;
b) as it relates to the total network of higher education institutions and to those non-formal types of education and training which fulfil similar functions;
c) in terms of formal regulations and criteria for admission as well as of the actual behaviour and strategies of the individuals in response to these regulations;
d) as encompassing a wide range of policy instruments, including admission regulations and practices, student financing schemes, information and guidance services, designed to avoid serious imbalance between supply and demand in the context of national priorities such as equity, efficiency or employment considerations.

THE ISSUES

Discussion of specific issues in the area of access to higher education can be organised under five broad headings:

---

2. In Sweden this consideration lay behind the reforms of the early 1970s aimed at increasing adult participation. This country now faces the opposite problem, namely that of having to design an admission system which at least partially redresses the balance in favour of young qualified school leavers.

I.   Principles for the quantitative planning of higher education.
   II. Admission policies and the institutional framework.
   III. Changing links between secondary and higher education.
   IV. Access of new groups and new forms of attendance.
   V.   Co-ordinating admission and financing policies.

I. PRINCIPLES FOR THE QUANTITATIVE PLANNING OF HIGHER EDUCATION

Attention should focus on the political rather than the technical aspects of the planning process, in other words on the assumptions underlying forecasts of the quantitative development of higher education, and the targets and priorities set in normative plans.

How governments determine the total demand for various types of higher education continues to be a crucial planning issue. However, as new parameters acquire importance in the planning process and governments have to redefine priorities, a useful starting point for discussion is how policy-makers determine the extent to which this demand can and/or should be met and under what conditions. This entails examination of the methods and criteria by which different countries:

a) assess the overall quantitative evolution of their higher education systems and estimate its resource implications;
b) have established normative targets for the future growth of their higher education systems and how these relate to estimates of demand;
c) take steps to either restrain or encourage demand or channel it along lines which correspond to overall national priorities;
d) cope with sudden fluctuations in demand, such as a sharp rise or fall in the number of applicants.

In tackling all these questions, it is important that reference be made to the various categories of demand as defined and accounted for in the planning process in individual countries.

II. ADMISSION POLICIES AND THE INSTITUTIONAL FRAMEWORK[3]

It is frequently claimed that with shrinking college age groups and a certain stabilisation in participation rates, the issue of selection and problems of access in general will be less acute and politically sensitive in the 1980s than they have been in the past two decades.

---

3. See Part Two, "Access to Higher Education", Chapters I and II.

It is suggested here that even in countries which foresee a decline in enrolments or where total demand for higher education is expected to be met, access will remain an area of tension and social conflict and therefore a major political issue. This is so because competition for entry into certain sectors of higher education is likely to increase so that problems of reallocation and selection will persist. Also, as has been the case for some time in the United States, the central policy issue in European countries will not be so much how many enter higher education as who enters what type of institution or programme. The question of entry and the role of admission regulations and practices in shaping, monitoring and controlling demand will be discussed under Sections III and IV below. Here it is suggested that admission regulations be viewed primarily in relation to supply policies, that is, in terms of how they reflect and how they contribute to the pursuit of broader policies concerning the overall structure of higher education.

In this context, the following specific considerations will determine how access is regulated in different countries:

a) Whether the aim or policy is to develop "closed", "open" or "mixed" systems of higher education. In the case of rather "closed" higher education systems, limits or targets are set in terms of their overall capacity, and generalised numerus clausus may exist when demand exceeds supply. Educational policy in Denmark, Finland, Greece, Sweden and Turkey takes this approach. The degree of selectivity of this type of system can vary considerably depending on how the targets or supply limits are set in relation to estimated demand. In "open" higher education systems, free access is guaranteed to all candidates with formal qualifications (e.g. Austria, Switzerland, Italy). Here again, there are variations primarily due to the extent to which selection takes place before or after entry into higher education. In "mixed" type of higher education systems closed and open access institutions or programmes co-exist. The majority of Member countries follow this model, differences depending on the size and characteristics of the "selective" sector, the type of institutions or programmes which represent the open or elastic segment of higher education, etc.

b) Whether a policy of equality among similar types of higher education institutions or programmes is advocated (e.g. Sweden, Germany) or whether hierarchies are allowed to develop (e.g. France, United Kingdom, United States). In the past this question was mainly discussed in relation to the prestige gap between the university and the non-university sector. After years of expansion, an equally important policy issue is whether, and under what conditions, competition and prestige differences within each sector, i.e. universities, should exist. Of special interest and concern is the growing prestige gap between fields of study which appears to be developing in quite a number of Member countries, mainly as a result of the current employment situation but in certain cases also reinforced by admission policies.

c) Whether there is support for a comprehensive model of higher education which attempts to integrate short-cycle and long-cycle higher education courses within a single institution (diversification within institutions) or whether binary type policies (diversification among institutions) are favoured. Particularly in the case of the binary model, adopted with variations by most Member countries, a key policy question relates to the transfer of students in the course of their studies; this also involves greater co-ordination and rendering institutions or programmes more accessible at different stages beyond entry.
d) On viewpoints and policies concerning the access of adults to higher education and the degree of integration of initial and recurrent education : whether the emphasis on greater adult participation in higher education is understood as facilitating access of mature people to most colleges and universities (e.g. Sweden, United States); to particular programmes or institutions (e.g. further education in the United Kingdom, certain university programmes in France, Italy); to specially created non-traditional institutions (e.g. Open Universities in the United Kingdom, Germany, the Netherlands, Japan). Also, whether emphasis will be on allowing or encouraging adults to enrol in mainstream courses, or in separate study schemes within established institutions (e.g. extramural courses, continuing education centres).
e) On policies vis-à-vis the "weaker" or less attractive institutions or programmes of higher education which in the recent past have suffered most from the employment situation and slackening demand and are likely to constitute the vulnerable sector in the years to come.

Problems related to access to post-graduate education also merit examination, particularly as governments are likely to assume growing responsibilities in this area. Of particular concern is the future of research-oriented studies which, in many Member countries, face the prospect of severe budgetary cuts and corresponding reductions in the number of post-graduate students, particularly in certain disciplines. It is, however, an open question whether limitations in the student intake will lead to enhanced competition for entry and serve to improve or maintain the quality of the student body. Indeed, given the lack of financial support and of attractive career prospects, talented undergraduates may move away from research options. Another problem highlighted by the Swedish experience is that as more and more students enter universities without any intention of obtaining a first degree, the pool of qualified candidates for graduate courses may decrease considerably.

III. CHANGING LINKS BETWEEN SECONDARY AND HIGHER EDUCATION(4)

Many of the present difficulties in organising a smooth transition from secondary to higher education are due to the growing autonomy and often divergent development patterns of these two sectors over the past years. Differences in growth rates, recent drops in transfer rates from academic lines of study to universities and, in some countries, the increased participation of adults in higher education, are among the symptoms or causes of this trend. Policy statements and proposed reforms in a number of countries seem to point to a further uncoupling in the development of these levels in the coming decade, in particular between the traditional academic-oriented lines of study and universities. A major challenge in the coming years, therefore, will be that of ensuring a type of articulation between upper secondary and higher education which implies recognition of their common values, but also of their distinctive functions and objectives. Although responsibilities are shared, given the hierarchical power structure of education systems, decisions taken within higher education, and notably those pertaining to access, are likely to have a significant impact on the possibilities for such mutual adaptation.

Against this background, a set of questions and alternative policy options should be examined: What should be the role of upper secondary education in the selection process for admission to higher education? Can and should completion of secondary studies be dissociated from the concept of qualification (or even the right) to enter higher education? Should grades or other indicators of past performance be maintained as the unique or dominant criteria in the selection process? What are the advantages and drawbacks of the various meritocratic type procedures currently being used? What weight could be given to other methods and criteria in determining entry - for example subjective indicators such as motivation, initiative or other personal characteristics, work experience, socio-demographic characteristics of students, etc.? In particular, what lessons can be drawn from recent experience in Member countries with admission schemes aimed at reducing group disparities, such as quotas, affirmative action(5)? In countries where criticisms are voiced on the "quality" of secondary school leavers, what evidence is provided to substantiate the decline and what solutions are being proposed? What are considered to be the benefits as well as the drawbacks of having a more diversified student body, not only in terms of age but also of school background? What are the policies vis-à-vis provision of remedial education in higher education institutions? What have been the most successful schemes initiated by higher education institutions aimed at guiding and informing secondary school pupils before they have to make their choice of studies?

---

4. See Part Two, "Access to Higher Education", Chapters II and III.
5. Such as policies and specific measures designed to increase female participation.

IV. ACCESS OF NEW GROUPS AND NEW FORMS OF ATTENDANCE(6)

In spite of the rising interest in recurrent education schemes and the many formal policy statements in favour of greater adult participation in higher education, the proportion of adults enrolled at the tertiary level grew very slowly throughout the 1970s and remains practically nil for the more selective universities and fields of study. Significant exceptions are Sweden, the United States and, to a lesser extent, Australia, Canada and the United Kingdom.

The pace of change may well, however, accelerate in the coming decade. Whereas in the past pressure to increase adult participation stemmed primarily from groups outside the education system, a growing number of higher education institutions are now taking initiatives in this direction, not least because catering for a new clientele is seen as a way of compensating for slackening demand from the traditional college age group. Such institutions find themselves faced with the problem not only of coping with a different clientele, but increasingly of carrying through a dynamic policy aimed at attracting new groups. The development of a "marketing approach" to higher education in some countries, notably the United States, is a clear indication of this trend. The difficulties which this gives rise to in terms of maintaining entry standards and fair practices already anticipate some of the issues likely to be more generally confronted in the future.

The terms "adults", "new groups" or "non-traditional students" are rather too vague and a more precise categorisation is needed to facilitate policy discussion. Among candidates entering mainstream studies which qualify for credits and/or lead to formal qualifications, at least four groups can be distinguished(7). In all four groups, the particular problem of women calls for special attention.

The first group, typically found in European countries with streamed secondary education, includes young people having completed various types of terminal vocational studies which traditionally did not qualify for higher education. The general direction of reform is to maintain these programmes as they stand while affording leavers the possibility of entering higher education with or without additional qualifying requirements. A central question is whether to change admission regulations in order to promote the participation of this type of school leaver or to encourage their entry at a later stage on the basis of work experience(8).

The second group consists of mature students who do not have the formal secondary school qualifications for entry into higher education. Problems include: the type of extension and support

---

6. See Part Two, Chapter IV.
7. Australia suggests a different classification of mature age students: i) recyclers; ii) deferrers; iii) early school leavers.
8. Finland focuses on measures aimed at enlarging access from technical institutes to higher education.

services likely to enhance the chances of entry and success of this group; identifying and implementing suitable admission/selection criteria with due consideration to candidates' age, sex, work experience and background; evaluating existing national schemes in the light of subsequent performance, the advantages and drawbacks of greater diversity of the student body for this group as well as for the traditional students.

The third group is made up of young people who meet the formal requirements for entry, but who are non-traditional students in the sense that they combine, in a variety of ways, education and work (defined in a broad sense); for instance entry after a period in employment, alternating periods of study and work, combining the two simultaneously, etc. The proportion of young people who opt for such patterns of study has increased steadily over the past few years so that in a number of programmes they constitute the norm rather than the exception. The characteristics and implications of this gradual and largely unplanned development deserve special consideration in view of the fact that it essentially reflects the variety of individual responses - whether or not fostered by government policy - to the problems posed by the transition from education to work.
It could be argued that in the future some of the more significant changes in higher education will result not only or primarily from the presence of new groups but rather from the traditional young clientele which may well look for new forms of participation.

The fourth, and more heterogeneous, group includes various categories of adults who want to pursue post-secondary studies a few or many years after having completed their secondary education. With rising levels of educational attainment and changing lifestyles, this group could grow quite rapidly in the coming decades. In terms of access and selection, what weight should be given to their work or life experience in relation to their formal school qualifications? And, in the case of highly selective institutions, what policies should be adopted when such adults compete with young qualified school leavers without work experience?

These are some problems likely to confront higher education institutions as a result of the substantial increase in the participation of new groups and the changed situation which may arise. Issues and policies will, of course, vary considerably depending on whether adults represent 5, 25 or 50 per cent of the total student body in a programme. Secondly, a growing proportion of students may enrol in higher education without the intention - at least in the short term - of completing a degree. The existence of "single" courses in Sweden and their impact on the overall system of higher education is a significant example. Alongside the changes in curriculum content and in the organisation of studies, higher education institutions will find themselves under pressure to develop new delivery systems, that is new ways and means of teaching and of disseminating information.

V. CO-ORDINATING ADMISSION AND FINANCING POLICIES(9)

In the general context of growing government involvement in monitoring the development of higher education, financing policies and instruments acquire a strategic role. There has, of course, always been a close relationship between financing policies and admission policies. In view, however, of the wide range of objectives that such policies serve, particularly the need to reconcile efficiency and equity objectives, it is hardly surprising that admission policies and financing mechanisms often appear to be poorly co-ordinated.

One clear illustration of this lack of consistency is that, though a number of Member countries have changed their admission criteria in order to foster adult participation, the provisions for student grants are still largely framed to suit the traditional student, entering straight from school. Similarly, the general trend in the past few years to reduce selectivity in secondary education has not been matched by increases in financial aid to secondary school pupils to prevent low-income students from dropping out. There are also difficulties arising from disagreement about what the objectives imply: for example, does equity require that access be made more equal, or that the distribution of costs be more closely related to benefits?

Be that as it may, in the present situation of financial constraint, there are many signs that governments are becoming more aware that financing and admission policies must be viewed as a whole. Such questions as whether government subsidies should be given to students or institutions, whether students should receive grants or loans, or whether fees or fee differentials should be abolished or increased are seen more and more as directly related to selection procedures, the use of quotas in determining admissions, pass rates in final examinations or the need for a probationary year at the start of higher education. It can be assumed that pressure to make these relationships more explicit will grow, both within governments and the public as well as among the students themselves (in certain countries the courts are already active in this field) and that there will be a need for more careful analysis of how they operate as regulating mechanisms on both the supply and demand for higher education.

It can also be assumed that the majority of OECD countries will wish to maintain public financing as the major source of funding higher education and that there will be an actual decline in the growth of such funding. In these circumstances, one question which arises is: how can student-aid policies be adjusted to respond to changes in the composition of enrolments, with more adults and part-time students, as well as in relation to such new developments as paid educational leave? On this latter point, it is an open and politically delicate issue whether, as non-work and leisure time increase, adults wishing to use this opportunity for indulging in educational activities could not be encouraged to do so in ways which bring new resources into higher education.

---

9. See Part Two, Chapter V.

Theme 2

CHANGING RELATIONSHIP BETWEEN HIGHER EDUCATION
AND WORKING LIFE

THE CONTEXT

Possible implications of the changing employment situation on the future development of higher education have been outlined in the Overview where particular attention was drawn to two main features of the situation of young graduates[1]:

a) an increasing number of graduates will in future have to seek employment in non-traditional, lower level jobs;
b) the sharp decline in the recruitment into the public services and teaching implies that most young graduates will need to find employment in the private sector. Both of these developments will represent a major challenge for higher education, particularly in those countries which have not reached the stage of a mass system of higher education.

In response to the question of whether such changes will affect the overall demand for higher education, the argument put forward was that shifts in demand were more likely than a decline in enrolments. It was also suggested that the main issue is perhaps not so much one of expansion versus contraction, but of achieving a new balance and introducing the necessary qualitative changes into higher education.

The range of problems that come within this theme is, of course, much broader than those relating to the employment prospects of young graduates. They include such issues as:

- the contribution of higher education to scientific and technological development, and particularly the role it can play in the development of innovative industrial strategies;
- the response of higher education to new community needs and the further training needs of adults faced with technological change;

---

1. See "Employment prospects for higher education graduates", OECD document, Paris, 1981.

- strengthening liaison and co-operation between higher education institutions and the world of work in matters of teaching and applied research in order to improve the relevance of studies to employment;
- the overall planning of the future development of higher education, to take better account of changes in patterns of employment and working life.

In the past, under conditions of growth, developments in the above areas were easy to discern. They occurred as a result of policy action and grass-root initiatives. Growth made experimentation possible and this in turn facilitated change and innovation. The situation has now changed and there is uncertainty and differences of view about what may or should happen over the eighties. The period ahead will witness not only changes in patterns of employment and working life, but will also be one of financial stringency and there is a very real danger that it might be marked by contraction and decreased innovation. It should also be considered, however, as a period of necessary shifts in emphasis and of changing priorities, responding not only to temporary conditions, but also to longer-term needs, particularly those deriving from the structural changes which OECD economies and societies are currently experiencing. The discussion could serve to identify possible directions for such positive developments.

Account would of course need to be taken of differences among countries, depending on the stage of development of their education systems and on national perceptions of the role and place of higher education in society. Such differences will determine the way in which individual countries perceive the issue of the changing relationships between higher education and the world of work, an issue which will receive increased attention from both policy makers and higher education institutions in all countries in the eighties. How will the issue be interpreted and reflected in terms of policy and practice? Will the consequent re-orientation promote the pursuit of the broader and longer-term objectives of higher education?

ASPECTS AND DIMENSIONS OF THE PROBLEM

Given this diversity and current developments in national policies, it seems that the following aspects and dimensions of the problem are worth considering:

i) <u>employment as a parameter in the overall planning of higher education</u> - the initial education and training of young people as well as the further education of adults;

ii) <u>the employment relevance of higher education studies and the response to social needs</u> - an area where emphasis will be placed on the reform of studies and their structure, but also on the implications for higher education of developments in working life, particularly its response to new patterns of participation and the needs of adults already in employment;

iii) <u>the development of a new partnership between higher education and the world of work</u> - including initiatives that may be taken by the institutions to develop closer contacts with the realities of working life, as well as the contribution of the world of work, including the social partners, in enhancing such co-operation.

I. EMPLOYMENT AND THE OVERALL PLANNING OF HIGHER EDUCATION

The first question is whether the vocational dimension of higher education should be further strengthened. In recent decades, possibly in line with its expansion, there have already been signs of a move towards a more instrumental view of the role of higher education in society. Some would see all social institutions in this light. In many countries, however, emphasis on its cultural and social objectives continues to prevail while others may fear increased credentialism within the world of work. Other arguments are also put forward: higher education is considered as a preferable alternative to unemployment; the less vocational and less costly courses have acted as safety valves for variations in demand; and spending some time in higher education is a smooth way for individuals to adjust their aspirations to the realities of the world of work. Possibly the right approach to the problem is to look at the changing nature of the vocational dimension of higher education.

What would this mean in terms of overall planning of the system? As suggested in an OECD report(2), for a large number of graduates there may well be a further widening of the gap between education and training received and employment opportunities. Whilst in some countries, among which Japan and the United States, such imbalances seem to have been absorbed, in others the size of the gap and the numbers affected may become a matter of concern. A laissez-faire policy could perhaps be the most effective response to such changes, particularly in countries where the costs of higher education to the individual are high. In certain countries, such as Italy, however, such policies may lead to lower participation, a higher drop-out rate, increased unemployment, and, therefore, a waste of human resources and public money. As a result, governments may find themselves impelled to seek more interventionist and positive policies.

Apart from measures regarding the organisation and content of studies as such, which will be considered below, such policies could be along the following lines:

i) <u>Steering individual demand for higher education</u> with a view to guiding students towards more occupationally-relevant courses. This may imply restrictive measures concerning access to studies with poor employment prospects, or increasing the cost of such studies to the individual.

---

2. "Employment prospects for higher education graduates". op. cit.

The relative importance given to the development of the
university and non-university sectors of higher education
is a key element of such a policy. Another possibility
would be to develop more systematic information and
guidance policies and measures to steer students towards
courses with better outlet.

ii) <u>Encouraging institutions</u> to be more sensitive to employment/
working problems and to give priority to courses that
respond to the requirements of working life. This may
often take the form of <u>selective financial incentives</u>, but
may also affect the formal recognition of institutions and
grades by the state or professional associations.

iii) <u>Developing new forms of higher education</u>, particularly for
adults who have to adapt and contribute to technological
change. This may involve facilitating new patterns of
participation for students already in employment, as well
as developing innovative programmes such as single or non-
degree courses, or new types of training, in collaboration
with the social partners, as alternatives to more
traditional forms of higher education.

Emphasis will certainly differ between countries, according
to their experience, the degree of government influence over
institutions and the political commitment to change. Given budgetary
constraints, it will also differ according to the type of courses
considered and their cost. Italy, Japan and the United Kingdom drew
a useful distinction between courses supplying marketable vocational
training, those imparting skills that may be applied in a variety of
occupations and those providing general education. Of particular
concern here is the place of the traditional university and of some
of its departments, such as the humanities and the social sciences;
some countries might pay particular attention to the costs of such
disciplines as compared to those of shorter, more vocational courses,
or to other, less traditional types of training. Strengthening the
vocational dimension of higher education will certainly imply an
increase in costs. Some countries may also express special concern
for the situation of post-graduate studies and their potential for
research and technological development. In many countries demographic
trends may be a determining factor in policy options, since certain
problems may be seen as essentially transient.

II. ENHANCING THE EMPLOYMENT RELEVANCE OF HIGHER EDUCATION
STUDIES AND THE RESPONSE TO SOCIAL NEEDS

Many would argue that higher education has its own objectives,
and that the fortunes of its various disciplines should not be
affected by fluctuations in employment. On the other hand, others
might consider that the very growth of higher education has led to
an over-emphasis on the type of knowledge traditionally imparted by
its institutions, at the expense of other, equally respectable,
traditions of knowledge.

In addition, relevance can be viewed in a variety of perspectives, particularly as regards the initial education and training of young people. In the first place, countries have very different perceptions and traditions in regard to higher education. One can mention the British view of the trained mind or the German emphasis on the pursuit of pure knowledge; some countries place emphasis on the cultural, others on the vocational objectives of higher education. Second, a number of criticisms have been voiced, as in Norway, about the growing role of higher education as a screening device for the allocation of roles in society: the formal qualifications required are sometimes irrelevant, in the sense that they do not correspond to the actual skills needed for a given job. The view of employers on the required profile of candidates may differ widely: some place emphasis on general levels of ability, others on specialised skills. Finally, to the extent that the general skills needed in working life and outside are different, the increasing weight of leisure and non-work time in the life of individuals has to be considered when defining the relevance of higher education. The problem of improving the social and employment relevance of studies is, therefore, far more complex than the improvements or adjustments so far considered would seem to imply.

In addition to the now rather traditional complaints of the over-specialisation, isolation or the academic drift of higher education studies, the issue of relevance has aroused new and wider interest in view of narrowing employment outlets, in particular in the public services and education, and the need for adults to adapt to technological change. Special pressure might be put on particular institutions or disciplines, although it may rightly be argued that it is difficult to speak of vocational relevance for certain types of education that serve a wide range of interests and purposes. Where the general aim is to develop activities that are more relevant to working life, the following guidelines might be considered:

i) Placing more emphasis on technology and applied subjects, a trend that is already noted in government policies and in student demand, but one that may have to be stepped up. This may imply changes within departments, major reforms in the overall orientation of studies and efforts to motivate young students to enter such fields.

ii) Reviewing the content and structure of studies, with a view to avoiding a situation where substantial numbers of graduates leave the system with few usable skills. Such reforms should aim at imparting a more practical orientation to studies and making them more accessible to adult students. In addition, encouragement should be given to the integration of general and vocational studies rather than the substitution of one for the other(3).

---

3. See "The reform of studies and the state of research in higher education", OECD document, Paris, 1981.

iii) Fostering more flexible ways of participation in higher education, not only to ensure a more considered choice of subjects and better student motivation but also to promote a mutual enrichment of work experience and higher education studies and encourage a two-way adaptation process through the development of new combinations of work and study or recurrent education.

The case of the humanities and social sciences calls for particular attention. National reports and one of the Secretariat documents (4) on this subject point to the growing role which these disciplines will be called upon to play, particularly as part of broadly-based initial courses of higher education studies - a role which is increasingly necessary to maintain a healthy balance with highly specialised courses, especially in technologically-based degrees. Their essential role in developing perceptive, as opposed to purely thinking and analytical capabilities, is increasingly recognised both within higher education itself and in the evolution of job functions in all branches of economic activity. Some countries, such as Japan, clearly place special emphasis on the general education of young graduates.

III. NEW PARTNERSHIP BETWEEN HIGHER EDUCATION AND THE WORLD OF WORK

The moves suggested above, whether they refer to the overall planning of the system or the relevance of higher education, would already represent an effort by the system or its institutions to respond better to broader social needs. It would also be necessary to establish closer relationships with the world of work, particularly if higher education is to shift its emphasis towards the concerns of the private sector.

The recent CERI Conference on Higher Education and the Community (5) has illustrated and documented the development of such new partnerships and interactions, with special emphasis on the service function of higher education institutions. The main services that higher education renders to the community are its traditional roles of teaching and research. In addition to these, however, a number of innovative activities are being undertaken to meet demands mainly expressed at the regional or local level. The service function has always been, implicitly or explicitly, one of the functions of higher education, particularly mass higher education such as in the United States ; it now tends to receive increased emphasis in all systems.

Since these activities are launched mainly to respond to regional interests and through local initiatives, one may well expect a wide diversity of perceptions and achievements. There are strong arguments

---

4. See "The reform of studies and the state of research in higher education", op. cit.
5. See The University and the Community; the Problems of Changing Relationships, OECD/CERI, Paris, 1982.

in favour of such developments. They tend to build up closer links between higher education and community life, and this in turn may improve the image of higher education in society. When focused on concrete problems of special interest to a region or sector of economic activity, they help break down the isolation of institutions. This in turn may improve their teaching activities, often accused of being abstract or academic. Moreover, service to the local community may bring additional resources to the institutions. Such criticism as is voiced derives from the fear in certain quarters that higher education institutions may lose their autonomy if they engage in activities that are not directly related to their traditional roles. In particular, emphasis on applied or problem-centred research may well be at the expense of fundamental or basic research. The dispersion of efforts that this may imply could also be criticised on other grounds: such grass-root initiatives may appear to some as lacking in consistency and needing a degree of overall control. In fact, the accountability issue, especially in periods of financial stringency, may well leave scope for opposing arguments.

It would be surprising if, given the financial constraints, such a strong trend were not to persist throughout the 1980s. The conclusions of the CERI Conference spelled out future prospects in two broad respects:

i) greater involvement of higher education institutions in applied or problem-centred research in co-operation with or on behalf of public or private enterprises; this could also take the form of consultancy services, for instance smaller firms, in particular to facilitate technology transfers;

ii) greater participation in analysis and research to solve problems of interest to the local or regional community, and possibly actual participation in the implementation of relevant social programmes. Such activities might perhaps be more in line with the concern for the public interest prevailing in many higher education institutions.

What will be the precise commitment or responsibility in terms of governmental policy with regard to activities of this kind, which are initiated and conducted by the institutions themselves? The answer will certainly be very different according to country, in view of the very different relationships prevailing between governments and institutions. One point to be underlined, however, is the need to provide more flexibility in the regulations governing the employment of academic staff, if the latter are to participate actively in such innovative projects.

A broader issue is, of course, whether such internal initiatives, however welcome, suffice to ensure appropriate communication with the world of work and the community generally, particularly the private sector. Strengthening the links between higher education and the world of work is, of course, a much debated issue: it could be argued that this would amount to selling out higher education to private interests. On the other hand, it could be said that the present system is not properly balanced in that it overwhelmingly reflects the needs and ideas of the academic professions; that higher education, or at least the university sector, has largely become a self-justifying enterprise. Some countries no doubt count on the natural course of events to promote co-operation and provide the incentive for change. In other countries it may be felt that an organised framework is needed.

In which areas would such an organised partnership be most fruitful? The following areas are proposed:

i) Information, guidance and placement: this is an area where increased communication at central or local level would be highly beneficial. Some countries place emphasis on information given to students at the outset of their studies, others on briefing employers, launching graduates on the labour market, organising work experience schemes, with a view to encouraging employers to recruit graduates in non-traditional positions.

ii) Co-operation in research: this should extend beyond applied research, which responds to relatively short-term interests, to encompass strategic research(6), to promote industrial innovation and expansion. A reform of post-graduate studies could also be considered, under the joint auspices of higher education and industry.

iii) Participation of representatives of the world of work in course design and the exchange of staff between higher education and industry: such modes of co-operation already exist in some countries, particularly in such fields as medicine or technology. It is to be feared that current academic employment conditions might force academics to adopt a conservative stance, at a time when more flexibility would be welcome on many grounds; hence the necessity for innovative proposals.

Patterns of co-operation may be conceived in a variety of ways. Some feel that closer links between higher education institutions and other sectors may lead to increased bureaucratisation and to political criticism; others think that if efforts are focused on concrete and well-defined areas, this might provide incentives for more active participation. A key political issue is, of course, who finally controls higher education; an equally important question is how to devise modes of collaboration that serve to enhance the vitality of the institutions.

---

6. See "The reform of studies and the state of research in higher education", op.cit.

Theme 3

NEW PATTERNS OF AUTHORITY[1]

THE CONTEXT

Higher education institutions in OECD countries have had to face a formidable array of new pressures in recent decades; these have been outlined in the preceding Overview. The pressure of numbers has perhaps been the one which has presented the greatest challenge to the system as a whole and to individual institutions.

This relationship between quantitative development and governance is certainly a complex one. In very simplified terms two major impacts of expansion on patterns of authority in higher education may be identified. First, growth has stimulated public attention. Soaring costs, the large number of people affected, and the real or perceived importance of higher education for economic and social development have incited demands for public accountability. Second, growing size will create problems of co-ordination in any organisation.

The pressures on higher education, however, largely reflect broader trends in Member countries. Details aside, demands for participation and autonomy have been voiced in practically all countries and in most public service sectors. Interestingly, the higher education sector would often seem to have pioneered developments which later permeated through to the rest of society.

The traditional patterns of authority in higher education have varied greatly among Member countries as have their responses to the new constraints. Perhaps the briefest way to describe policy developments is in terms of <u>convergence</u>. Such convergence has occurred in two major respects.

First, in all OECD countries higher education now occupies a more prominent role on the political agenda than before the period of explosive growth in the 1950s and 1960s. There has been a considerable growth in administrative staff at both central and local levels. Specialised bodies have been set up for co-ordination and policy analysis.

---

1. For a more detailed review of trends see "New patterns of authority in higher education", OECD document, Paris, 1981.

Though higher education systems still vary greatly in their degree of centralisation and politicisation, the trend towards central co-ordination has been pervasive, even in countries where the autonomy accorded to higher education institutions has been greatest, such as the United Kingdom and the United States. In some of the more centralised systems - good examples are France and Sweden - attempts have been made to decentralise the decision-making process.

The second major trend has been towards participative forms of governance in higher education. Here, it is in Western Europe that the changes have been by far the most dramatic. The advent of mass higher education in combination with student unrest signalled the decline of the traditional "professors' university". Its autocratic structure of authority was particularly ill-suited to mass institutions. It had to give way to some kind of "group university". Comprehensive reforms in most countries of Western Europe created very complex decision-making structures with "graded" voting rights for all groups within the institutions. Changes were much less dramatic in the non-European systems. Here, the trend towards more participatory governance has not taken the form of elaborate systems of formal representation but, rather, has manifested itself as more intensified consultation on an ad hoc basis. Still, it seems safe to say that the trend has been present in all Member countries.

THE CENTRAL CHALLENGE: NEW PARTNERSHIPS

As in other policy sectors, governments in OECD countries have experienced the reality that policy formulation with respect to higher education is one thing, implementation often quite another. It may even be argued that policy implementation in the area of higher education is particularly difficult, due inter alia to its susceptibility to market forces (both on the input side - student demand - and the output side - the labour market), and its peculiar organisational characteristics which will be discussed below.
With the creation of elaborate systems of representation and participation at regional and institutional levels in many countries, problems of implementation may even have been aggravated, since governments now have to cope with a much larger number of legitimised interest groups. It has, for example, been reported from a number of countries that, contrary to the expectations of many reformers, "external" representatives who were supposed to act as instruments of government vis-à-vis institutions have, instead, taken on the role of eloquent defenders of their institutions.

Governments cannot resolve the major policy issues in the area of higher education governance without reference to basic value positions concerning the nature of higher education as a social institution and the legitimacy of various interest groups in determining its future. In this, due account should be taken by policy makers of the experience of the 1960s and 1970s. Above all, it is important for them to realise that there are difficult trade-offs to be made between democracy and efficiency, and that there are important problems of implementing reforms in higher education.

There is no simple way around the basic dilemma between the urge to reform by way of central policy-making and the wish for an autonomous and pluralist system of higher education. It is a question of finding the right balance.

The Conference, therefore, provided an opportune moment for taking stock of the experience of the last fifteen years or so with various forms of participatory governance of institutions of higher education in Member countries. Of particular interest are: attempts at central and regional co-ordination - now they have operated, with what effects, at what cost and what they promise for the future; how, within the context of legal and constitutional realities, a new division of responsibilities between governments and institutions could be defined; ways and means of developing new partnerships in higher education so that institutions can be both assisted and encouraged to move forward in new directions and assume new functions commensurate with needs.

Four broad themes are proposed below within which specific issues can be discussed. These are:

I. The special position of higher education within the social and ideological polity.

II. Changes in the connotation and application of the concept of autonomy.

III. Changes in participation and the decision-making process.

IV. The perennial dilemma between democracy and efficiency.

THE ISSUES

I. DOES HIGHER EDUCATION DESERVE SPECIAL TREATMENT?

The debate surrounding problems of governance in higher education has pointed to its eminently political and ideological nature. Policy positions are often linked with general views on the proper role of government in society. Interestingly, however, it is argued quite frequently that higher education is special in the sense that it deserves other arrangements in terms of governance than those which apply to most other policy sectors. In what respects is higher education regarded as unique?

Most arguments in this vein seem to be elaborations of two basic observations. First, the very nature of academic work is said to necessitate special considerations with respect to governance. The primary tasks of the academic enterprise have been the creation and dissemination of often highly abstract and esoteric knowledge.

The discipline was the basic organisational unit in such a setting. The disciplines divide the academic profession into tens or even hundreds of sub-professions with very little in common. Disciplines create criss-crossing patterns of communication and authority which defy the formal organisation of the institution and the system.

Second, it is argued that higher education should perform a special role in cultural development. The independent criticism provided by academics has been a prominent feature of Western civilisation. And it is equally vital today to the health of pluralist democracy. Society needs disinterested social criticism inspired primarily by a search for truth, even if the boundaries between objective views and political ideology are not always easy to delineate. Only strong and independent institutions can be expected to perform this function effectively.

The counter-arguments in response to the view that higher education is so special that it deserves special treatment in terms of governance are many and varied. In brief, they may be summarised as follows: while it may well be true that higher education and research have unique features, this is not sufficient to motivate exception from ordinary political accountability. Academics are of course professionals, and as all professionals they should have an important say in matters related to their specialist field. But in matters such as allocation of resources between disciplines and institutions, content of vocational training, etc., they are no better equipped than others to decide. Here, the broad interests of pluralist democracy should participate in decision-making; and while academics must certainly be accorded an important role in cultural development, this role is for every citizen to play and not just for a privileged elite. Besides, there are many historical examples of academics who, instead of being social critics, have sided with the Establishment of the day.

Furthermore, the different treatment accorded to different types of higher education institution is fuelling the debate. For example, universities are said to have a separate global or national vocation, the prime purpose of which is the production of knowledge on a universal scale. Their true environment is the international scientific community for whom their output is intended and to whose judgement they defer; for example, university research workers are answerable only to their peers and therefore deserve special treatment.

On the other hand, other post-secondary institutions have a special assignment and must adjust to local and regional economic and vocational realities. Such institutions can scarcely shake loose from an environment on which they depend for their resources. This is to perpetuate the system set up in the 1960s to diversify the aims and functions of the different levels of higher education institutions. Polytechnics in the United Kingdom, Community and Regional Colleges in the United States, Colleges of Advanced Education in Australia, Regional Colleges in Norway, and many others, are regional in scope, mainly because of the vocational nature of their training. They respond to local economic needs, provide recurrent education and carry out applied research for the benefit of the local community.

Furthermore, special treatment means also more prestige. New types of courses for non-traditional students, particularly short and part-time courses, carry low prestige within higher education. The same could be said about fundamental versus applied or problem-oriented research.

II. WHAT DOES AUTONOMY MEAN TODAY?

There can be no policy discussion on higher education governance without first attempting to elucidate the very concept of autonomy. At the outset, it is necessary to state clearly:

i) the various connotations attached to the concept of autonomy;
ii) who is to enjoy autonomy;
iii) in relation to whom it is to be enjoyed;
iv) the extent of autonomy in specific areas.

On the first point, as a report from Spain suggests, the idea of parity of control on the part of teachers and students that first emerged at the beginning of the century in the Argentine University of Cordoba and which largely inspires the current Latin-American concepts of university autonomy, has little to do with the form of governance of any of the American universities with more solid traditions of autonomy. Furthermore, the meaning of autonomy changes according to whether it concerns privately-owned or public universities. Let us say at this stage that autonomy implies the power to make independent decisions, the extent of which may vary considerably from one country to another.

On the second point, there is often considerable confusion: it makes a world of difference whether the concept applies to the institution or only to full professors.

On the third point, it seems reasonable to focus on the relationship between the State or central government and the institutions. However, one should be aware of the importance of other relationships. For hundreds of years, the Church was the main counterpart to universities in many OECD countries. Today, regional and local authorities, private corporations, professions, unions and other interest groups all serve to impair the autonomy of higher education institutions. It should be noted that from this standpoint some aspects of the latter's activities are more important than others. In the normative literature on university autonomy, the following key areas which relate to societal objectives are frequently cited: finance, curricula and examinations, staff selection and employment conditions, student admission and research.

Finally, the degree of autonomy in specific substantive areas can and does vary immensely between systems. Nowhere is the autonomy of institutions vis-à-vis the environment "total". It also varies in relation to the different institutions themselves according to the aims and functions which are assigned to them.

Higher education institutions, particularly the universities, have now to respond to new social, economic and cultural pressures and the specific needs of society and of the communities in which they are located. This means that the more higher education turns toward the society, the more it will itself be affected by the decisions, inequalities and conflicts which, in varying degrees, disturb society as a whole. The traditional concept of autonomy - to develop a free zone, away from the currents of opinion, a neutral territory in which researchers may enjoy total freedom of expression - must therefore be reviewed. Within the concept of autonomy, the accent is no longer so much on independence as responsibility; autonomy should be increasingly seen as the link which ensures that information is transmitted freely, and as a way of "negotiating" on an equal footing, the planning of teaching and research activities. As the Trade Union Advisory Committee has noted(2), "the concept of the autonomy of the Universities has to be developed in a way which extends the possibilities to interact with the community as a whole, in a democratic way". It is not so much a matter of safeguarding and preserving the traditional autonomy, but of transforming it in order to bring more objectivity and knowledge to the social system.

Such a change implies that the previous legal concept of autonomy - which was defensive in nature - should give way to another, with institutions mobilising their resources in response to vocational training needs within the region or undertaking research for public or private bodies. But as was revealed by discussions at the CERI Conference on "Higher Education and the Community: New Partnerships and Interaction", in 1980, higher education institutions will be unable to serve society unless they can fully exercise their critical function, retain their objectivity and assert their professional authority to carry out analyses on a scientific basis. In other words, higher education institutions must be guaranteed the necessary independence and status if they are to serve the community in the fullest sense.

III. PARTICIPATION AND THE DECISION-MAKING PROCESS

Most university governing boards in OECD countries are made up of elected or nominated members who represent both the academic and non-academic community. Both BIAC (the Business and Industry Advisory Committee) and TUAC (the Trade Union Advisory Committee) would wish to see a good balance between representatives of teaching staff and students on the one hand, and unions, industry and local/regional authorities on the other.

---

2. Views expressed by TUAC at the International Conference on "Higher Education and the Community: New Partnerships and Interaction", OECD/CERI, Paris, February 1980.

Problems are posed by both of these categories. In the first case, it is often claimed that participation by the various university groups has resulted in institutional paralysis; a number of reasons have been cited: the influence of professors who are mainly concerned with the welfare of their own departments; the lack of interest on the part of some faculty, students and service personnel; the use of the decision-making body for radicalising and politicising the university; the difficulty of translating policy decisions into resource allocation decisions, etc.

As far as the "external representatives" are concerned, they tend to be confined, at least in certain countries, to committees concerned primarily with finance and administration and they have no say in matters of curricula, research or staff appointment. Furthermore, they are usually local personalities from business firms, the municipal or regional authority or the professions - virtually all graduates of higher education. Paradoxically, their presence on university boards may well serve to strengthen the elitist aspects of higher education. In particular, the role of the professions in controlling certain branches of higher education has recently come to the fore in a number of countries. This being said, particular mention should be made of the special case, and one which often goes unremarked, of univeristies (as in the United Kingdom or the United States) where the external representatives include "laymen".

Which internal and external interest groups should be represented in the decision-making process and why? In what fields: management, curriculum review and development, programme planning, academic standards, teaching evaluation? How can allowance be made for the interests of the various groups in society - enterprises, trade unions, local/regional authorities - through new forms of participation and negotiation? To what extent should these external representatives participate in formulating curricula and research policy?

Research provides a good example of such problems. The establishment of research priorities is not an accustomed task for higher education institutions, and whilst it seems to imply a valuable concern for a measure of self-determination there is the undoubted problem of how it is to be done. It may, for example, require that the central authority be strengthened at the expense of traditional departments or faculties. It will be necessary to decide whether research committees within institutions should have responsibility for allocating research appropriations available (whether or not the amount is known beforehand) and if so, on what criteria. If there are to be procedures of this kind, it will need to be considered whether a single institution possesses the breadth of expertise to make objective judgements of scientific excellence across all the fields of science. There is the question of whether such a research committee should have the right to vet all applications by faculty members to outside sources of research funds which would constitute a considerable erosion of traditional independence. Whilst difficult issues of this nature inevitably arise, the desirability of institutional planning of this kind is increasingly being debated.

Finally, with respect to participation in higher education, it seems useful to policy discussions to bear in mind the important distinction between formal and informal participation. The real influence of the various interest groups can, of course, not always be gauged from formal positions. This does not, however, warrant the conclusion that the mode of participation adopted is unimportant; on the contrary, it may well make the difference between reasonably efficient decision-making and deadlock.

IV. TRADE-OFF BETWEEN DEMOCRACY AND EFFICIENCY

All parties should recognise that in the end any model of governance must represent a reasonable trade-off between democracy and efficiency. Both aspects are important, and not necessarily incompatible, if it is accepted that the issue is ultimately settled with recourse to basic value positions. But this does not imply that it is not worthwhile investigating the specific nature of that trade-off in higher education or analysing the current situation in different systems and institutions.

It should be possible to agree that, irrespective of their specific contents, teaching and research are the primary tasks of higher education, and constitute its raison d'être as a separate social institution. Other activities are secondary in the sense that they must be judged in terms of their contribution to the creation of a supportive environment for teaching and research.

A problem which, though not unknown in other types of organisations, seems particularly acute in higher education is gauging whether or not the institution is fulfilling its primary functions. While the need for performance criteria is generally recognised, attempts to establish a productivity function in higher education have borne out the complexity of the problem: and results have been disappointing. Without going further into the matter, mention should be made of one major implication: while in a car factory it should be possible - though difficult - to establish some kind of systematic relationship between "democracy" and "efficiency", this would appear virtually impossible in higher education. Here, one has to settle for very crude observations, almost exclusively related to "inputs" rather than "outputs".

Two additional observations are called for; both relate to the widely held fear in some higher education institutions in OECD countries that "democracy" has reached a point where "efficiency" is threatened. First, in several countries, and in particular those with the most "democratic" models of governance, a growing opinion argues that governance is so time-consuming that it "crowds out" (to use a popular term) teaching and research. Even staunch proponents of participatory governance are increasingly beginning to wonder whether the price is worth paying. In many institutions priority is now assigned to an intensive search for time-saving mechanisms. It is felt that the large number of endless committee meetings are wasting everybody's time. Perhaps it is time to end the control of everybody by everybody else?

Second, there is evidence from some countries that in the 1970s the number of administrators and support staff has grown much faster than the number of teachers or researchers - or students, for that matter. This can of course be interpreted in a number of ways. Some institutions were probably "under-administered" after the student boom during the 1960s. And much which passes for "bureaucratisation" is the inevitable consequence of growing size and complexity. Somewhat paradoxically, decentralisation has obviously caused some of the "bureaucratisation" in countries which have attempted it; France and Sweden are cases in point.

However, there is also the ominous possibility that democracy breeds bureaucracy. Apart from being time-consuming for teachers and researchers (and all others involved), participatory decision-making is cumbersome in a number of other ways. The result is "inefficiency" which must in some manner be compensated. Decisions must often be made quickly and authoritatively. If the representative bodies cannot perform, somebody else must. Ample evidence from some systems of higher education indicates that a combination of bureaucrats and activist professors are dominant, while representative bodies are becoming merely "ornamental".

These are issues on which clear-cut decisions and recommendations cannot be easily arrived at. Discussion of them, however, in an international context, may be particularly rewarding for all those concerned, both the policy-makers and those responsible for the day-to-day running of institutions of higher education.

Theme 4

FINANCING AND REDEPLOYMENT OF RESOURCES

THE CONTEXT

The great expansion in higher education expenditure during the 1960s and early 1970s had its roots in two widely held beliefs. One was that higher education helped to promote social equality by acting as a vehicle of social mobility. The second was that higher education helped to promote economic growth and social development by making the labour force more productive. This led to what in some respects was a "laissez-faire" attitude to planning higher education provision. Places were made available mainly on the basis of expressed student demand in the belief that, by acceding to this demand, equality would be promoted and a more productive and wealthier economy would result. The precise mechanisms by which these beliefs were translated into plans for higher education and then into political action differ between OECD countries but the general relationship was widely accepted throughout the OECD area.

Basing provision on student demand worked reasonably well as long as student numbers were growing. Although the pattern of higher education may not always have achieved optimal efficiency, the availability of incremental resources each year meant that most claimants were at least partly satisfied.

However, by 1980, most OECD countries had experienced several years of stagnation or even contraction in public expenditure on higher education[1]. This trend must clearly be linked to the general economic situation and the pressures on public expenditure. However there has also been a levelling off in demand for higher education with, in addition, the prospect of very slow growth in demand in most countries during this decade. Both population trends and apparent student demand seem to point in this direction. Any policy of basing overall resource provision simply on crude estimates of student numbers is thus of doubtful viability. For, if the level of public resources allocated to higher education continues to be linked to the level of enrolments of young people, then higher education may well no longer be able to fulfil some of its fundamental tasks, such as research, or respond to new demands, such as more extensive adult education.

---

1. See "Higher education expenditure in OECD countries", OECD document, Paris, 1981.

With respect to financing, therefore, it seems that higher education has now reached a turning point and that new ways will have to be sought to facilitate a shift of emphasis in its activities and to stimulate its quality and vitality. Equally, it will be necessary to re-consider the mechanisms of its financing and how they affect the distribution of social demand.

THE ISSUES

The following issues merit special consideration:

- Principles for planning the development of higher education
- The financing of higher education in the 1980s
- Encouraging vitality in higher education and problems of staff development.

I. PRINCIPLES FOR PLANNING THE DEVELOPMENT OF HIGHER EDUCATION

The most fundamental policy planning problem for higher education in the 1980s is to decide what guidelines should replace or supplement the principle of acceding to student demand. It seems essential therefore to review possible criteria and to suggest which are the most appropriate in the likely socio-economic conditions of the 1980s. Many countries began to impose a numerus clausus on all or some of their higher education faculties in the 1970s though this action was often no more than a crude attempt at limiting public expenditure rather than based on a coherent plan for the development of higher education.

New criteria for the long-term development of higher education must be worked out in the light of the following considerations:

a) The belief that higher education contains the key to social equality or to economic growth is now widely disputed. The research evidence is at best contradictory and calls for clarification.

b) Current political priorities in many OECD countries seem to place both economic growth and social equality lower down the list than was the case in the 1960s. Some consideration needs to be given to the implications of this for higher education and also to the possibility of a revival of one or both of these aims as a high political priority.

c) Many of the earlier planning criteria treated higher education as if it were a homogeneous linear activity. This notion is no longer valid - if it ever was. Higher education serves many functions for many people.

If social demand, particularly the demand from young people, can no longer be considered as the sole or main criterion in planning, then others must be used in determining the appropriate provision of public resources for higher education. Since such resources are limited, it might be useful to think in terms of priorities, though countries may formulate their public priorities in different ways: the following aspects merit consideration:

   i) the balance between research and teaching;
  ii) the balance between higher education for young people and further education for adults;
 iii) emphasis on responding to social demand or on preserving excellence;
  iv) the relative importance accorded to the vocational dimension of higher education;
   v) the concentration of resources on selected sectors or institutions or a wider spread.

II. THE FINANCING OF HIGHER EDUCATION IN THE 1980s

In a period of financial stringency, a sensible starting point is to ask what gains can be made in the use of the resources actually available to institutions of higher education through more effective management. The question itself is controversial since, despite the steady increase in enrolments in recent years, resources have been declining and were already felt to be insufficient in 1975. The experience of Denmark, however, shows that reform of financing and planning methods can be fruitful. Traditional financing methods did not allow expenditure to be analysed by category and actual use, while a method involving institutions' participation and co-operation should provide for better management. Activities under the IMHE Programme show that higher education institutions have every interest in managing their resources more effectively and the capacity to do so(2).

Secondly, the aim must be to facilitate the redeployment of public resources within institutions, between similar or comparable institutions, as well as between the various sectors of higher education. The Danish reforms are designed with this in mind. Policy planning and selecting priorities is one thing, implementation quite another. Even if basic principles can be established, a fundamental problem for both governments and institutions will be selecting the criteria for assessing the viability of their activities. Given the range of functions, this is not easy. Student demand and costs are obvious indicators. However, other criteria are also relevant.

---

2. Programme on Institutional Management in Higher Education, "Ten years of service to universities", OECD/CERI, Paris, 1980.

For example a high cost activity which is unpopular with students might make claim for increased resources on the basis, for example, of research output, or institutions might point to the successful entry into working life of their graduates. In the 1970s, many United States institutions were obliged to undertake such analyses and to develop new methods for evaluating alternative uses of available resources.

A third question is whether private financing should be sought. This issue is not very relevant to countries such as Japan or the United States where, traditionally, private higher education has an important place. In Europe, however, higher education is essentially financed from the public purse and the question of private funding is a very sensitive issue in countries where higher education is considered as a public service. At this turning point in the history of higher education, however, it is necessary to follow some new paths; in terms of financing, this implies an internal redeployment of resources and other sources of funds. One possibility would be to develop a private higher education sector which, backed up by a system of loans or grants would allow students a wider choice and oblige higher education institutions to become more competitive. Large enterprises could also create their own universities, an example being the Toyota University in Japan. Contributions from firms to public institutions for the further training of their staff could constitute another source of funds, as is already the case in Germany. Although it has been shown that even today a substantial portion of the real costs of higher education are met from private sources[3], there may be a case for letting students contribute a larger share of the costs of their education, be it in the form of fees, various forms of loans, graduate tax, etc. The possible effects of schemes based on this principle would require detailed assessment of their implications.

Consideration should also be given to the question of what financing mechanisms are most appropriate for different activities of higher education institutions. New forms of aid for young part-time students could be envisaged; adult students could be at least partially financed by social transfer schemes, such as paid educational leave, this in turn being partly financed by employers. Another possibility would be to call on employers who take on highly specialised post-graduates or who benefit from applied research to provide a greater contribution.

The financing of university research warrants special consideration. Financing based on the number of enrolments may no longer be appropriate in the 1980s. If this criterion were to be maintained, the resources which universities allocate to research within their normal operational budgets would decrease, at least in those sectors where the number of students is declining. Under these conditions, one question is whether research and teaching can be treated separately in planning resource allocation among and within institutions of higher education. A policy which treats the two

---

3. "Higher education expenditure in OECD countries", op. cit.

aspects separately is being considered in a number of countries, and has already been adopted in Sweden, in order to maintain the level of research funding. There are, however, considerable risks in implementing such a policy which should be carefully examined. Another question is whether governments should make special funds available for "refinancing" or "recapitalising" university research and for replacing obsolete equipment. Greater efficiency in the use of resources could perhaps be achieved if research policies of governments and institutions were better co-ordinated, but the problem of course is how to ensure such co-ordination.

Recourse to external funding for university research, in particular from private sources, is no new phenomenon. In some countries, however, growing dependence of this type of finance is causing concern for the future of fundamental research as the trend is to shift resources to short-term and applied research. One problem is how to develop, in co-operation with industry, strategic research aimed at promoting technological and industrial innovation. Academic institutions could undoubtedly make a major contribution in this type of activity which represents a middle ground between research of purely scientific interest on the one hand, and research of no more than short-term industrial interest on the other(4).

III. ENCOURAGING VITALITY IN HIGHER EDUCATION AND PROBLEMS OF STAFF DEVELOPMENT

Whatever changes take place in methods of finance and even if there are substantial increases in demand from new groups of students, slow growth seems to be the most optimistic prospect for the 1980s. This is likely to give rise to a number of planning problems at the institutional and system level.

The emergence of surplus capacity in higher education will have far-reaching effects. Competition between institutions will become more acute. Attempts by institutions and vested interests within them to maintain their position may well be dysfunctional from the point of view of the system as a whole and often even from the viewpoint of their own long-term interests. In particular, innovation of all kinds is likely to suffer.

However, the most intractable planning problems are likely to arise from the rigidities of staff structures. Even if new kinds of students can be attracted, flexibility in staffing will be essential if institutions are to adapt to the needs of this new clientele.

A major concern in this respect will be to develop new attitudes among teaching staff at all levels and to enhance their morale and enthusiasm. Lack of career prospects, limited opportunities for

---

4. See "The reform of studies and the place of research in higher education", op. cit.

research, the need to take up activities which do not carry the same prestige as their traditional tasks, are leading to discouragement and tension in the academic world. Since a major objective is to preserve the vitality of the staff and their capacity to respond to new needs, it is important to demonstrate the positive aspects of the shift in priorities.

In particular, it will be necessary to offer wider possibilities for career development and enrichment. The further education of adults faced with new functions and technologies alongside the development of closer links with the world of work and the local community could offer such opportunities. A certain amount of additional training may be necessary for this to be realised. In the field of research, the ageing of teaching staff and the lack of renewal are threatening the intellectual vitality of many higher education institutions. Measures have already been taken in some countries to encourage young people to pursue an academic career, (for example the Heisenberg programme in Germany). It should be noted that higher education is not alone in facing a situation of limited prospects for career promotion and staff mobility. But higher education should not only look at ways in which the other sectors of the economy have coped with this type of problem; it should also seek ways and means of co-operating with industry and the services likely to bring a positive and mutually beneficial response to the problem.

In some countries at least, it would seem that the central problem is that of introducing greater flexibility into staff recruitment and employment at a time when the current trend is, conversely, towards greater employment protection. It would be desirable to develop a greater degree of permeability between institutions and between the various types of higher education, but also between higher education and the different sectors of the economy, in order to promote a diversification of career opportunities.

To a large extent, however, such developments will be determined by decisions affecting the total level of resources made available to higher education and their distribution between its various sectors, functions, institutions and fields of study. It seems essential that in taking such decisions, due consideration be given to the long-term objectives of higher education, in order not to destroy its capacity to respond to changing needs and to fulfil its fundamental functions in society.

CONCERNS AND DILEMMAS IN THE YEARS AHEAD

"At the beginning of the 1980s the overriding concern... seems to be how to sustain public confidence in and support for a system which, in most countries, is no longer growing in such a way as to ensure its continued dynamic evolution... In many countries there appears to be a crisis of confidence which is approaching alarming dimensions. Unless new policies are rapidly conceived and implemented there may be a real danger, over the longer term, that the potential of higher education for supporting countries' economic vitality and the welfare of their citizens, through cultural, scientific and technological development, could be seriously and perhaps irretrievably compromised".

(From the Chairman's concluding remarks)

The role and functions of the universities

It was clear throughout the discussions in the Conference that the crisis to which the Chairman referred in his concluding remarks is not merely one of public confidence vis-à-vis the performance of higher education; it is also, and perhaps more fundamentally, an internal crisis of purpose, that is one which touches on the very nature of individual institutions, their roles and functions and their place in the total higher education system. In this, a reappraisal of the special position of the university appeared as crucial.

In a period of growth colleges and universities could absorb new functions relatively easily. New demands were usually accompanied by additional resources so that on-going activities were rarely reduced or eliminated. The situation now is quite different. In the first place, the extended period of growth and the diversification which went with it have led to diffusion of mission and purposes of higher education institutions. There is consequently a need for clarification, if only to avoid that such diffusion is not interpreted as mere confusion. Second, against continuing pressures on higher education to assume new roles, budgetary constraints, and in certain cases slackening student demand, necessitate decisions about the contraction or elimination of programmes. Such decisions require an examination of purposes on the part of government policy-makers and the institutions themselves, in that they imply not just choice among programmes, but options affecting the fundamental role of the different sectors of higher education.

In the late 1960s and the early 1970s, short-cycle or non-university institutions were the ones which had the greatest difficulties in defining their own mission and identity within the academic community. By now - and this came out quite clearly in the Conference - it is the university sector which in many Member countries constitutes the focus of greatest concern. Frequent criticisms vis-à-vis higher education - such as lack of responsiveness to new demands, in particular those stemming from the employment world and from the surrounding community, declining quality and vitality, inability to reconcile traditional value and functions with the requirements of mass education - are being primarily directed to the universities.

This must be seen in the context of two additional considerations relating specifically to the position of the universities: first, recognition of the reality that in many counties the universities, because of their strongly entrenched position as the keepers of academic standards, are the pace-setters for the entire system and there are limitations to any policy for reform which attempts to by-pass them; second, the real danger, strongly voiced at the Conference, that the essential qualities of higher education institutions might be impaired by over-responsiveness to assumed outside needs and pressures. Recognising that the term "essential qualities" applies differently to different institutions, the fact remains that the main concern here is with those qualities which traditionally have been associated with the functions and role of the university.

It follows from the above that an essential element in the discussion of future higher education policies would involve a subtained effort to reappraise the position of the universities.

Access to Higher Education

Delegates at the Conference recognised that decisions concerning the overall intake of higher education and the way students are distributed among the various options will continue to be of strategic importance, not only for higher education, but for overall educational policy.

The following problem areas emerged from the discussions as calling for further study and consideration:

i) The relationship between secondary and higher education

The main need which was seen here was for closer co-ordination of policies vis-à-vis the two levels; otherwise the severe strain which already exists will tend to sharpen, particularly in European countries, where the trend is to set limits to the overall intake capacity of higher education. Specific issues which were considered to merit further study included: balance to be achieved between the various self-sufficient or internally defined objectives of secondary education and those which are more or less imposed by higher education institutions through their entrance requirements; the question of who should decide on the basic entrance qualifications to higher education and, when entry standards are not met, who should bear the main responsibility for remedial education; what should be the degree of uniformity of entrance requirements among and within different types of institutions and programmes; what value is to be assigned to vocational and practical talents.

ii) <u>Alleviating the impact of restrictive policies on the chances of under-represented groups</u>

In several countries the proportion of higher education students from low socio-economic origins seems to stagnate, and even to decline in some of the more selective and prestigious institutions. Cuts in student aid schemes or reforms in admission policies without careful consideration of their equity implications carry the risk of further deterioration of the situation of these groups. Increase in the participation and improvements to the educational careers of women in higher education (including a more balanced distribution by sex in certain fields of study) as well as the participation of mature students were clearly seen as a high priority in most Member countries. Equally important, in a selected number of them, is the improved participation of minorities and groups from sparsely populated areas.

iii) <u>New forms of participation</u>

The discussion also pointed clearly to the changes that were needed in higher education as a result of the increased presence of new groups, but also of the growing demand both from such groups and the traditional young clientele for new forms of participation in the light of new life patterns. The development of part-time studies, of schemes which combine, in a variety of ways, work and education, whether offered in conventional or in non-traditional higher education institutions, distant learning and open universities, and other opportunities opening up by new technological developments, were seen as specific topics calling for closer investigation.

<u>Changing links between higher education and working life</u>

As usual in discussions on this topic, it was easy to reach general agreement on the need for closer links between higher education and the world of work: there was far less consensus as to the ways and means of how this could be accomplished. The discussion around what importance should be assigned to manpower forecasts in higher education planning revealed both widely differing viewpoints and a strong ambivalence among educational decision-makers. Distrust and scepticism were frequently combined with the belief, or the wish, that certain types of manpower planning can be used in providing a broad steer to the higher education system. The real question which participants seemed to be addressing was that of the type of information on employment trends which could be most helpful as guidelines for quantitative planning and also as a basis for student counselling and information.

There was great interest in and support for the view that the way to improving the relationship between higher education and the world of work lay in qualitative changes in the nature of higher education.

The greatest challenge was seen to lie in reforms in the organisation and content of studies, particularly in disciplines where it is highly probable that graduates will have to seek new or different employment outlets. Many of the issues and dilemmas in the organisation of undergraduate curricula provide concrete illustrations of the problems of defining the mission and purpose of the universities referred to above. On the one hand, it is essential that degree level programmes maintain the standards and research basis defined and required by the academic world; on the other, such programmes are under growing pressure to provide a type of knowledge, methods of work and ethos which are less "academic" and more compatible with the requirements of changing work and life patterns. In this respect, a major need is to ensure that the rapid development of a new technological culture and the impact of technological change on the economy and on jobs are effectively reflected in higher education courses, leading to a pragmatic redefinition of "liberal" or "general" education commensurate with the functional requirements of employment conditions in modern societies.

Although the papers and discussions of the Conference focused on undergraduate education, there was widely expressed interest in the examination of similar problems at the post-graduate level, which in some countries has been the sector most seriously affected by current demographic and socio-economic trends.

Discussions of measures aimed at facilitating closer interaction between higher education and the world of work, reflected greater confidence in pragmatism and grass-root initiatives than in strict principles or global policies. A number of recent developments were identified which could provide effective avenues for such co-operation. Examples in this direction are the growing demand for work-study schemes, increased participation of adults, employment of outside people as part-time teachers, development of transition courses, of graduate placement schemes, continuing and post-experience courses. A number of other measures, such as the participation of outside groups in boards of higher education institutions and the encouragement of research contracts with industry, although more controversial, also aroused great interest. There was, indeed, a shared feeling that there is ample room for experiment and innovation in this area and that in this connection the experience of the non-university sector and non-formal education and training schemes would be of particular interest.

Governance and Power in Higher Education

A trend which was repeatedly noted in the Conference discussions was the move in most Member countries during the 1970s towards increased direct involvement of governments in the affairs of higher education. In general, this involvement is being viewed as a necessary, if not always desirable, development. More recently, however, criticism has been voiced about the possible negative effects of certain forms of government control.

In recent years, the academic community has come to recognise both the urgent need for changes in order to maintain the credibility and vitality of their institutions and the fact that such changes can only be accomplished through shared responsibility between governments and institutions. A central question now is how to define and organise such government/institution partnership in pursuit of this common objective. It was generally agreed that governments would have to envisage new approaches implying less top-down authority and allowing for more grass-root initiatives. As stated by the General Rapporteur, "rather than seeking its objectives by direct intervention in the decision-making of institutions, governments will need to develop more indirect incentives for institutions themselves to respond in creative and effective ways".

Discussion of participation and the internal decision-making process of higher education institutions was clearly influenced by the experience of the 1970s with participatory forms of governance and by the impact on universities of recent pressures that they be more responsive to the diverse needs of society. The move towards more democratic or representative decision-making bodies is not being basically questioned, but delegates stressed the need to develop models of internal governance which better reconcile, or at least represent a reasonable trade-off between, democracy and efficiency requirements.

Strong interest was expressed in issues related to the participation of external groups in the decision-making process whether at institutional, regional or central level. The presence of new partners is seen as inextricably linked with the new functions which institutions are called to perform, with particular pressures for closer relationships to the region and surrounding community. A central issue for higher education institutions is how to strengthen these links without surrendering essential commitments to academic freedom and the advancement of knowledge.

Obviously, who decides what these essential commitments are depends on the type of higher education institution. Even more so, it depends on the subject matter concerned and is, therefore, related to the political question of who defines and controls the quality of higher education studies: i.e. in the words of the General Rapporteur: "who will set the rules by which the effectiveness of higher education programmes is to be judged and who will monitor or evaluate the quality of these programmes." Whereas in the past criticism was essentially addressed to the dominance of strictly academic criteria in the assessment of higher education programmes, it was clear from the discussions at the Conference that the pendulum is swinging rapidly in the opposite direction. More and more importance is being assigned to the immediate employment value or social relevance of academic programmes, with the result that the locus of judgement on the quality of the work of higher education institutions is shifting, perhaps excessively, outside the institutions themselves.

Financing and Redeployment of Resources

It is hardly surprising that problems related to sources and methods of financing of higher education occupy a prominent place in government agendas for the 1980s. Indeed, in most Member countries one of the few certainties about the coming years is that resource constraints and financial cutbacks will provide the background against which problems of higher education will have to be resolved.

There was a general feeling at the Conference that the time is opportune to examine in a more systematic way various possibilities for a more diversified pattern of revenue sources. This is a topic of growing interest, even though few of the European Member countries would be ready to accept any major departure from the traditional public service and publicly financed nature of higher education provision. A first question is whether certain groups of students, e.g. some categories of adults, part-time students, foreigners, graduate students, should bear a greater share of the cost of their education, particularly in the form of fees. This issue must, of course, be seen in close relation to policies vis-à-vis student support schemes, in particular with the question of financing through student loans. Debates are also going on as to the extent to which institutions should be encouraged, if not required, to seek other sources of finance. In addition to the issue of fees are the various types of contracts with both private and public groups for teaching (e.g. continuing education), and research as well as different services to the community. It was generally recognised at the Conference that the implications of more "market oriented" higher education institutions should be carefully studied before developing strong incentives in this direction.

Of equal importance were questions of how available resources can be used more effectively through improved planning and management at the institutional level. Close reference was made in this connection to the work being done within the Organisation under the Programme on Institutional Management in Higher Education.

Recognising the strategic role of financial policies and practices in shaping demand for and success in higher education, delegates highlighted the need to examine how different financing measures contribute to enhance or inhibit the participation of under-represented groups. Among the various target groups identified, particular interest was shown for certain categories of adults, e.g. adults without formal entry qualification, unemployed or under-employed adults, women, etc.

There was general agreement that maintaining the vitality of institutions was very closely related to maintaining the vitality of teaching and research staff. Resource stagnation, rigidities of tenure, lack of opportunities for young staff, declining research capacity, were all seen as interrelated factors which affect the intellectual morale of higher education institutions. It was generally recognised that the analytical bases for closer study of these issues hardly existed, though a few brave initiatives were beginning to appear in some Member countries.

STATEMENT BY THE GENERAL RAPPORTEUR

Michael O'Keefe[*]

The purpose of this statement is to identify and discuss a limited number of overall themes and key points of view which emerged from the discussions at the Conference. It is not in any way an exhaustive summary of the discussion.

The background papers and discussions by the delegates identified numerous forces which are likely to affect higher education over the next two decades. Some of these forces come from outside the institutions themselves. Discussed in detail in the background papers, these include a decline in the number of young people, a levelling-off of the past growth in participation rates for higher education, stagnant or declining economic conditions, a lessening of the public's confidence in education, and increases in governmental actions which affect colleges and universities. As the papers establish, and the discussion confirmed, these factors are familiar to most of the Member countries and were the common basis on which a detailed and mutually beneficial discussion of higher education issues took place.

A second set of forces which were identified are those which are internal to colleges and universities themselves. Some of these are deeply rooted in the traditions of the academic enterprise itself, having evolved from the Middle Ages to the present as essential elements of the university as we know it. These traditions include, for example, the independent professoriate and tenure, both closely related to our modern concept of academic freedom. Another characteristic of the modern day university - one which developed more recently - is the structure of the disciplines and the resulting departmental fragmentation of campuses. Most of these characteristics reflect a traditional (and strongly held) view that academic decisions and the responsibility for maintaining the integrity of the enterprise belong in the hands of those most qualified to judge such matters, namely the academics themselves.

Beyond the intrinsic characteristics of the university-based intellectual enterprise are others which, as the Chairman pointed out in his remarks, emerged as responses to the pressures and forces brought to bear on higher education during the growth period of the 1960s and the 1970s. During those decades, a larger and more diverse

---

[*] Vice-President, The Carnegie Foundation for the Advancement of Teaching, United States.

student body entered higher education institutions. Increases in the number of minorities, lower-income students, adults and part-time students led to shifts in both the perceived mission of particular institutions as well as the nature and structure of instructional programmes. In the United States, for example, a large number of two-year Community or "Junior Colleges" were established to serve this new student population. In some countries, the influx into higher education institutions of less well-prepared students led not to the more rigid application of entrance criteria but rather to the creation of courses of instruction which were, in effect, remedial in nature.

These forces - both external and internal to higher education - provided the backcloth to the detailed discussions by participants of their implications for the future development of higher education. The central issue on which all agreed was that, because of the decline in the numbers of students, increase in older and part-time students, the prospect of limited or even declining resources committed to higher education, and increasing expectations by society, colleges and universities must effectively address more immediate problems, and that this will place greater stresses on the institutions of higher education. In turn, many of the traditional mechanisms by which institutions are governed may not be able to respond to these new stresses either rapidly enough or to the degree necessary to meet the changing needs of society. Unless institutions themselves can take the leadership and make those necessary changes, many participants felt, governments themselves will have to do so.

In discussing this central issue, three critical and interrelated questions emerged which, in my view, encompassed the essential concern of the Conference, and on which the present report is based. First, who will ultimately make the changes in higher education that are going to be required in the next decade; and with what participation by those who will be affected by the decisions? Second, how can the quality and vitality of our post-secondary institutions be maintained as they respond to these forces? And, third, what are the essential missions both of the entire post-secondary sector and of individual institutions, given the changing conditions and demands of society? The ultimate answers to these questions will determine whether higher education systems in the Member countries emerge from the decade of the 1980s stronger after the challenge that will have been faced or weakened and diminished in the roles they play in the societies of the future.

WHO WILL DECIDE?

One of the trends of the 1970s which was noted in the discussions was the movement in most Member countries toward an increasing engagement of governments in the affairs of higher education. This shift was the result of a number of factors, among them the rapid increase in the numbers of students leading to an increased need for centralised national or regional planning, a reduction in the level of confidence in education, and increased pressures by the public for accountability on the part of institutions. Given likely trends for the future decade, it was generally felt that the shift of decision out of institutions and into the hands of external policy-makers is more rather than less likely to continue. Declining enrolments and shifts in the kinds of programmes students want could lead to excess capacity both within and for overall systems. In the view of many in the government, the need for the efficient and effective use of resources in a time of retrenchment will require increased centralised planning and decision-making.

From this perspective, institutional leadership, left to its own initiatives, will be either unwilling or unable to make the difficult decisions necessary in the coming decade. In the extreme, for example, there is little confidence that an institution - particularly a governmentally supported one - would voluntarily decide to close its doors. Traditional decision-making mechanisms within the university are also expected to have difficulty in dealing with the problems presented by programmes or departments which must be eliminated and the tenured faculty assigned to them. If the natural conservative tendencies of the internal academic governance process are to be overcome, those with this view would conclude, a decision-making body external to the institution will have to either make or force the necessary decisions.

On the other hand, college and university administrators and members of the faculty view recent increases in outside involvement in their decisions with growing concern. The possibility of future increases in that involvement causes genuine alarm within the institution. As higher educators see it, an erosion of authority at the institutional level will seriously compromise the traditional concept of academic freedom, ultimately undermining the quality of intellectual inquiry which takes place in higher education institutions. The traditional autonomy of higher education is seen not as an accident of history but as the necessary precondition for a productive and creative intellectual enterprise.

In the course of discussions, it was argued that each of these points of view has some merit. Admitting this, it was recognised that governments face a difficult dilemma. Stated somewhat in the extreme, if governments do not act, the problems will be dealt with either ineffectively, inappropriately, or not at all. If, on the other hand governments do act aggressively to deal with the problems, that very action may seriously undermine the capacity of institutions to serve society in the very ways needed to discover effective solutions to the problems of society. The challenge then - for both institutions and governments - will be to find ways to get institutions to change, to attend to new tasks and priorities, without at the same time undermining their capacity to make their essential contribution.

How can we escape this dilemma? If we are to do so, different behaviours than have been in evidence in the past will be required on the part of both governments and higher education institutions. In the first instance, government will need to better appreciate the essential nature of the intellectual effort and its ultimate incompatibility with bureaucracy. The flame of intellectual creativity does not burn well when heaped with procedures, regulations, planning, evaluations and the ubiquitous tool of bureaucracy, paperwork.

But if this is so, how then should governments proceed? This question was explored in detail in the discussion of new patterns of authority. The general conclusion was that new approaches by governments will need to be developed. Rather than seeking its objectives by direct intervention in the decision-making of institutions, governments will need to develop more indirect incentives for institutions themselves to respond in creative and effective ways. For example, if institutions which cut back or eliminate unnecessary or low quality programmes lose all the resources freed up by that action, there is little or no positive motivation to take such steps. If, on the other hand, such an institution could retain some of those funds for other newly emerging institutional priorities, its leaders would have the opportunity for positive as well as negative leadership.

Careful consideration of the incentives given to institutions by governmental policies will be especially necessary during the coming decade. But escape from the dilemma will also require changes on the part of colleges and universities. Most urgently, institutions will need to deny - not by words but by their very actions - the premise upon which government will base a shift of responsibility from institutions to itself, namely, that unless forced to do so, colleges and universities cannot and will not respond effectively to these problems. It should not be denied: it is difficult for institutions to take an aggressive role in seriously modifying their own missions, programmes, and procedures, particularly when resources are scarce. Yet, it is also urgent that they do so. As the holders of the academic traditions of our societies, those who work in our colleges and universities are probably best qualified to determine how those traditions can and should be altered to meet new conditions and needs. And if the leaders of academe do not move to meet these challenges, two consequences are likely. First, public confidence in higher education institutions - already on the decline - is likely to fall even further. The public will read defensiveness and reluctance to change as simple self-interest and a rejection of responsibilities to the society at large. And second, governments will be forced to assume the responsibilities refused by the academic community, resulting in a further loss by the colleges and universities of power over their own affairs.

An important distinction must be kept in mind. Some decisions which will be faced in the next decade - by their very nature - will need to be made by agencies external to the institutions themselves. For example, dealing with an excess in the number of institutions in a country or region will require analysis, planning, and decisions that are made across, and therefore outside institutions. A number of participants explicitly recognised that governments will need to be ready to make firm, if courageous, decisions to close down institutions which, because of declining enrolments and resources, cannot hope to maintain adequate quality. Not to do so was viewed as an invitation to deterioration in quality and a serious disservice to society.

Other issues, however, will emerge within institutions which are closely linked to important academic concepts and the traditions of self-government. Ideally, these are issues which institutions themselves should address. Two important examples which were explored in the discussions were tenure and the disciplinary and departmental structure of the institution. Many felt that, given the likely conditions in the 1980s, these are two sources of rigidities which could hamper effective responses to new challenges.

The granting of tenure is one of the important means by which those who have established their academic qualifications are assured the independence to explore, research, and teach as they will in substantial immunity from coercion of punishment by society. Tenure is viewed by many as the single most important element in preserving academic freedom. Most would recognise its crucial role. Yet, with the coming decline in students exacerbated by sizable shifts in what students wish to take, tenure is likely to come under considerable stress. In some cases, programmes, departments and even entire institutions will need to be closed. If so, what is to befall the senior tenured faculty in those programmes? In limited instances individuals may be able to retrain into closely allied fields for which student demand is still high. Most of the time, however, this will neither be possible nor very effective, and faculty will need to be let go completely. Probably far more widespread will be a dramatic reduction at many institutions in the number of young faculty who can be hired. With declining enrolments and a stable faculty body, there will be little or no opportunity for the traditional renewal of academic departments by the influx of highly productive, freshly trained young people. As a result, the academic quality and vitality of many departments and institutions may gradually if almost imperceptibly decline. If so, what is to be done and what role will changes in the concept or application of tenure play in the solution? And, more importantly, who will it be who will seek out and implement those solutions?

Another aspect of colleges and universities which is likely to need re-examination during the next decade is the organisational separation into disciplines and departments, and the ways in which that separation constrains the ability of researchers to address problems society wants and needs solved. As one of the delegates put it, society has problems but colleges and universities have departments, and there may be a serious mismatch between the two. In some countries, it was reported, a decreasing proportion of total research funds are being allocated to universities. The shift is apparent not in the support of basic research, but for those monies directed toward development and practical problem-solving. The reasons for the shift appear to be varied. The problems society wants solved may not be problems that academics like to spend their time solving; they may be too practical, or simply uninteresting to the academic mind. Or, the urgent problems of society may be so intractable that academics - exercising their academic freedom - choose to address other more simple problems. Or it may also be that the traditional structures into which academics have sorted themselves prevent the emergence of approaches to solving these problems. To the extent the latter is the case, higher education is faced with a clear challenge. Will it stand by as its role as problem-solver for society (and with it some of higher education's authority in society) is gradually yielded to other institutions? Or can institutions overcome the separateness imposed by their own structures and discover ways to organise, synthesise, and apply the findings of many disciplines to the complex problems of our modern society?

These are examples of the issues which colleges and universities will need to face over the next decade, if they are to take a hand in helping governments escape from the dilemma of too much control frustrating the very purposes of their own actions. Many argued that institutions can meet this challenge - indeed, it would be inaccurate to suggest that some institutions have not already shown extraordinary leadership in doing so. But, it was also the sense of much of the discussion that such leadership will need to be much more widespread and more willing to deal with issues which cut very close to the essential elements and interests of the institutions.

HOW CAN QUALITY AND VITALITY BE MAINTAINED?

The inevitable question of quality in research and teaching has already entered into this report. Almost everyone, both academics and government officials, can reach agreement that the preservation of quality in our educational programmes - whatever the financial or demographic constraints - is of paramount importance. However, as the discussions proceeded it was evident that the "quality" which can be affirmed as a commonly held goal is more complicated and potentially controversial than it might appear. Three further issues lie hidden behind the easy use of this term. First, what is quality in a higher education institution? That is, how can we tell if we have quality programmes? Second, who will define quality, or, in more practical terms, who will set the rules by which the effectiveness of our higher education programmes is to be judged? And, third, who will monitor or evaluate the quality of academic programmes?

A statement of the essential element of quality in an academic programme, as was the case in the discussion, is likely to be strongly coloured by the point of view of the speaker. Academics, especially those on university faculties, are likely to insist that the ultimate and determining criterion to be applied to their professional work is the production of quality research. And this judgement is to be rendered, not by the citizenry or its governmental representatives, but rather by the researcher's own peers. In this view, teaching is a subordinate activity, and the production of journal articles, presentations at scholarly meetings, and the number of Nobel prizes are the primary indicators of a vital academic enterprise. It should be observed that it is this concept of academic excellence which, almost universally, has embedded itself in the judgements made in the granting of the doctoral degree and of tenure. Most young academics are strongly socialised into this definition of quality in post-secondary education as they are trained and sorted into their places on the faculties of higher education institutions. Others, outside higher education, place greater or equal emphasis on different measures. Government planners and representatives of business and industry stress the importance of the production of well-trained individuals who have been socialised into the needs of the workplace and who can fulfill the manpower needs of the economy. In this view, quality teaching is far more important, as is the synthesis of field of knowledge and practical training in advanced and specialised intellectual skills. While not of necessity incompatible with the conduct of quality research, these criteria are clearly different. In some areas, the judgement of the quality of the work of higher education institutions has formally moved outside the institutions themselves. For medical professionals, lawyers and, increasingly, engineers, standards are established by professional guilds and associations, and enforced by certification tests which potential practitioners must pass before becoming professionally active. Such tests have as much, if not more, influence on the curriculum of colleges than do faculty or administrators.

To these more formal or professional ways of defining and judging the quality of higher education might be added the highly informal judgements made by society at large. One of the realities of higher education in many of the Member countries is a reduction in the respect for the sector on the part of the general public, a situation which in a time of fiscal restraints can have serious effects on institutions. At least in part, this may represent a feeling that colleges and universities should, but do not, provide practical problem-solving services to the communities in which they reside. Or, perhaps it represents a judgement by the graduates of our institutions (who, ironically, today represent a larger proportion of the population than they did when higher education was more favourably viewed) that the programmes they experienced were not as relevant to their later personal or professional lives as they had expected. It may be that with so many admitted into the temple, the mystery is gone, the secrets are out, and former respect and awe have given way to a more cynical view of the virtues and vices of the priesthood.

WHAT ARE THE MISSIONS OF HIGHER EDUCATION?

A discussion of the nature of quality in higher education leads immediately to questions of the roles or missions in our societies of colleges and universities. In most countries the rich diversity of views on how quality is to be judged has resulted in a complementary diversity in types of institutions as well as the acceptance of a variety of missions within single colleges or universities. In most countries, the range of purposes society assigns to higher education has been matched by the range of institutions. More and more students with non-traditional needs and qualifications have entered post-secondary studies and, in response, institutions or programmes were created to meet their needs. In many ways, this was a positive development and should be applauded as a strength, not a weakness. However, it also created a problem which will need to be dealt with during the 1980s. As the missions of post-secondary education evolve and expanded, the boundaries between the traditional college and newer forms became less and less clear. Variety became diffusion, if not sometimes confusion, of purpose and mission. And, now, as society turns a more harshly critical eye on all of its institutions, that diffusion of purpose could easily become the target of criticisms and the basis for adverse policy decisions.

It was clear from the discussion that the question of mission in higher education will need to be addressed more carefully during this next decade than ever before during the past twenty years. In a period of growth, colleges and universities had the luxury of being able to absorb new missions relatively easily. New students and new programmes may have caused opposition from some of the more grumpy and traditional faculty. However, since new demands were usually accompanied by additional resources, ongoing programmes of the institutions did not have to be reduced or eliminated. As a result, opposition was usually easily overcome. New roles and missions were added, but not at the expense of anything else. Now, however, we face a dramatically different situation. New problems are emerging and along with them new roles of higher education. But at the same time resources are not expanding. New missions can only be embraced at the expense of other, older, activities. For some institutions, the picture is even more grim. Resources will actually decline. Activities and programmes will need to be reduced or eliminated. Either situation will require a careful examination of mission by institutions themselves and government policy-makers, if these decisions are to be made well. The choices higher education faces in the 1980s will be choices not just among programmes but choices affecting fundamental purposes. This reality will present leaders in higher education with another potential loss in authority and control. Unless they can establish a clear sense of mission for their institutions, one which responds to the evolving needs of society during a period of limited growth, society, in the person of its governmental representatives, is likely to do so for them.

A final observation on the mission of higher education emerged with great force from the discussions. Many delegates commented on the need to reaffirm the importance to society of the role of colleges and universities beyond that of basic research. In the coming decade, the assimilation and synthesis of more and more complex bodies of knowledge will be a more important service to society than ever before. And, along with that synthesis will be the urgent need to transmit it much more effectively, not only to future generations of young people, but also to the broader society. Inundated as we will continue to be by information, our most crucial need will be to learn how to sort, assimilate, and use it effectively. Teaching us how to do this is a role which higher education can perform for society but must do so with far greater emphasis than it has in the past.

Ultimately, it may be on this issue that higher education itself will be most severely tested. The synthesis of bodies of knowledge, excellent teaching, and certainly the "popularisation" of knowledge are not accorded high status by much of the academic community. The value structures hidden within the processes of graduate education and advancement within the profession do not encourage talented young people to engage in these activities rather than in basic research. Yet society needs and wants these services and is likely to put great pressure on higher education to perform such tasks. If higher education cannot or will not respond, society will find other ways to create other institutions to meet its needs, probably to its own detriment as well as to that of higher education.

CONCLUSION

The next decade will confront us all - leaders in higher education and in government - with serious challenges concerning who will exercise power and authority in higher education, what quality is and how it will be preserved, and what the new and evolving roles of higher education will be. The conditions which can be foreseen for the 1980s are expected to make these issues both more important and more difficult to deal with. It is possible that the future will bring increased conflict between higher education and the government, as priorities shift and values collide. Purposes and roles may become more rather than less confused and we may witness a gradual decline in the effectiveness and importance of our colleges and universities. If this prospect is to be avoided, leaders in education and government will need to understand clearly where they are headed, and they will have to exercise courage and sensitivity in the decisions they will be making. If they can do so, higher education of the future is likely to be stronger and more vital than it is today. It is this second vision for which the delegates to this Conference hoped and to which they appeared committed.

Part Two

ACCESS TO HIGHER EDUCATION

Chapter I

STRUCTURE OF HIGHER EDUCATION PROVISION:
THE HERITAGE OF THE 1970s

1. LIMITS TO GROWTH OF HIGHER EDUCATION

This chapter will focus on some of the more significant structural and qualitative changes that have occurred in post-secondary education in recent years, as compared with the pattern of development which prevailed in the 50s and 60s. It should be stressed from the outset, however, that many of the critical problems and issues facing post-secondary systems in the early eighties are not all that different from those already identified and discussed before the onset of the economic crisis.

Some of the dilemmas with which policy-makers in the field of higher education find themselves permanently confronted were summed up in the general report to the OECD Conference on Future Structures of Post-Secondary Education, held in 1973, in the following terms:

"This new goal structure for post-secondary education, superimposed on its traditional functions, gives rise to a number of critical areas of tension around which much of the current debate on the future of higher education revolves. Such tensions exist, for example:
- between the requirements of excellence and of egalitarianism;
- between the structure and size of individual demand for higher education and of labour market requirements;
- between the aspirations and interests of the different groups involved in higher education;
- between the aspirations and expectations of individuals and the prevailing socio-economic constraints in terms of availability of resources, academic attitudes, institutional hierarchies, established cultural and social value structures striving for self-perpetuation. (1)

---

1. Policies for Higher Education, General Report, Conference on Future Structures of Post-Secondary Education, OECD, Paris, 26-29 June 1973.

The new social and economic context has undoubtedly led to changes in priorities, to a number of problems being viewed in a different light and has heightened certain conflicts and tensions; but basically many of the current issues in higher education are bound up with the structural and qualitative changes brought about by the extraordinary expansion of this sector during the two preceding decades.

The crisis of the 1960s, at least in most European countries, was in large part due to the lack of an adequate institutional framework to cope with the growing and increasingly diverse student population. But while it takes time to develop structures in response to new pressures, it takes even longer for people to fully grasp the implications, for the individual and society as a whole, of post-secondary systems which in a few years more than trebled their population with enrolment ratios exceeding 15, 20 or 25 per cent of the relevant age group. There is a still greater time lag before this awareness is translated into changes in the attitudes, expectations and behaviour of the groups most directly concerned with the advent of mass higher education: young people and their parents, teaching staff and employers as well as educational policy makers and government authorities.

While the terms "steady state" or "zero growth" may serve to typify the situation during the 1970s (particularly in highlighting the changed pattern vis-à-vis the period of growth in the 1960s) it is important to remember that in the majority of OECD countries the overall growth of the post-secondary sector has continued, albeit at a much slower pace, during this decade (2). Many of today's problems stem from the need to pursue the slow process of internal organisation and consolidation of mass systems in a far less propitious socio-economic context faced with the problem of promoting the necessary readjustments in attitudes and behaviour.

Past OECD work in the field of higher education consisted essentially in analysing and comparing the main quantitative trends and structural reforms of the 1960s and in making some prognoses about future patterns of development, particularly in countries where mass higher education was a comparatively new phenomenon (3). The conceptual framework used for these analyses and forecasts was drawn in large measure from the elite-mass-universal access model originally presented by Martin Trow (4). According to this theory of stages of development, structural reforms in the United States were typical of a country passing from a mass system to a stage of quasi-universal access, while in Western European countries reforms were designed to cope with the transition from elite to mass higher education, seen as an ineluctable development in an assumed context of steady growth.

---

2. See Statistical Annex.
3. (a) Towards New Structures of Post-Secondary Education, OECD, Paris 1971; (b) Policies for Higher Education, OECD, Paris 1974; (c) Towards Mass Higher Education: Issues and Dilemmas, OECD, Paris, 1974.
4. Trow, Martin: "Problems in the Transition from Elite to Mass Higher Education" in Policies for Higher Education, OECD, Paris, 1974.

The Trow model was no doubt extremely useful as a framework for the study of post-secondary systems in a comparative perspective and in providing a basis for a more global and coherent analysis of a variety of dimensions within the field of higher education which are often treated in isolation. However, as with the majority of forecasts made in the mid-1960s, it proved less successful in terms of predicting developments in the 1970s.

Obviously no one could have been expected to foresee the oil crisis and the economic recession or their subsequent effects on education. But the fact remains that, at the time, much of the comparative work in education was over-concerned with identifying similarities in patterns of development. Essential differences among OECD countries, in particular those relating to the structure of their educational systems and prevailing attitudes to education, tended to be neglected.

Martin Trow has himself recently made an interesting critical analysis of his conceptual scheme, pointing to a series of factors which may help explain why European systems did not develop as foreseen in the early 1970s (5).

In the present report the argument is put forward that a key factor and one which past forecasts did not take sufficiently into account is the basic organisational features of the education and training provision for 16-19-year-olds in individual countries, in particular the various forms of secondary education. The impact of quantitative growth of secondary schools on the development of the higher levels has been recognised for a long time; but far less attention has been focused on the organisation and functions of secondary education; on the specific selection and orientation procedures used, on how these affect demand for higher education and consequently the size and structure of post-secondary systems. Some of these aspects will be reviewed in Chapters II and III; at this stage it is useful to point to those characteristics of European secondary systems which can help account for some of the "unexpected" trends in higher education during the 1970s and throw some light on prospects for further development in the coming years.

In the 1960s the view was held that with the continuous expansion of secondary education in Europe the growth in private demand for higher education would be such that European countries would find themselves faced with the need to set up mass post-secondary institutions functionally equivalent to the community colleges in the United States, Canada and Japan. At least two features distinctive of many European upper secondary schools help explain why higher education did not expand as rapidly as foreseen or follow the United States model of development. These are:

a) the modal age of secondary school leavers;

---

5. Trow, Martin: "Elite and Mass Higher Education: American Models and European Realities", in Research into Higher Education, Processes and Structures, NBUC, Stockholm, 1979.

b) the existence of lines of study as basic units of organisation at the upper secondary level, and in particular the existence of a rather large technical-vocational sector at this level.

a) The modal age of secondary school leavers

Since educational structures and reforms tend to be perceived as an integral part of more global social policies concerned with the needs and problems of specific age groups, the age distribution of the population receiving a particular level or type of education is a significant indicator in attempting to foresee its future development. This refers not only to shifts in the balance between mature and young students but more importantly in this context to differences between countries in the age composition of young students pursuing their initial education.

As the following table shows, while the majority of 18-year-olds in the United States and Japan are enrolled at the tertiary level, in many of the European countries the same age group tends to be heavily represented at the secondary level. This phenomenon is most evident in Austria, Western Germany, Netherlands and Switzerland as well as in the Scandinavian countries, where a similar trend - though far less pronounced - can also be observed for 19-year-old students. As was pointed out in a previous OECD study (6) these differences do not necessarily imply that all European students have more years of formal education before entering higher education (this is only true for Germany); in some cases they are due to late school entry age (Scandinavia), while in others they are explained by the large number of students who repeat grades (France). They do, however, point to the significant fact that, under present schooling conditions, even were European countries to aim at achieving United States enrolment ratios for their 18- and even 19-year-old population, this would not lead to a similar expansion in their post-secondary systems.

b) Streaming in upper secondary education

Whatever the differences in rates of expansion and in the types or pace of reforms, the curricula and structure of studies in the last years of secondary education in all Western European countries continue to be organised around a varying number clearly defined and highly structured lines of study. In all of them a clear distinction is drawn between long cycle - usually transfer oriented - and short cycle - usually terminal oriented - lines of study, as well as between general, technical and vocational sectors. Even in Sweden (7), one of the European countries which most strongly advocates the development

---

6. Selection and Certification in Education and Employment, Part I, OECD, Paris, 1977.
7. Reviews of National Policies for Education: Educational Reforms in Sweden, OECD, Paris, 1981.

Enrolment Rates of 18- and 19-year-old Students

Country	18-year-old Secondary Education	18-year-old Higher Education	19-year-old Secondary Education	19-year-old Higher Education
Australia(1979)(4)	6.6	12.9	1.4	13.3
Austria(1977)	40.9(1)	4.1	13.1(2)(1)	7.9
Canada(1977)	20.9	19.4	4.0	24.3
Denmark(1977)	54.1	0.8	41.7	4.0
France(1976)	23.9	10.4(3)	7.6	13.6(3)
Germany(1978)	60.9(1)	0.9	29.1(1)	4.3
Greece(1975)	25.5	9.4	18.5	14.9
*Japan(1976)	3.6	40.1	--	40.9
*Netherlands(1976)	32.3	6.0(5)	14.8	9.3(5)
*Norway(1976)	47.4	0.7	23.0	5.0
Spain(1977)	19.8	14.5	12.2	15.0
Sweden(1978)	35.2	0.9	10.9	4.5
United Kingdom(1977)	35.4(1)	7.3	23.3(1)	12.4
*United States	16.1	32.2	3.6	36.9

* Educational Statistics in OECD Countries, OECD, Paris, 1981.
1. Full and part-time students.
2. 1976
3. Including the "classes préparatoires" to the "Grandes Ecoles".
4. Not including apprenticeship.
5. Not including university-type higher education.
Source: Statistical Annex.

of "comprehensive upper secondary education", or the United Kingdom(8), where various types of comprehensive upper secondary schools co-exist (i.e. tertiary colleges, sixth form colleges) this concept is in no way understood as implying the abolition of different lines of study. In spite of the differing and evolving interpretations within the European context, the comprehensive principle when applied to the upper secondary level is primarily understood as the elimination or attenuation of hierarchical and status differences among rather well-defined streams, greater flexibility between lines of study and above all, the integration of most or all options within a single type of upper secondary school.

Thus, contrary to the comprehensive systems in North America where most options prepare or qualify for further studies, European countries have maintained a rather large vocational sector at the upper secondary level in preparing pupils for a final professional qualification(9) and only exceptionally qualifying for direct entrance to post-secondary studies.

Both the presence of an older student body and the organisation of studies on the basis of streams implying in many cases a substantial degree of specialisation, point to the fact that European upper secondary schools are fulfilling a number of functions which in the United States are being assigned to the first years of post-secondary education. There is evidence of this in the field of both general and technical education. Young people having obtained their academic secondary school certificates in France, Germany, United Kingdom or in the Scandinavian countries and who want to pursue higher education studies in the United States are granted equivalences which allow them to take the four year Bachelor's degree in three years, or even less - depending, of course, on the entry standards of the particular institutions(10). Also quite a number of professional qualifications which in Europe are obtained at the end of secondary schooling, require several years of post-secondary education in the United States.

This type of functional equivalence between institutions that are formally classified under different levels of education highlights the weakness of international comparisons which analyse in relative isolation a single level of education or a specific sector of the educational system.

Whether the continuous growth of enrolment rates of the 16-19-year group in Europe will lead to a closer resemblance between European upper secondary systems and the North American senior high school model is a moot point. Expansion and diversification in response to common pressures and objectives must inevitably lead

---

8. G. Neave, How They Fared: The Impact of the Comprehensive School upon the Universities, London, 1975.
9. See Chapter II.
10. Such an opportunity is also granted to a small percentage of American high school students who pass a special examination.

to a certain convergence at least in terms of the problems and issues being faced by most OECD countries. On the other hand, with the economic recession and the calling into question of past patterns of growth at the post-compulsory level it could be argued that Western European countries may seek other models of development in the coming years.

In this, Western European countries may well have derived benefit from the experience of countries which preceded them in the process of educational expansion. In the United States, for example, a frequent claim in past years has been that the rapid growth and democratisation of education has impaired the quality of secondary education. Even admitting that a larger proportion of pupils from the less privileged groups and with lower levels of academic ability could well bring about such a result, there are many who question a policy of devoting substantial resources to remedial education at tertiary level rather than improving standards and performance at high school level. One consequence of this practice has been that more and more young people have had to take a 13th and 14th year of education in order to attain the minimum standards or basic skills traditionally associated with a secondary level education.

In recent years this line of criticism has gained momentum and at present there seems to be a strong movement in the United States in favour of devoting far more attention to the social and educational problems encountered at the senior high school level (11).

In most European countries the policy is to encourage participation at the upper secondary level. However, a major concern is that of avoiding that upper secondary education be considered only, or even primarily, as an intermediate or incomplete stage requiring the immediate pursuit of post-secondary studies. As at present in the United States, there is a strong move in favour of setting or maintaining minimum standards for the completion of this cycle. At the same time efforts are being made to strengthen the professional orientation and relevance of the various options provided in contrast to past trends of adding more years of study as a requirement for entry into certain occupations and professions. The rapid development of schemes enabling young people in post-compulsory schooling to combine education, training and work are also likely to affect demand for higher education.

Whether these are temporary measures largely conditioned by present concern over youth unemployment, or whether they reflect a more profound change in educational philosophy, is unclear. What is clear, however, is that both the quantitative and structural changes at the upper secondary level call for much closer scrutiny and attention, in view of the crucial role they play in shaping the future of higher education.

---

11. It is interesting to point out that the U.S. Carnegie Council for the Advancement of Teaching, which for many years has assigned top priority to higher education, is now paying greater attention to secondary education.

2. STRUCTURAL REFORMS OF HIGHER EDUCATION

In comparison to the previous decade, the 1970s appear as a period of considerable stability in terms of structures of post-secondary education(12). Whether this stability is only apparent in the sense that the structural reforms have been far less dramatic and less visible or whether it also involves a general slowdown in the pace of internal change and innovation at this level of education, is a matter for debate. Judgements are likely to vary as much from country to country as within individual countries, depending on which groups are expressing their views as well as on the sectors or higher education which are under scrutiny.

To a large extent, the apparent stability of recent years can be seen as a natural follow-up to the wave of expansion, sweeping reforms and the creation of new types of institutions, i.e. short-cycle institutions, open universities, which characterised the 1960s and early 1970s. After the widely publicised debates on general policies and the actual formulation and approval of reform proposals concerning major sectors of higher education, came the period of detailed implementation with its attendant problems, problems which, most often, had to be tackled at the level of the individual institutions and departments of staff as well as student relationships.

Thus, in areas such as internal management, access conditions and criteria, structure of studies, organisation of curricula, much effort and ingenuity was required to translate into practice the terms of reference and broad principles formulated at the political level in earlier years. Additional difficulties stemmed from the fact that the socio-economic context of Member countries changed radically between the time when these major policies were formulated and the time of their actual implementation. Much of the criticism and impatience on the part of outside groups, and even of public authorities, vis-à-vis the performance of higher education institutions reflects a lack of understanding of the difficulties involved in implementing these reforms. There is also a tendency, at times, to underestimate the significance and long-term consequences of grassroot or internal changes within individual colleges and universities.

The fact that reforms in higher education during the 1970s seem to have mainly taken the form of slow incremental changes and focused more on internal and qualitative aspects than on overall structures - i.e. as M. Trow puts it, on the "private lives" rather than on the

---

12. The reference throughout the report to the 1960s and 1970s should not be interpreted as covering exactly each decade. The 1960s is understood as the period of growth and expansion lasting in most Member countries up to the early 1970s. The 1970s encompasses the period marked by the onset of the economic recession, i.e. 1973/74.

"public lives"(13) of higher education systems - makes broad characterisations of national policies during this period particularly difficult.

At the risk of oversimplifying the discussion an attempt will be made to identify some of the more significant trends in higher education during the 1970s, comparing them when possible with those prevailing during the 1960s. The main features of the scenarios of the 1960s and 1970s which account for many of the differences have been repeatedly stated and will not be discussed again here. Given that the trends and reforms are typically the result of the interplay of a variety of pressures and circumstances in which casual relationships are difficult to discern, the emphasis of the present review will be on the type and direction of change rather than on the complex dynamics of how the different changes came about.

Changes in the institutional framework of higher education systems will be examined under the following headings:

- New hierarchies in post-secondary education;
- Internal reforms within universities;
- Reorganisation of the non-university sectors;
- Continuing education: the expanding sector of post-secondary education.

a) New hierarchies in post-secondary education

During the 1960s, a major concept in the analysis of the quantitative and structural development of post-secondary education was the distinction which was established between university-type and non-university type higher education. This classification served to highlight the existence and increased significance of a wide range of post-secondary institutions which, given the traditional view of equating higher education with university studies, had been disregarded in earlier investigations. Studies of the dichotomy between the "noble" university and the "less noble" non-university components of

---

13. See M. Trow - "The Public and Private Lives of Higher Education" in Daedalus, Winter 1975. Public life is defined as comprising all the plans and decisions affecting colleges and universities made by people other than teachers and students. It includes public discussions and governmental decisions about the support, organisation and structure of higher education; the hearings of legislative committees; the work of coordinating commissions and state departments of higher education and much (but not all) of university administration.
Private life of higher education is what actually happens in the classrooms, libraries, the laboratories, at the desks and in the offices, the moment-by-moment, day-to-day activities and interactions of teachers and students engaged in teaching and learning.

higher education pointed to the hierarchical structure characterising most post-secondary systems. They also paid special attention to the problems faced by many post-secondary institutions which were striving to become fully recognised members of the higher education world while at the same time being under strong pressure to develop a distinctive role (14). This characterisation between the "noble" and "less noble" sectors seems far less obvious now than a decade ago. Firstly, in most Member countries the expansion of higher education has in itself led to a much wider variety of university and non-university type programmes and institutions, generating greater diversity and prestige differences within each. Recent developments affecting both the supply and demand for higher education may have further contributed to accentuating some of these "internal" hierarchical differences: introduction of <u>numerus clausus</u> in certain universities or departments witnessing a <u>growing competition</u> for entry with open access policies being maintained in others; widening disparities in the employment prospects of graduates from different fields of study, some witnessing high rates of underemployment or even unemployment while others have guaranteed entry into occupations or professions with hith income, prestige and power; renewed government concern for developing a small number of well-financed and staffed centres of excellence sheltered from the impact of demand, etc.

Secondly, it should be recalled that at the root of the "noble" (university)/"less noble" (non-university) distinction was the traditional <u>academic value</u> system dominant at the time. This placed at the top of <u>the prestige ladder</u> theoretical and so-called disinterested studies plus the training for certain established professions, while relegating to the lower rungs programmes primarily concerned with the imparting of knowledge and skills usable directly in a wider range of occupations. It was clear, even then, however, that "prestige and quality" differences will always exist among individual institutions and in this sense more and less noble universities or colleges; what is important is that these differences do not apply to whole categories of institutions e.g. university versus non-university sector(15).

Actual developments have followed at least partially this postulate, perhaps at a faster pace than was expected some years ago. With the changing labour market situation the dominance of strictly academic criteria has declined at the same time as growing importance is being assigned to the relative employment value of different types of higher education. Thus a different order of preferences seems to have emerged: the ranking of institutions and programmes in the new pecking order is still conditioned by their academic standing but also, and to a far greater extent than in the past, <u>by their perceived job relevance</u>.

---

14. <u>Short-Cycle Higher Education: A Search for Identity</u>, OECD, Paris, 1973.
15. <u>Towards New Structures of Post-Secondary Education</u>, OECD, Paris, 1971, p. 37 (document for general distribution).

The growing importance assigned to the immediate employment value of higher education institutions is having a number of effects on both supply and demand and these will be discussed throughout the report. In terms of the pecking order of the various components of national systems of higher education the following developments are of particular significance:

i) the traditional university model has lost some of its attraction and prestige; this has also meant that other higher education institutions have been less prone to copy universities and that problems of academic drift have somewhat subsided;

ii) hierarchical differences among programmes within the university as well as the non-university sectors have sharpened to an extent that some of them have acquired greater significance than the previous binary university/non-university distinction. Within each sector some departments or institutions are witnessing growing competition for entry whereas others are recording declining enrolments and empty places;

iii) directly related, a number of short-cycle programmes or institutions, especially those with a professional orientation and providing a certain guarantee of employment are listed higher in the order of student preferences than some university programmes with less professional relevance or leading to employment outlets which are saturated.

The resulting situation is illustrated in the following graph showing the standing of different types of higher education programmes in terms of their academic and employment dimension(16). It should be interpreted merely as an analytical schema designed to illustrate the above argument and facilitate discussion of some of the implications of current trends.

Bearing in mind the far greater complexity of the institutional network in each national context and the variations among countries it could be useful to examine within each system recent changes in the relative position of different options and their likely mobility in the future.

Listed on the upper right-hand side of the graph are a selected number of university-type institutions or programmes ranking high on both dimensions, usually strongly selective, performing the traditional functions of higher education (strong concentration on research and post-graduate education and training for high level professions). Whatever scenario is chosen for the coming decades, the future of this "noble" sector seems to be relatively well-assured from most points of view (student demand, institutional prestige, government support). The notable exception for some of them would be perhaps that of maintaining a strong research capability.

---

16. As will be seen in other sections of the report the employment value is in a way a less rigid and more subjective dimension than academic standing. It is more likely to change over a relatively short time span and be more affected by the individual or group characteristics of those involved in the assessment.

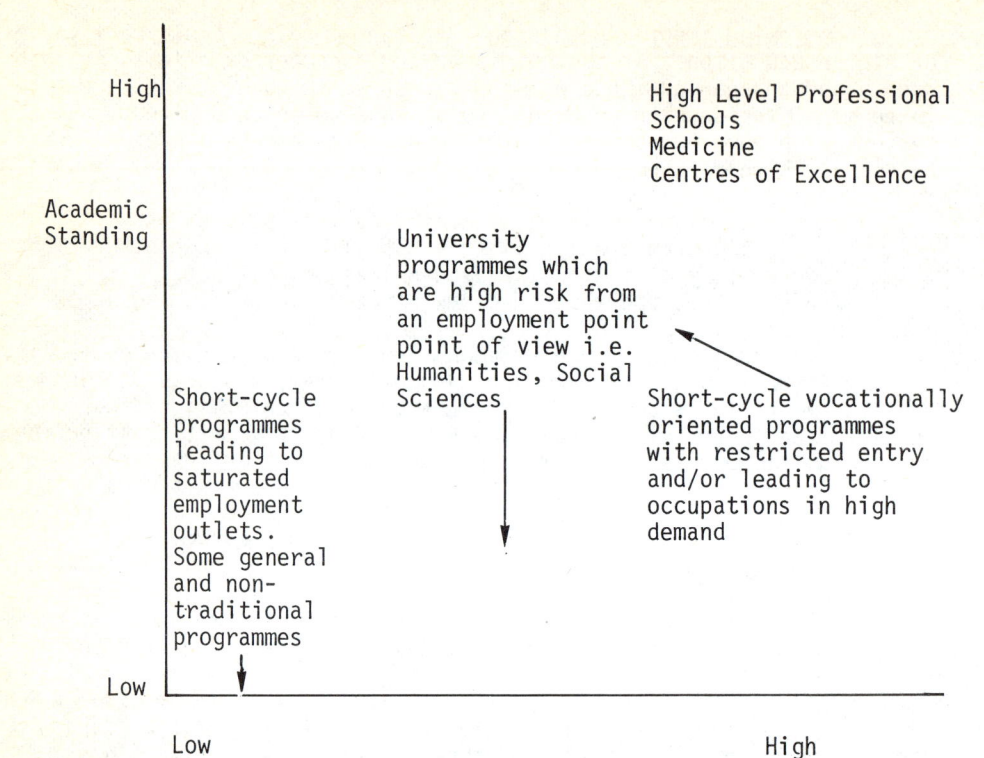

```
High |                                    High Level Professional
     |                                    Schools
     |                                    Medicine
Academic                                  Centres of Excellence
Standing |
     |              University
     |              programmes which
     |              are high risk from
     |              an employment point
     |              point of view i.e.
     |              Humanities, Social
     |  Short-cycle Sciences       Short-cycle vocationally
     |  programmes                 oriented programmes
     |  leading to                 with restricted entry
     |  saturated                  and/or leading to
     |  employment                 occupations in high
     |  outlets.                   demand
     |  Some general
     |  and non-
     |  traditional
     |  programmes
Low  |_____↓_____
        Low                                      High
                    Employment value
```

Of particular interest to the present discussion is the situation of those university programmes (centre of the graph) which have traditionally had a high academic ranking and prestige but which under the combined effects of massive expansion, the declining employment value of their degrees and consequent changes in student choices, risk becoming increasingly unattractive options. The situation of such university programmes - more often found in the fields of humanities, social science and pure science - becomes even more critical when in addition to the problems created by lack of employment outlets, they constitute the main or only open access sector of higher education and are thus perceived both as high "risk" options and as "safety valves" for the overall system. Now that they have lost some of their attraction and prestige these programmes are recruiting a larger proportion of poorly motivated students: those previously rejected by other selective institutions; those who enrol fully aware of their slim chances in the competition for entry into the prestigious higher education fields; students accumulating credits while awaiting entry into other selective university courses; young secondary school graduates "biding time" for lack of job opportunities, etc. In addition, the trend among senior academic staff members to neglect or abandon undergraduate programmes coupled with the increasing difficulty of teaching a highly heterogeneous student body - in terms of motivation, ability, socio-demographic characteristics - render the task of maintaining high academic standards increasingly difficult.

There is the additional danger that this deteriorating climate will increasingly discourage talented young people with a genuine interest and a sense of vocation from enrolling in the humanities, social sciences and pure sciences. This may have serious consequences for these areas of knowledge, which may gradually find themselves deprived of new talent, creativity and research capacity.

From the point of view of general higher education policy, the problem is not so much the emergence at the tertiary level of a consumption-oriented or of a "low employment value" sector - a trend which may be considered acceptable, even desirable in some countries - but the fact that once certain disciplines or university programmes are deemed to have low employment value they risk being further downgraded by a diminution of their academic standing. In this respect, specific types of government measures, such as the reallocation of resources in favour of options with immediate employment value, may further aggravate this situation.

Employment policy measures aimed at improving the career prospects of these young graduates both in traditional and new sectors are of course of key importance. Equally important would be educational policy measures aimed at preventing employment considerations from reinforcing what appears to be a widening gap or segmentation between disciplines or areas of university study.

Similar hierarchical differentiations are also emerging within the enlarged and diversified network of post-secondary institutions outside the university sector; these will be further discussed under sections (c) and (d). Suffice it here to add that, in recognising the need to increase the employment relevance of many higher education programmes, governments and institutions should be fully aware of the dangers involved in adopting a too narrow or short-term employment perspective. Policies for higher education in the 1980s cannot ignore developments extending into the 1990s and beyond, which may entail drastic changes in the size and composition of the labour force and have very different implications for higher education.

b) Internal reforms within universities

The need to ensure greater diversity of provision at the post-secondary level remains one of the major concerns of educational policy. During the 1960s the prevailing policy was that the most viable - and for many the most desirable - strategy for achieving greater diversity was to develop options and schemes outside the realm of the university. For some it was a question of protecting universities from the dangers inherent in mass education, for others it was the lack of capacity or unwillingness of universities to adapt to the new requirements, in short their "resistance to change"(17)

---

17. Reference to the universities' resistance to change should not necessarily be understood as implying a negative value judgement. In many cases such resistance has protected universities from certain pressures or temporary fashions likely to undermine their capacity for high-level performance.

which justified the adoption of diversification strategies which essentially aimed at bypassing them.

Moreover, during the earlier period of rapid growth the academic world itself had no strong incentive to undertake major internal reforms in response to either employment needs or individual demand. In spite of government efforts to divert demand to other post-secondary programmes, students continued to opt for university, whatever the field of study or the standing of institutions, so that eventually governments had to devote additional resources to this sector to accommodate demand. On the employment side too, university graduates maintained their advantage in terms of recruitment and promotion whereas graduates from short-cycle institutions often had considerable difficulties in achieving adequate recognition.

With the plummeting of confidence in the universities in the 1970s the urgency of certain internal changes became more manifest to institutional leaders and academics. In a far more vulnerable position than in the past, with less access to scarce financial resources in a period of rising costs and prey to growing external criticisms, universities were gradually led to become more responsive to the needs of clientele and to the new socio-economic circumstances.

i) The Comprehensive University: A fading idea?

Strategies aimed at the internal reorganisation of universities are of course bound up with the particular traditions and structure of university systems in each country. It is interesting to note, however, that in their attempts to ensure greater diversity, few universities have adopted the comprehensive or multi-purpose model which attracted considerable interest in the late 1960s[18]. It will be recalled that a fundamental characteristic of the comprehensive model as defined at the time was the merging of short- and long-cycle programmes within one single institution.

Only very few examples can be found in the early 1980s of fully integrated comprehensive universities[19] i.e. those which have a combined curriculum in the first years of study designed both for students pursuing short-cycle programmes leading to a professional qualification and for those aiming at full degrees.

In Germany six integrated comprehensive universities exist (1 in Hesse and 5 in Nordrhein-Westfalen)[20]. However, in all of them integrated programmes represent scarcely more than a third of their

---

18. See "Towards New Structures of Post-Secondary Education", OECD, Paris, 1971.
19. The term comprehensive university and the distinction between integrated and cooperative models are used according to the definitions established in Germany in the early 1970s and adopted by the 1976 Framework Act for Higher Education.
20. L. Cerych, A. Neusel, U. Teichler, H. Winkler: Erfahrung, Hemmnisse, Zielwandel, Frankfurt & New York, Campus 1980.

total provision. In addition, none of these German Gesamthochschulen includes an old-established university; they were initially set up by merging teacher training colleges (Pädagogische Hochschulen) and higher technical schools (Fachhochschulen) and only later developed full university programmes.

In the OECD area as a whole, a fairly common model is the cooperative comprehensive university as it is known in Germany, which implies coexistence of different types of higher education institutions under a single administrative umbrella without integration of their programmes. This is the case of the IUTs (Instituts Universitaires de Technologie) in France which administratively are part of the universities but function quite separately and differ considerably from the other departments or faculties (U.E.R.s - Unités d'Enseignement et de Recherche) in terms of their teaching and organisation. Interestingly enough, they are subject to special regulations putting them under closer government control than the university departments.

It is in Sweden where the idea of setting up comprehensive universities or higher education institutions has received the strongest political support during the 1970s(21). The 1977 Reform formally abolished the distinction between university and non-university higher education and advocated a unitary policy. However, whereas considerable progress was accomplished from a planning and administrative point of view relatively little seems to have been done in terms of the actual integration of university and non-university type programmes or courses.

In some respects the cooperative comprehensive model as defined above differs relatively little from the policy advocated by countries of ensuring closer coordination between the various sectors or institutions of higher education within a region even when these remain under separate administration. Indeed, the general trend seems to be to maintain the specificity or distinctiveness of each type of institution in terms of education provided while strengthening their links so as to promote closer coordination and planning of provision in different geographical areas, make better use of scarce resources and enhance student mobility.

Designing systems of transferable credits between universities, and even more, between different sectors and types of higher education institutions(22) can be seen as a way of promoting an approach to diversity which favours the movement of students between programmes whilst enabling institutions to maintain their distinctiveness(23). However, the slow progress made in improving

---

21. Educational Policy and Planning: Goals for Educational Policy in Sweden, OECD, Paris, 1980.
22. R. Premfors: "Integrated Systems of Higher Education: Sweden". Report presented at the Conference on Comprehensive Universities, New York, December 1980.
23. In the United Kingdom there is strong support for development of credit transfer schemes. Similarly in the Netherlands, see: Opening Up Higher Education, Policy Statement concerning Higher Education in the Netherlands, Ministry of Education and Science publication, 1978, p. 27.

this type of student mobility, especially in European countries and in Japan, poses at present a serious problem and can be expected to remain a major policy issue in the years to come. A highly diversified structure is bound to become a rigid hierarchy if students' choices are irreversible or if many of the options provided are perceived as blind alleys.

Thus, rather than developing sub-degree-level work and organising short-cycle, vocationally-oriented programmes of a similar type to those existing in other post-secondary institutions, universities tend to focus primarily on the reorganisation and diversification of degree level programmes and post-graduate studies. Increased efficiency, greater social and employment relevance of first and higher degree programmes and more flexible arrangements for the pursuit of university studies appear to be among the central concerns of recent reform proposals.

ii) Organisation of University Studies in Cycles

The trend towards organising university studies into consecutive and more sharply differentiated cycles constitutes the initial approach to coping with the massive expansion of recent decades. Such a policy has been more frequently taken in continental European countries where universities, committed to open access and having degree programmes which last from 4 to 7 years(24), had to operate an orientation and/or selection function explicitly or implicitly after entry. The first cycle, generally labelled introductory or orientation, offers a general type of education in which research activities are kept to a minimum and teaching is predominantly carried out by junior staff members. In France, for example, in the early 1970s, a first cycle of 2 years' duration leading to a diploma (DEUG) was set up within a large number of university programmes. The government's idea was that this diploma was to have both a terminal and a transfer orientation. However, in practice it was never considered by the staff or the students as a terminal qualification but rather as the basis for selection and streaming into the next cycle culminating in either a "licence" or a "maîtrise". A similar first cycle exists in Yugoslav universities; in Belgium the first cycle or candidaat lasts 2 years but has no terminal or professional orientation. In the Netherlands the recently voted Higher Education Bill envisages the introduction of a preliminary year followed by an examination which has a "threefold function of orientating, selecting and advising another course" (25).

---

24. In some countries such as the Netherlands and Germany there is no distinction between undergraduate and post-graduate studies. This distinction will be introduced in the Netherlands in 1982.

25. Opening Up Higher Education, Policy Statement concerning Higher Education in the Netherlands, Ministry of Education and Science publication, 1978, p. 27.

In addition to its explicit function of orientation, the first cycle or propaedeutic years in universities have often been implicitly assigned a "cooling out" or selective function, particularly in countries where universities had open access. A number of their characteristics show that they were designed primarily as an <u>introductory and selective phase of a full degree programme</u> (and less as a terminal diploma or an orientation phase). Firstly, rather than adapting first-year courses to the incoming students, their traditional characteristics were often maintained; sometimes selection was reinforced through difficult examinations or the introduction of selective subjects, i.e. emphasis on mathematics during the first years of many social sciences programmes. Secondly, little attention was paid to orientation beyond the options provided by the institutions and even less to the preparation of those who would have preferred to leave after the completion of the first stage. As a consequence, universities witnessed high drop-out rates during the first years of study while the majority of students who completed the first cycle aimed at a full degree(26).

Future efforts at enhancing the value of two-or three-year university programmes, or even at shortening the duration of studies leading to a first degree, may suffer the consequences of past attempts of subdividing degree courses without paying sufficient attention to the needs of those who leave after completing the first years of study. Lack of a more positive orientation at this level tends to reinforce the view, especially among young people pursuing their initial education, that programmes of shorter duration within universities, even when sanctioned by a diploma, are essentially incomplete degrees or an administrative device designed to render selection or dropping out a less traumatic personal experience. (As will be seen later, it is doubtful whether the introduction of a modular structure of studies in some European universities, whatever their other advantages, has basically modified this point of view).

In the majority of Member countries - whether or not a system of cycles has been introduced - the trend has been to <u>emphasize the cut-off point between first degree programmes and post-graduate studies</u>. This has again led to reforms aimed at strengthening the terminal orientation of first degree programmes, at a better adaptation of curricula and the structure of studies to the employment situation and, in many cases, at reducing the research orientation of undergraduate studies. Very often, these reforms have been accompanied by more stringent selection policies for entry into post-graduate education.

Indeed, whereas in the 1960s post-graduate studies in a number of countries expanded at an even faster rate than undergraduate courses, in some of them the growth of such courses has been quite seriously curtailed in the course of the 1970s(27). Seen from a

---

26. Some illustrative figures on dropouts during the first year of university studies are given in Chapter II.
27. See Statistical Annex, Table A-3.

research perspective, this trend reversal is even more dramatic since, in some countries at least, the post-graduate level recruits a growing proportion of professionally rather than research-oriented students. Serious cuts in the resources assigned to research training and activities, together with the slow turnover due to the age composition of the staff - mostly recruited in the 1960s - poses a very serious problem for the future of this level as well as for the research enterprise as a whole whose dynamism and vitality to a large extent depend on the renewal of its work force(28).

iii) <u>Development of Modular Courses</u>

Another way in which universities have attempted to respond to the more diverse needs of the student body has been through <u>the development of modular courses or an aggregative pattern of studies</u> (29) as a means of facilitating the preparation and transition to employment of young people who are in their initial training and who could eventually decide to interrupt their studies after one, two or three years of university education. Few universities have so far adopted this pattern of studies. Up till now at least, the emphasis has been either on reorganising degree level studies or on fostering the participation of new groups, in particular adults already in employment.

When the focus is on the first function, as for example in France where a modular system ("unités de valeur") has been introduced within the mainstream of many university programmes and applies to all students pursuing undergraduate studies, modules are organised and perceived primarily as part of a full degree and in general have not resulted in stronger vocational or terminal orientation of the first years of study. On the other hand, when modular courses are introduced essentially as an alternative to full degree programmes and are mainly designed for adults, e.g. the single courses in Sweden, they tend to be structured as self-sufficient or independent units. It is possible that as a growing number of students enter the mainstream of universities without the intention of completing a full degree those distinctions may become increasingly blurred. However, this still leaves open the question of whether the future trend will be towards a stronger terminal or vocational orientation of the first years of university studies. For the moment, the trend in quite a number of countries is to maintain the general orientation of the first years of university studies and facilitate the transfer of young students completing the first years to other post-secondary institutions where they can obtain a middle-level qualification fairly rapidly or enrol in a vocational course likely to enhance their employment prospects.

---

28. "The reform of studies and the state of research in higher education", OECD document, Paris, 1981.
29. For the main characteristics of such a model, see <u>Selection and Certification in Education and Employment</u>, OECD, Paris, 1977.

iv) <u>Shortening the formal and real duration of university studies</u>

Shortening the formal and real duration of university studies has been a matter of particular concern in many of the continental European countries e.g. Denmark, Germany, Netherlands, where long-cycle studies leading to a first degree usually take 6 to 9 years. Measures aimed at improving the efficiency of university studies - understood in this context as increasing the proportion of students who both complete their studies and do so without delays - have been more rapidly introduced, if not always with great success, than the actual shortening of university programmes. The introduction of restricted entry, the development of credits transferable between institutions, certain changes in student aid schemes designed to encourage students to proceed at the established pace can be seen as responding to these efficiency requirements. In spite of the fact that changes in student participation and the diversity of attendance patterns have rendered the definition and measurement of efficiency more complex, the persistence of a wide gap between the number of new entrants and the number of first degrees awarded x years later remains a key problem in many European universities.

The shortening of the formal duration of first degree university programmes appears to be an even more difficult enterprise. Although on the agenda for reforms in some countries where it has been scheduled as a priority for a number of years (e.g. U-90 in Denmark, 1978 Bill in the Netherlands, Federal Frame Law in the Federal Republic of Germany), by the end of the 1970s little progress had been achieved. Only recently, and after long negotiations, has the Dutch Parliament approved a Higher Education Bill which stipulates that most first degree university programmes will take four years (doctoral stage) (as opposed to 5 or 6 years in existing programmes) with a 2-year post-graduate stage(30).

Since the real duration of studies in the Netherlands is on average 7 to 9 years the law also stipulates that students will be allowed a maximum of two additional years, i.e. six years in all, to complete their first degree.

Resistance to shortening of university studies comes from both within the university and from the professional associations. The latter fear that the value of university degrees will be further undermined and that these shortened degrees will not be given adequate recognition in employment. In Germany, employers have opposed the <u>Wissenschaftsrat</u> proposal to shorten university courses.

It is interesting to note that when new degrees are introduced in each country they are set up so that they correspond as closely as possible to the traditional ones. Sociology and political science, for example, take 6 or 7 years in Denmark, 4 years in France, and 3 years in the United Kingdom. Understandably, this is considered

---

30. <u>Opening Up Higher Education</u>, op.cit.

essential in ensuring the social and economic status of the new professions but at a time of strong financial constraints this monolithic structure may well contribute to blocking the development of new programmes within the university sector.

v) Diversifying modes of attendance

One recent reform to which universities appear to be increasingly committed is that of promoting <u>more flexible and diverse arrangements for the pursuit of university studies</u>, in particular part-time courses. Recognising that most programmes have been traditionally designed for a small proportion of young people who had the time and opportunity to stay on at university full-time for many years, efforts are now being deployed to respond to a clientele for whom such arrangements are ill-suited or represent a major obstacle to their further education.

A key policy issue in the 1970s was whether the provision of more flexible schemes on a larger scale, in particular distance learning, should be taken over by the established universities or by specialised institutions set up for the purpose. Initially quite a number of OECD countries, e.g. Germany, Japan, Spain, Netherlands, favoured the second option, influenced by the success of the Open University in the United Kingdom; others like Australia, with a long tradition of part-time adult education, and Sweden, opted for diversifying provision within the existing framework. More recently, even in countries where special "non-traditional" institutions have been set up, there seems to be a growing disposition on the part of universities towards facilitating part-time attendance and developing schemes which allow for an alternation between studies and work. As discussed in Section (d) an essential consideration is that of maintaining levels of participation and resources. However it is possible that whereas during a first phase the Open University in the United Kingdom may have inhibited reforms within established universities, its subsequent success in paving the way for part-time studies and in establishing their respectability may prove to have an opposite stimulating effect on the traditional university sector.

As shown in Table A-4 of the Statistical Annex in the few countries for which information is available, the number and proportion of part-time students has increased over the past decade. This table, however, does not provide a true picture of the growing diversity in patterns of attendance, a trend difficult to discern in many of the national statistics(31), particularly in countries where no clear distinction is made between full-time and part-time enrolments. In France and Italy, for example, where all university students are listed as full-time, surveys show that a considerable number of students - varying according to fields of study and location of university - are engaged in some type of work, including full-time employment.

---

31. See Chapter III.

A French survey based on a national sample of higher education institutions(32) shows how the proportion of students who combine studies and work is increasing:

PERCENTAGE OF UNIVERSITY STUDENTS DECLARING THEMSELVES AS BEING IN PAID EMPLOYMENT

	1977	1979
Students in full-time employment	5.4	6.4
Students in part-time employment (working regularly)	15.0	18.8
Students in part-time employment (working irregularly)	18.6	24.3

PERCENTAGE OF STUDENTS WHO ARE EMPLOYED AT LEAST PART-TIME OR OCCASIONALLY(1)

	73(2)	77(2)	79(2)
1. Law and Economics	35.4	39.9	44.4
2. Letters and Social Sciences	34.8	47.0	59.9
3. Sciences	31.9	31.2	40.5
4. Medicine, Dentistry and Pharmacy	21.2(3)	34.0	48.8
Total University	32.2	38.9	49.5

1. National Survey: "Les Etudiants".
2. 73 = Students engaged in paid employment (irrespective of type) during the week of survey.
77+79 = Students in paid employment on a full-time or part-time basis, regularly or otherwise.
3. Medicine only.
Source: Jarousse, Evolution du Comportement des Etudiants, op.cit., p. 9.

In some countries courses are increasingly being organised in evenings, weekends and during holidays. An Italian survey(33) gives a rough idea about the percentage of new university entrants who do not work or plan to work while pursuing their studies.

---

32. Survey undertaken by the "Guide de l'Etudiant" 1977 & 1979. Source : J.P. Jarousse, Evolution du Comportement des Etudiants, CREDOC, Paris, December 1980, p. 17.
33. ISTAT, Indagine speciale sulle caratteristiche degli studenti universitari iscritti al I° anno di corso, Rome, 1977.

Discipline	Proportion who declared they did not work and did not intend to seek work
Mathematics	56.6
Physics	36.0
Chemistry	53.2
Geology	36.5
Computer Studies	45.6
Natural Sciences	50.4
Biology	54.4
Pharmacy	55.2
Medicine	66.1
Engineering	50.4
Architecture	38.5
Agronomy	39.8
Veterinary Medicine	48.7
Economics and Commerce	29.8
Politics	22.3
Sociology	22.4
Law	37.2
Letters	48.1
Literary Subjects	45.1
Philosophy	40.7
Pedagogics	42.0
Modern Foreign Languages	44.4
Foreign Languages	46.2
Psychology	33.1
Total (All subjects)	44.4

The steady increase in the number of part-time students combining studies with work, other social activities or leisure reflects perhaps a certain loss of confidence in the economic value of the studies being pursued. Unsure as to the social and economic returns on their "investment", students tend to be less motivated to complete their courses rapidly; they are keener to enter the world of work or engage in low and even unpaid activities when openings are available. The fact that young people participating on a part-time or more irregular basis tend to be pursuing studies with poor employment prospects would seem to confirm this argument.

It may well be that somme of the more significant changes in higher education in the years to come will derive not so much from the presence of new groups but rather from the traditional young clientele seeking forms of participation.

vi) <u>Increasing the employment relevance of university programmes</u>

The need to increase <u>the employment and social relevance of university first-degree programmes</u> is mentioned by most Member countries as a major consideration in many proposals and actual reforms of the structure and content of university studies. Despite this common concern there is no consensus on how this objective should be translated into practice. The controversy and confusion surrounding this issue are to a large extent due to the fact that it touches on the fundamental question of the function of the various types of undergraduate studies and more specifically on the complex relationship between higher education and employment. The very different ideological viewpoints which prevail, coupled with the multiple definitions and interpretations of certain key concepts such as "employment relevance" and "employment needs", particularly in regard to the qualitative aspects, add to the difficulty of finding satisfactory solutions.

An idea which enjoys a considerable measure of support and which has been the guiding principle in recent plans and reforms(34) is that of organising degree courses so that they respond to the needs of more broadly defined occupational sectors. This has meant advocating reforms in quite different directions, depending on the orientation of traditional programmes of study and the objectives pursued. In the case of certain types of professional training, in particular where the market for graduates is considered to be nearing saturation, there are claims in favour of broadening the curricula and introducing a more comprehensive type of education aimed at preparing future graduates for a wider range of jobs. The reform of many Colleges of Education into more comprehensive or polyvalent Institutes or Colleges of Higher Education illustrate this trend.

In a growing number of countries reforms in the content and structure of studies with a view to enhancing the employment and social relevance of professionally oriented programmes are being seen as a means of changing and diversifying the profile of established professions so that they better respond to new societal requirements. This is in particular the case of the service professions i.e. health, social services, teaching(35).

At the other end of the spectrum are a variety of university degree courses, primarily in the Humanities, Social Sciences and Natural Sciences faculties which, after a period of very rapid expansion in response to individual demand and employment needs in the public sector, in particular those of the education system itself,

---

34. As in Sweden and Denmark.
35. See <u>The University and the Community: the Problems of Changing Relationship</u>, OECD/CERI, Paris, 1982.

are now under strong pressure to change and/or strengthen their professional orientation, given the serious contraction in these employment outlets(36). Arguments in favour of an increased "professionalisation" of university studies, introducing courses likely to facilitate transition to the world of work, or better suited to employment prospects inside and more importantly outside the public sector, focus primarily on programmes for which enrolment is traditionally highest particularly among women (see table).

PROPORTION OF UNIVERSITY STUDENTS ENROLLED IN THE HUMANITIES & SOCIAL SCIENCES (1977)

	Total Enrolments			Female Enrolments		
	Humanities[1]	Soc.S.	Total	Humanities	Soc.S.	Total
Australia	36.2	17.6	53.8	56.4	16.1	72.5
Canada	43.2	13.4	56.6	49.7	14.1	63.8
Finland(2)	29.7	26.0	55.7	21.0	46.5	67.5
Germany	37.6	13.9	51.5	58.0	10.5	68.5
Ireland(2)	39.8	12.3	52.1	65.3	5.4	70.7
Japan	23.9	"	"	"	"	"
Netherlands	18.0	22.9	40.9	31.7	19.1	50.8
Spain(2)	30.6	12.6	43.2	51.3	8.7	60.0
Switzerland	23.5	21.5	45.0	40.8	24.0	64.8
United Kingdom	24.9	20.5	45.4			

1. Humanities, Fine Arts & Education.
2. 1976
Source: Educational Statistics in OECD Countries, OECD, Paris, 1981.

c) The consolidation and reorganisation of the non-university sector

During the 1960s efforts to widen the range of options at post-secondary level led governments to focus their attention on a variety of institutions already providing advanced-level training but which were at the periphery of higher education. Some of them were in between the secondary and the post-secondary levels, others were labelled post-secondary as opposed to the higher education and university sector. In general, they constituted the peak of the

---
36. See "The reform of studies and the state of research in higher education", op.cit.

technical vocational sector leading to middle-level qualifications and represented the main post-secondary options for pupils completing secondary technical education.

The need to expand provision and set up alternatives to full degree programmes for the growing number of secondary school graduates qualifying for higher education and to enhance the status of technical education were among the pressures which led governments to reform, upgrade and integrate these institutions within more largely defined higher education systems. Similar considerations were behind the creation of new short-cycle institutions and other non-traditional programmes which flourished in the late sixties(37).

Evidence for some OECD countries on the growth of the non-university sector over the past 15 years and on the proportion of students entering this sector is given in the Statistical Annex.

Figures should be interpreted with caution, particularly those concerning European countries where the majority of institutions in the non-university sector have restricted entry. Indeed, in many cases, the decline in rates of growth during the 1970s may be due less to a falling off in demand than to a slowdown in the expansion of places. Claims that competition for entry into post-secondary technical education has increased in recent years would confirm this interpretation.

As indicated above, until the early seventies short-cycle institutions tended to favour a pattern of development likely to increase their standing within the academic world. However, they often ended up by losing out both ways: on the one hand they seldom succeeded in achieving true parity of esteem within the academic world; on the other, because they neglected some of their traditional functions, they came to be viewed by outside groups, in particular employers, with increased scepticism.

As a result of this development coupled with changes in the employment situation and in patterns of demand, short-cycle institutions are tending to become less concerned with academic status and in recent years many of them have strengthened the vocational orientation of their programmes.

It is too early to say whether the move towards greater distinctiveness has helped these institutions in finding a new balance and in consolidating their place and identity within the higher education world.

In general it could be said that the narrower the gap or social distance between institutions in the non-university sector and the universities the more intense and persistent will be the concern over parity of esteem and the "identity crisis". In particular, Teacher

---

37. OECD, Short-Cycle Higher Education: A Search for Identity, op.cit.

Training Colleges in many Member countries, some of the Junior Colleges and 4-year general programmes in Japan and the United States, different types of Polytechnics in Europe, Colleges of Advanced Education in Australia are faced with the dilemma of whether to strive for upgrading and risk becoming weak of second choice university-type institutions or professional schools, or to develop a different orientation emphasising differentiation rather than equality. Choice of strategies vis-à-vis the future development of these intermediary type of institutions is of key importance, if, with the expected reduction of college age cohorts, they are to strengthen or maintain their competitive position within the overall post-secondary system.

Indeed, in recent years, these intermediary type of institutions seem to have experienced more difficulty in adapting to the new pressures and constraints than the more vocationally-oriented short-cycle schemes. The latter, having less chance of competing academically, traditionally more receptive to externally defined employment and community needs and often receiving strong public and private financial support, appear to be having an easier task in attracting clientele and gaining outside recognition. In fact, many of them could be criticised on different grounds, namely that they are too employment oriented and thus tend to take <u>the success of their graduates in finding immediate employment</u> as the overriding criterion for institutional performance.

Although some governments are being held responsible for promoting such a narrow employment perspective, the trend towards increased vocationalism to a large measure reflects changes in private demand. In the United States, for example, where the development of post-secondary education is particularly sensitive to changes in student preferences, the balance between general and vocational programmes in Community Colleges has changed considerably. Whereas in 1971 42% of all Associate Degrees awarded corresponded to vocational programmes, the proportion rose to 57% in 1978(38). Enrolments in post-secondary vocational courses receiving federal aid nearly quadrupled in 8 years from 593,000 in 1968 to 2,169,100 in 1976(39). In France a marked preference for post-secondary technical education has been observed in recent years. Schools for high-level technicians which were to be phased out not only continued to expand but experienced a sharp increase in demand (in 1978 there were ten applicants per place in some sections). In Norway, a growing number of qualified secondary-school leavers from academic streams are enrolling in vocational secondary schools. In Sweden a similar trend can be observed. In Germany the proportion of students with secondary school academic qualifications (Abitur) enrolling in apprenticeship schemes rose from around 3 per cent in the early 1970s to 10 per cent in 1977(40).

---

38. National Center for Education Statistics: <u>Digest of Education Statistics</u> - Washington, Volumes 1977/78 <u>and 1980.</u>
39. <u>The Condition of Education</u>, 1978 Edition, p. 156.
40. Der Bundesminister für Bildung und Wissenschaft, <u>Berufsbildungsbericht 1978</u>.

The growth of privately-financed vocational colleges catering for qualified school leavers or adults with equivalent qualifications poses the problem of setting norms for their accreditation, that is of defining the type of professional orientation and minimum standards required for their inclusion and/or recognition within the formal post-secondary framework. The use of narrowly defined academic criteria within the formal education sector may result - as has already been the case in some countries - in the emergence of further development of training schemes outside the control of Ministries of Education and a corresponding loss of political support and resources for the formal sector. On the other hand, the question remains as to what extent educational authorities should give way to pressures in favour of narrowly oriented or increasingly specialised vocational studies which aim primarily at facilitating placement of graduates in their first jobs.

The search for strategies which enable the more immediate "transition" employment requirements to be reconciled with the broader longer-term consideration of the life-time career of individuals - the most important and uncontested function of educational institutions - is one of the more difficult challenges confronting educational authorities and institutional leaders.

d) Continuing Education: The Expanding Sector of Higher Education

Whereas during the late sixties and early seventies the predominant trend was to set up special institutions or schemes catering for the non-traditional clientele, in more recent years conventional universities and colleges have shown growing interest in, or at least greater responsiveness to, the needs of adult students. True, the existence of extra-mural courses, extension activities or even external degrees is by no means a new phenomenon, particularly in universities and colleges with an Anglo-Saxon tradition. What is of more recent date is the growing proportion of adults enrolled in mainstream courses leading to recognised qualifications. Perhaps of even greater significance in terms of potential for the future, is the greater interest and efforts on the part of universities and colleges to provide in a more systematic way continuing education courses which respond to the specifically defined requirements of certain groups e.g. short courses or special training schemes organised in cooperation with or under the sponsorship of professional groups, trade unions, enterprises, government agencies and other groups in the surrounding community.

In the majority of cases - the notable exception being the United States - these courses are a relatively new departure and considered as a clearly distinct and peripheral activity; nevertheless they represent one of the few growing enterprises in the higher education world. The consequences of declining birth rates, the need to use available physical resources as well as tenured teaching staff and growing financial constraints are among the forces likely to impell higher education institutions to develop further these types of activity. Also, with the generalisation of shorter working hours and early retirement, there may be growing opportunities for attracting new groups for whom education will represent a form of consumption.

The development of such variety of courses and schemes primarily intended for adults, but also for groups of young people seeking more flexible arrangements, could well lead to radical changes in attitudes to the approach and organisation of post-secondary education. While such courses no doubt respond to the various claims in favour of greater openness and a better adaptation of the formal system to a recurrent or lifelong pattern of education, their development would need careful monitoring so as to avoid inherent dangers to the traditional core functions of academic institutions. Most higher education institutions in OECD countries are still highly unlikely to run such a risk and deserve encouragement in facilitating access to adults and in promoting services to the surrounding community. A different situation pertains in the United States, which is by far the most advanced OECD country in terms of non-traditional provision both in respect of the variety of schemes and the numbers of participants. Recently, observers in that country have expressed their concern over some ethically dubious practices developed by certain colleges and universities in their efforts to enrol new students in non-traditional programmes as well as in conventional degree programmes(41). The fear is that in a period of intensified competition for enrolments such as will be faced in the coming 15 years these practices risk becoming more frequent, thus compromising the integrity of academic life and contributing to a gradual erosion of confidence in and public support for higher education institutions.

---

41. Fair Practices in Higher Education. A Report of the Carnegie Council on Policy Studies on Higher Education. Jossey-Bass Publishers, San Francisco, 1979.

Chapter II

ADMISSION POLICIES

The 1970s were a period of significant changes in admission policies. These were due as much to "outside pressures", linked to the economic situation as to "internal" forces consequent on the extraordinary growth of education and the emergence of new ideas about the type and direction of growth of formal education. While financial and employment factors certainly played a part and appear to have played a key role in influencing private demand for post-secondary education (1), many of the recent proposals or actual reforms have their origins and support in broader educational and social considerations. Closely linked to quantitative developments, such considerations often reflect different approaches to some of the perennial problems of educational policies, most notably that of selection within formal educational systems.

Given the well-known fact that selection within formal education is a continuous process and that all educational systems fulfill at one stage or another a major selection and allocation function, it is essential that the debate on admission policies at the post-secondary level be set in a wider system perspective. Even when a distinction is drawn between systems in which universities select at entry and those where universities are open to all those who apply - a distinction which is now much more difficult to make - it is important to bear in mind that this implies fundamental differences between systems with different strategies and modes of selection.

Although recognising that in practically all OECD countries, compulsory education still retains a selective function, even in comprehensive systems, the present chapter will take as its point of departure the transition from compulsory to post-compulsory education (2). The first part of the chapter - <u>selection before entry</u> - briefly reviews trends in participation rates at the upper secondary level which may help explain differences between countries in their approach and policies vis-à-vis access to higher education. The second and main part of the chapter - <u>selection at entry</u> - examines recent trends and

---

1. <u>Individual Demand for Education: Analytical Report</u>, OECD, Paris, 1978.
2. For a thorough analysis of developments in basic education see: <u>Compulsory Schooling in a Changing World</u>, OECD, Paris, 1983.

reforms in admission policies in various Member countries, focusing in particular on the articulation between secondary and higher education, on policies concerning the access and distribution of students throughout the total range of higher education institutions and on the issue of selection within the university sector. The third and final part - <u>selection after entry</u> - examines briefly what happens to students once they are admitted to higher education, comparing in particular programmes and institutions with different degrees of selectivity at entry.

1. SELECTION BEFORE ENTRY

Over the past two decades many Member countries have extended the period of compulsory schooling while practically all countries witnessed a steady increase in participation rates at the post-compulsory level (3). However, the same indicators which provide evidence of progress accomplished reveal the substantial differences in patterns of development across the OECD area. Table 1 gives an approximate picture of the transition from compulsory to post-compulsory education: whereas in the late 1970s in the United States, Canada and Japan practically the totality of the age group continued beyond compulsory schooling, in other countries, such as Austria, Denmark, France, Sweden, United Kingdom, participation rates dropped by more than 25% between the last year of compulsory schooling and the first year of non-compulsory education. In Spain and Portugal departures begin earlier: around 13% of children do not comply with the legal requirement of compulsory school attendance.

Table 2 on enrolment rates in the 16-year age group also gives a rough indication of the proportion of young people staying on beyond compulsory schooling (4). Throughout the late 1960s and the 1970s enrolment rates for this group increased in all Member countries. This table confirms the top ranking of Japan, the United States and Canada, which together with the Netherlands and Germany have the highest enrolment ratios for this age group; in the latter country, however, 36% of 16-year-olds attend formal education on a part-time basis. In a second group of countries - Austria, Denmark, Norway, Sweden, Switzerland and the United Kingdom - between 15% and 30% of 16-year-olds were out of formal education in the mid- or late 1970s whereas the percentage of abstentions increases to around 40% in Greece, New Zealand and Italy and exceeds 50% in Portugal.

As seen from Table 3, in some countries the high participation rates of 16-year-olds is at least partly explained by the fact that a high proportion are still in education corresponding to compulsory schooling: 70% in Denmark, 60% of boys and 47% of girls in the Netherlands, around 25% in Canada, Germany, Switzerland and the United States.

---

3. <u>Compulsory Schooling in a Changing World</u>, op. cit.
4. In most Member countries the age at which compulsory schooling ends is 15 or 16. <u>Ibid</u>.

Table 1

HISTORICAL DEVELOPMENT OF ENROLMENT RATES DURING THE
LAST YEAR OF COMPULSORY SCHOOLING (c) AND THE FIRST YEAR OF
NON-COMPULSORY SCHOOLING (n.c.)

(1900 - 1977)

Percentages

Country	Year	1900 B G	1910 B G	1920 B G	1930 B G	1940 B G	1950 B G	1960 B G	1970 B G	1977 B G
Austria	c						99.7	99.7	99.7	99.8
	n.c.						77.8	88.2	70.0*	72.8
Belgium	c						◄——— All young people were attending school ———►			100 100
	n.c.						70.3 67.6	79.1 73.7	89.9	
Canada	c				96.0 96.0	95.3 95.4	96.2 95.7	98.0 98.0	100 100	100 100
	n.c.				86.5 85.6	84.4 85.0	92.1 90.7	86.6* 86.4*	98.3 98.0	92.1* 92.1*
Denmark(1)	c			◄——— All young people were attending school ———►					72.8* 82.7*
	n.c.		11.0 8.0	13.5 12.0	18.0 16.0	22.0 21.5	29.1 31.5	60.0	77.8 84.7	
Spain	c							68.6 58.3	87.6 80.2	86.7 85.4
	n.c.							45.7 33.5	55.4 44.3	79.5 75.7
Finland(2)	c					92.3	98.5	98.5	99.6	99.7
	n.c.									
France	c	95.0	98.0	98.0	98.5	97.0*	98.0	97.4	76.6 84.8	91.2
	n.c.	34.5	41.0	50.0	60.0	43.0*	50.0	68.3	59.0* 66.4*	70.8
Ireland	c							94.8 96.0	97.2 96.4	95.6
	n.c.							67.0 70.6	85.4 84.1	86.4*
Italy(2)	c	50.7 47.3	54.8 51.5	59.4 55.8	78.3 73.6		83.4	88.8	98.4	105.4 105.0
	n.c.									
Japan(3)	c	90.6 71.7	98.8 97.4	99.2 98.8	99.5 99.5	99.6 99.6	99.3 99.1	99.9 99.9	99.9 99.9	99.9 99.9
	n.c.									
Norway	c							98.0	77.6(3)	97.5 80.0*
	n.c.									
New Zealand	c	59.9	72.4	85.9		93.7	96.0	95.4	99.8	99.5
	n.c.	26.1	34.8	49.4	66.2	71.3	64.7*	77.2	86.8*	88.8
Netherlands(2)	c	85.2 79.6	88.7 85.9	88.9 86.7	96.8 98.6	97.2 97.5	95.5 97.0	98.0 99.2	99.5 99.6	97.8 97.3
	n.c.				87.2* 81.7*	90.5 86.5	71.1* 67.6*	84.9 77.1	96.8 92.8	86.6* 80.6*
Portugal	c					39.2	72.8(2)	89.3	87.3	87.5
	n.c.					35.2	60.9	71.2	60.8*	70.9
United Kingdom	c								100.5 100.4	100.1 100.2
	n.c.								72.2 71.4	61.0* 53.3*
Sweden(2)	c			79.5	86.3	87.8	84.3	88.4	93.8	97.8 97.4
	n.c.								70.5*	76.6 74.0

1. Except for the final two years, the figures relate to the whole of pupils in a given year of studies in relation to the population whose age formally corresponds to this year of studies.
2. Overall rate for the population of compulsory schooling age; for the Netherlands from 1900 to 1920 and for Sweden from 1920 to 1960.
3. Enrolment rates for the population whose age corresponds to primary schooling from 1900 to 1940 and to first-cycle secondary from 1950 onwards.
4. A 9-year period of compulsory schooling had already been introduced by 85 per cent of local authorities.
N.B. The asterisks indicate that compulsory schooling was extended.

Source: Compulsory Schooling in a Changing World, op. cit.

103

Table 2

EVOLUTION OF ENROLMENT RATES IN THE 16-YEAR AGE GROUP

Percentages

	1965	1970	Latest Year(2)
Australia	-	55.1(4)	59.1(4)
Austria	20.7	-	82.8
Canada	-	85.6	83.6
Denmark	-	-	85.1
France	52.3	62.6	72.0
Germany	92.9(27.5)(1)	94.6(34.8)(1)	96.7(61.8)(1)
Greece	-	54.4	58.7
Ireland*	-	55.1(1)	68.6
Italy	33.2	46.9	53.4(3)
Japan*	-	78.8	91.6
Netherlands	B 88.4(71.7)(1) G 65.3(54.7)(1)	B 95.3(80.8)(1) G 89.6(70.0)(1)	B 97.0(89.1)(1) G 95.7(86.7)(1)
New Zealand*	-	55.7	65.7
Norway*	-	-	80.1
Portugal*	-	25.7	37.2
Spain	14.0	29.4	50.3
Sweden*	-	70.3	77.9
Switzerland*	-	-	76.3
United Kingdom	-	B 75.0(42.0)(1) G 61.1(41.0)(1)	79.7 (B 57.9)(1) (G 62.9)(1)
United States*	-	92.7	91.3
Yugoslavia	56.3	-	75.1

1. Figures in brackets refer to full-time pupils only.
2. Latest year available for each country is given in Table 3.
3. Slight differences between these rates and those listed in Table 3 are due to the different sources used.
4. Not including apprenticeship and TAFE.

Sources: For countries marked with an *: Education Statistics in OECD Countries, OECD, Paris 1981. In these countries except for Switzerland part-time enrolments are not included. Lack of data is of particular significance in the case of Australia and New Zealand. For all other countries Secretariat data are drawn from national statistics.

Table 3

ENROLMENT RATES IN THE 16- AND 18-YEAR AGE GROUPS
BY LEVEL AND TYPE OF EDUCATION

Percentages

		Compulsory Education	Non-Compulsory Secondary Education	of which Technical and Vocational	Higher Education	Total*
Australia (1979)	16	1.8	56.9	-	0.4	59.1
	18	-	6.6	-	12.9	19.5(2)
Austria (1977)	16	-	-	66.5	-	82.8
	18		40.9	34.1	4.1	45.0
Canada (1976)*	16	23.4	63.4	-	1.7	88.5
	18	1.1	19.9	-	18.6	39.7
Denmark (1977)	16	69.3	15.8	5.0	-	85.1
	18	1.1	53.0	30.3	0.8	55.3
France (1979)	16	6.1	65.9	29.5	-	72.0
	18	-	26.0	6.7	11.2	37.2
Germany (1979)	16	22.6	74.1	50.8	-	96.7(61.8)(7)
	18	0.5	69.4	51.8	0.9	70.8(27.9)(7)
Greece (1975)	16	-	58.7	9.7	-	58.7
	18	-	25.5	11.3	9.4	34.9
Ireland (1975)*	16	10.8	57.1	-	0.1	68.6
	18	0.1	14.0	-	13.0	27.2
Italy (1975)	16	2.5	50.9	-	-	53.4
	18	0.3	31.6	-	4.4	36.2
Japan (1976)*	16	-	91.3(6)	-	-	91.6
	18	-	3.6(6)	-	40.1	43.9
Netherlands (1979)	16	B 58.3(34.2)(3)	38.7(4)	15.0(4)	-	97.0
		G 47.2(22.5)(3)	48.5(4)	20.6(4)	-	95.7
	18	B 8.5(5.3)(3)	33.9	16.7	9.7	52.1
		G 4.1(1.6)(3)	27.0	13.7	8.2	39.3
New Zealand (1976)*	16	3.0	61.9	-	-	65.7
	18		6.9	-	11.1	18.2
Norway (1976)*	16	7.9	71.7	32.2	-	80.1
	18		47.4	16.0	0.7	48.4
Portugal (1975)*	16	2.8	34.4	10.4	-	37.2
	18	1.0	25.5	9.8	2.7	29.2
Spain (1978)	16	-	50.3	13.9	-	50.3
	18	-	20.4	6.9	12.2	32.6
Sweden (1978)	16	5.0	72.9	-	-	77.9
	18	-	35.0	-	0.8	35.8
Switzerland (1976)*	16	23.1	51.8	40.6	-	76.3
	18	0.4	62.5	48.9	-	63.9
United Kingdom (1977)	16	34.5	34.8	9.1	-	61.0(79.7)(5)
	18	-	12.1	5.7	6.7	18.8(42.7)(5)
United States (1976)	16	22.3	67.9	-	0.6	91.3
	18	1.2	14.9	-	32.2	51.0
Yugoslavia (1975)	16	16.7	58.4	29.8	-	75.1
	18	-	49.5	35.4	NA	

1. In some countries the total includes a small percentage of pupils in special education.
2. Not including apprenticeship and TAFE.
3. Figures in brackets refer to enrolment rates in vocational education at this level.
4. Includes part-time students not classified by type of school: 7.9% boys and 9.0% girls.
5. Figures in brackets include full-time and part-time students.
6. In Japan 33% of 16-year olds and 1.7% of 18-year olds are in secondary technical courses Type A.
7. Figures in brackets refer to full-time pupils only.

Sources: For countries marked with an (*): Educational Statistics in OECD Countries, OECD, Paris 1981. In these countries except for Switzerland part-time enrolments are not included. Lack of data is of particular significance in the case of Australia and New Zealand. For all other countries, Secretariat data are drawn from national statistics.

Table 4

EVOLUTION OF FULL-TIME ENROLMENT RATES IN THE 17-YEAR AGE GROUP

Percentages

Country		Total Secondary A*	Total Secondary B*	Total Non-Compulsory Secondary Education	Total	Female Secondary A*	Female Secondary B*	Female Non-Compulsory Secondary Education	Female Total
Australia	(1971)	-	-	28.4(1)	-	-	-	24.4(1)	-
	(1976)	-	-	31.2(1)	40.0	-	-	30.9	40.3
Austria	(1970)	16.1	8.8	24.9	24.9	14.4	10.4	24.8	24.8
	(1976)	20.9	7.8	28.7	28.9(4)	20.5	10.1	30.7	30.8
Canada	(1976)	-	-	54.7	-	-	-	55.2	68.5
Denmark	(1970)	25.1	7.9	33.0	-	-	-	-	-
	(1976)	27.9	18.8	46.8	47.5	-	-	-	-
France	(1970)	20.8	10.4	31.2	45.6	23.0	10.7	33.7	48.6
	(1976)	26.7	15.0	41.7	53.5	-	-	-	-
Germany	(1971)	16.5	5.5	22.0	22.9(5)	14.1	6.0	20.1	20.7
	(1976)	-	-	30.0(1)	30.8(5)	-	-	30.6	31.3
Greece	(1972)	40.0	8.8	48.8	48.9	40.8	1.6	42.4	-
	(1975)	43.5	9.6	53.2	53.2	45.6	1.3	47.0	47.0
Ireland	(1971)	-	-	34.8	36.8	-	-	39.4	43.3
	(1975)	-	-	42.7	46.0	-	-	48.8	51.4
Italy	(1972)	-	-	38.1	38.6	-	-	33.7	34.1
	(1975)	-	-	42.6	43.2	-	-	39.1	39.5
Japan	(1970)(2)	-	-	74.7	74.8	-	-	74.9	75.0
	(1976)	88.1	-	88.1	88.4	-	-	-	-
Netherlands	(1970)	16.8	21.1	37.9	41.5(6)	15.1	16.5	31.6	34.6(6)
	(1976)	18.3	14.2	32.5	63.6(6)	18.6	15.2	33.8	56.6(6)
New Zealand	(1970)	-	-	23.2	27.1	-	-	17.2	23.1
	(1976)	-	-	32.4	35.4	-	-	29.6	33.6
Norway	(1976)	34.5	28.8	63.3	64.0	37.0	28.5	65.5	65.9
Portugal	(1970)	10.5	11.1	21.5	22.8	9.6	8.1	17.7	19.1
	(1975)	19.6	10.6	30.2	32.9	19.3	8.9	28.2	30.5
Spain	(1970)	9.8	4.7	14.5	22.1	8.2	1.5	9.7	16.8
	(1975)	19.0	4.5	23.4	36.7	17.7	2.5	20.2	32.6
Sweden	(1976)			60.7	61.7			60.1	61.1
Switzerland	(1976)(3)	9.4	58.8	68.2	72.0	7.9	48.7	56.6	60.4
United Kingdom	(1970)	-	-	20.3	25.9(7)	-	-	19.3	24.8(7)
	(1976)	21.0	9.7	30.7	31.3(7)	20.8	11.5	32.3	32.9(7)
United States	(1970)			70.1	82.3			70.2	81.5
	(1976)			74.0	84.6			69.2	79.4

* Secondary A: General or technical education offers pupils, upon completion, a relatively good chance of continuing their studies in a higher education establishment.
* Secondary B: General or technical education, after which pupils have little chance of continuing to higher education.
1. Total Secondary school.
2. Estimations.
3. Includes part-time pupils
4. If part-time studies are included the enrolment rate is 73.0%
5. "   "   "   "   "   "   " 74.5% in 1970 and 85.1 in 1976.
6. "   "   "   "   "   "   " are 76.6% for boys and 41.8% for girls in 1970 and 83.3% for boys and 64.9% for girls in 1976.
7. "   "   "   "   "   "   " are 66.6% for boys and 46.4% for girls in 1970 and 61.6% for boys and 54.0% for girls in 1976.

Source: Educational Statistics in OECD Countries, op. cit.

Indications of the evolution of upper secondary education in the OECD area are shown in Table 4 listing total and female enrolment ratios for 17-year-olds, the only age group which in practically all Member countries is typically found at the post-compulsory secondary level. In all countries there has been an increase in participation rates, at least up to 1976; but in some countries they are considerably lower than for the 16-year age group and the potential for growth remains quite high (5). In spite of the increase in female participation, enrolment ratios for girls remain below average in more than half of the OECD countries for which information is available. This is particularly the case for Switzerland and to a lesser extent Greece, Netherlands and the United States. Higher than average female enrolments are found in Ireland and Norway as well as in Austria and Germany though in the latter two countries the picture may be biased by the lack of information on part-time students.

Data on actual departures in the course of upper secondary studies for a few countries - as presented in Table 5 - are not very conclusive: in Australia retention rates in the 10th year of education have increased over the years, particularly for girls. Retention rates increased in France; the same in Canada between 1965 and 1970 but, as in the United States, declined slightly in the early 1970s.

Another rough indication of retention rates in upper secondary education is provided in Table 3 which compares enrolment rates for the 16-year and 18-year age groups. The information must be interpreted with caution since it refers to two different cohorts in a given year and departures may be due to a whole range of factors. As discussed in Chapter I, in most non-European Member countries - and to a lesser extent in France and Spain - the majority of young people complete secondary education when they are 17. However, the large differences in enrolment rates between the 16-and 18-year age groups, even in the European countries - a drop of up to 40%-50% in many of them - indicate that quite massive departures take place at this level. In some cases this may be due to successful completion of short vocational courses before the age of 18, in others to a move from full-time to part-time study schemes as students grow older which is not reflected in the statistics because of lack of information. An equally plausible explanation is that as compulsory education becomes more comprehensive and a larger proportion of young people stay on, selection increases during the last years of secondary education (as in the United Kingdom). Small differences in participation rates between the two age groups in Portugal, Spain and Italy - countries with the lowest enrolment rates in the 16-year age group - and large differences in the more advanced countries such as the Netherlands, Norway and Sweden, would tend to support this argument.

---

5. For some countries, in particular Austria, Denmark, Germany and the Netherlands, figures in Table 4 cannot be compared with those in Table 3 since the latter does not includes part-time students. Footnotes to Table 4 give enrolment rates for these countries which take account of full and part-time students.

Table 5

RENTENTION RATES IN THE DIFFERENT TYPES
OF 2nd CYCLE SECONDARY SCHOOL
1965-1979 (1)

Percentages

	1965 M	1965 F	1970 M	1970 F	1975 M	1975 F	1976 M	1976 F	1977 M	1977 F	1978 M	1978 F	1979 M	1979 F
AUSTRALIA — as a percentage of the number of pupils beginning secondary school														
10th year			78.7	76.2	82.0	82.2	86.5	86.7	87.1	88.3	88.3	89.5	88.5	90.4
11th year			46.0	38.7	48.2	47.1	51.4	52.6	50.3	54.4	51.1	55.8	50.4	55.8
12th year			31.1	23.7	34.1	31.6	34.6	35.3	34.0	36.6	33.1	37.3	32.4	37.2
CANADA — as a percentage of the number of pupils enrolled for 5th grade three years previously														
12th year	63.4		76.0		67.8		69.8				71.8(2)		72.3(2)	
UNITED STATES — as a percentage of the number of pupils entering 5th grade														
High school graduates	73.2		75.0		74.4		74.9		74.4					
FRANCE — as a percentage of total population aged (3)														
15 years			81.2		91.7		92.6		91.2		71.6		–	
16 years			62.9		69.6		70.6		70.8		54.3		–	
17 years			44.1		49.9		51.7		52.7		27.8		55.4	
18 years			24.9		25.2		26.2		27.0				29.0	
UNITED KINGDOM (England and Wales) — as a percentage of the number of pupils aged 13 (1965 and 1970) or 14 (as from 1975) two to four years previously – secondary schools only.														
State-aided schools														
15 years old	40.5	39.6	55.1	54.6	–	24.2	–	25.9	–	26.8	23.4	25.6		
16	23.9	21.8	32.4	31.7	23.1	18.0	24.5	18.8	24.7	19.5	18.5	19.1		
17	12.5	10.2	17.7	16.9	17.6	5.2	18.4	5.4	18.9	5.9	6.5	5.7		
18	5.1	3.2	6.6	4.8	6.4		6.5		6.8					
Non-State-aided schools														
15 years old	89.0	87.6	93.7	88.9	–	61.6	–	–	–		67.3			
16	76.2	62.7	80.0	67.2	77.2	52.6	68.6	57.2	68.2	57.7	57.3			
17	51.0	34.4	57.7	44.6	61.8	14.0	57.2	16.9	17.8		17.3			
18	17.3	8.4	18.7	11.2	19.1									

1. Or the nearest year to that mentioned.
2. Based on projections.
3. Excluding higher education but including the preparatory classes for the "Grandes Ecoles" and the higher technicians sections.

Source: National Statistics.

Table 6

DISTRIBUTION OF QUALIFIED SECONDARY SCHOOL LEAVERS BY TYPE OF SCHOOL COMPLETED 1965-1978 (1)

Percentages

	1965 M	1965 F	1970 M	1970 F	1975 M	1975 F	1976 M	1976 F	1977 M	1977 F	1978 M	1978 F
GERMANY			(1971)									
General			12.1		15.0		16.1		17.5		18.1	
Technical leading to higher			3.2		7.0		7.6		7.4		6.8	
Vocational PT			72.9		64.9		64.5		63.7		61.5	
Other vocational			11.8		13.2		11.8		11.4		13.5	
CANADA												
- High school	..	..	..		83.8		..		..		..	
- Other	..	..	..		16.2		..		..		..	
SPAIN												
- University foundation course	34.5		..		62.6		58.7		..		..	
- Vocational training	35.3		..		13.3		22.2		..		..	
- Teacher training colleges	16.3		..		6.7		5.4		..		..	
- Other	13.8		..		17.4		13.7		..		..	
FINLAND												
- General	20.6		22.3		25.6		..		..		..	
- Vocational	79.4		77.7		74.4		..		..		..	
FRANCE												
- General (Bac.)	29.1	36.7	35.1		27.2	37.2	28.1[2]	37.1[2]	26.5[2]	36.4[2]	26.1[2]	35.5[2]
- Short vocational	70.0	61.2	55.9		62.9	30.1	61.4	49.2	62.8	48.9	62.6	49.6
- Long technical	0.9	2.1	9.0		9.9	12.7	10.6[2]	13.7[2]	10.7[2]	14.7[2]	11.3[2]	14.9[2]
GREECE												
- General	71.9		67.5		58.9	82.0	57.9	80.6				
- Technical and vocational	28.1		32.5		41.1	18.0	42.1	19.4				
ITALY												
- General	23.6	16.6	15.9	18.0	16.8	20.8	16.8	20.2				
- Teacher training colleges	3.8	35.8	3.0	35.1	1.7	22.5	2.0	21.7				
- Technical	43.7	20.7	65.3	26.7	63.0	33.5	62.5	34.4				
- Vocational	28.9	26.9	15.8	20.2	18.5	23.2	18.7	23.8				
UNITED KINGDOM - School-leavers according to highest pass levels												
GCE A level/SCE F grade	17.4	14.2	18.9	16.8	17.8	16.1	17.8	16.0	17.4	16.0		
GCE O level/CSE/SCE O grade	22.2	25.0	23.8	25.1	31.1	36.3	32.7	37.8	32.4	38.0		
No high passes	60.4	60.8	57.4	56.0	51.0	47.4	49.5	46.2	50.3	45.8		
YUGOSLAVIA												
- General	21.8		23.3		23.9		25.1					
- Teacher training	3.3		2.9		0.6		0.7					
- Technical	28.1		25.2		29.3		29.5					
- Vocational	46.7		48.7		46.2		44.7					

1. Or the nearest year to that mentioned.
2. Including secondary school-leaving certificates.

Source: National Statistics

Of special interest to this report are participation rates in the various types of upper secondary education. As seen in Tables 3 and 4, Austria, Germany and Switzerland have a very high proportion of the 16-18-year age group in vocational secondary education, that is in lines of study which prepare for a professional qualification and do not normally lead to or qualify for higher education. Similarly, the Scandinavian countries (6), France, Netherlands, and Yugoslavia have a relatively strong vocational terminal-oriented sector which enrols around 30% of the 16-year-old group.

Table 6 shows the distribution of qualified school leavers according to the type of school completed. By the mid- or late 1970s pupils having obtained a professional qualification represent 75% of all qualified male school leavers in Germany, 74% in Finland, 50% in France and 45% in Yugoslavia.

Comparing the earlier tables with Table 7 it will be seen that the size of the vocational sector in individual countries tends to determine the proportion of young people who obtain the formal qualifications for entry into higher education. Austria, Germany and Switzerland, with high enrolment ratios for the relevant age group but enrolling a majority in vocational education, rank relatively low in terms of secondary school graduates qualifying for higher education. The same is true even in countries where vocational education grants qualifications for entry into higher education (e.g. Sweden) since everywhere the policy is that this type of education should maintain its "terminal" employment orientation (as opposed to a "transfer" higher education orientation). On the other hand, countries which have emphasised the development of general education (e.g. Belgium, France), or which have a large technical sector granting the same rights to higher education as the traditional academic sector (Italy), compare more favourably in terms of qualified school leavers than of enrolment ratios.

In terms of the proportion of young people of the relevant age group qualified to apply for or to enter directly higher education, some of the Mediterranean countries and certain European countries with large vocational terminal-oriented sectors appear to have the most stringent "selection before entry" within the OECD area. Similarly, the European countries, Australia and New Zealand, would seem to be far more "selective" than the United States and Japan.

Useful as this type of analysis may be to a review of admission policies and the demand for higher education it is only one of many criteria for comparing and assessing secondary systems. Value judgements about educational performance require thorough analysis of the social and economic implications of different types of secondary school systems and of the political philosophies underlying them, often lacking in this type of international comparison. It may be useful

---

6. Evidence for Sweden is given in K. Härnqvist: Individual Demand for Education, op. cit.: in 1975 45% of pupils entering the upper secondary school were new entrants to 2-year practical lines of study.

Table 7

RATIO OF QUALIFIED SCHOOL LEAVERS FROM SECONDARY (A)
TO RELEVANT AGE GROUP (1975/1976)

COUNTRY	TOTAL
AUSTRIA	19.4
BELGIUM	33.2
FRANCE	25.5
GERMANY	19.4
ITALY	36.8
JAPAN	85.9
NETHERLANDS	25.8
NORWAY	30.5
SWEDEN	21.4
SWITZERLAND	8.4
UNITED KINGDOM	19.9
UNITED STATES	74.6

Sources: - For relevant age group, see: Educational Statistics in OECD Countries, OECD, Paris, 1981.
- For number of qualified school leavers, see: L. Cerych, S. Colton, J.P. Jallade, Student Flows and Expenditure in Higher Education, 1965-1979, Institute of Education, Paris, 1981.

here to briefly recall how views evolved in the course of the 1970s regarding systems with a Germanic tradition of education and training; essentially in Germany, Austria and certain Swiss cantons.

At the time, this model of education and training came under severe criticism. The rigid binary division between a rather small academic-type secondary school sector and a large hierarchically structured technical/vocational sector seemed to function almost too perfectly as a social selection mechanism. The "creaming off" of a relatively small segment of the school population at a very early age was seen to imply that selection into those streams of secondary education which open up the greatest number of educational and professional choices is largely based on the social and cultural background of the pupils.

With the changing economic and employment situation has come the awareness that the social selectivity and the rigidity of these systems may have been somewhat exaggerated. First of all, the existence of large technical and vocational sectors with highly articulated cycles means that they recruit a relatively large and heterogeneous population in terms both of social and educational origin and that there are considerable chances of upward mobility within the technical sector itself. Secondly, in systems with a German tradition enrolment in technical education does not carry the same connotations of underachievement or failure as in Latin or Anglo-Saxon countries. Moreover, technicians appear to enjoy a substantially higher economic and social status. Finally, the success of Austria, Switzerland and Germany in maintaining low levels of youth unemployment and in ensuring a smooth transition from school to work has further contributed to renewed interest in and positive appraisal of a number of features of these systems; though the performance of upper secondary education systems cannot of course be judged on this criterion alone.

2. SELECTION AT ENTRY

a) Changing links between secondary and higher education

The number of qualified school leavers, in particular those coming from general streams, has been perhaps the single most important factor in determining rates of growth in higher education (7). This correlation between the development of secondary and higher education was especially close during the period of rapid expansion but loosened up during the 1970s.

Government policies at the post-secondary level have no doubt contributed to some uncoupling of the two levels. However, an important factor behind this trend is the fact that from around the mid-1970s many Member countries have witnessed a fall or levelling-off in the number of young qualified school leavers from academic-type streams applying to enter post-secondary education. Given the sample of countries represented, Table 8 below is not very conclusive; however it is well known that in Germany there has been a significant decrease (from 87% in 1971 to 68% in 1980) in the number of Abitur holders planning to enrol directly in higher education; a similar although less pronouced trend is reported for Italy, Japan, Netherlands, Switzerland, Yugoslavia and others. Also relevant, at least in some countries, has been the gradual increase in the number of mature students (see Table 9). Finally, it is becoming increasingly common, particularly in the United States and Sweden, to postpone entry into higher education (see Table 10).

b) Restricted and open access sectors of higher education

The majority of OECD countries have developed post-secondary systems which include a mix of selective and open access institutions

---

7. Development of Higher Education 1950-1967: Analytical Report, OECD, Paris, 1971. Towards Mass Higher Education: Trends, Issues and Dilemmas, OECD, Paris, 1974.

or programmes (8). A more accurate and pragmatic description would be that of a continuum - often a hierarchy - of options with different degrees of selectivity at entry. Practically everywhere, institutional differentiation in terms of access conditions have roughly corresponded to the binary distinction between university and non-university type higher education. However, within this broad pattern different combinations can be found.

Whereas in non-European Member countries, Greece, Ireland, the United Kingdom and Yugoslavia, the universities represent the selective sector, in most continental European countries the opposite is the case: the majority of university faculties maintain an open access policy while all other higher education institutions apply, in varying degrees, restrictions at entry. This has been the case not only in the small sectors of élite institutions such as the French Grandes Ecoles or certain professional schools in the European countries (engineering, veterinary science, etc.), but also in the majority of less prestigious short-cycle post-secondary institutions where interestingly enough entry restrictions have never been seriously questioned. A first reason is that they accepted candidates from technical streams whose credentials qualified for, but did not grant automatic right of entry into higher education; a second is that from the start their functions were closely geared to more specific manpower requirements, or at least to broadly defined employment needs and hence served to legitimate their restrictive practices.

These variations, which must be seen in conjunction with the traditional differences in the structure of secondary education systems, have obviously conditioned the way in which countries have coped with the expansion in demand during past decades. Recent efforts directed at a more balanced distribution of students within post-secondary education must be seen against this background. In the non-European Member countries, the development of a non-university sector with relatively open access, such as the Junior and Community Colleges in Canada and the United States, has been used as an explicit strategy to facilitate rapid expansion and diversification of post-secondary education and protect the more prestigious long-cycle institutions. Universities and many 4-year colleges could therefore continue applying selective policies with no major risks of creating tensions due to unsatisfied demand. The 1960 Master Plan for Higher Education in California, for the first time in history, guaranteed a place in a Community College for every high school graduate or person over 18 otherwise qualified and gave Community College graduates preference in transferring into the University of California(9).

---

8. As will become more apparent in the course of the report, the term "open access" has not the same meaning in all countries. It is far more narrowly defined in Western Europe than in the United States, Canada or Japan. In the former, "open access" is meant to apply only to qualified secondary school leavers from academic or general streams who seldom represent more than 25% of the age group.

9. C. Kerr, "Higher Education: Paradise Lost ?", in Higher Education, Vol. 7, No. 3, Elsevier, Netherlands, August 1978, p. 267.

Table 8

RATES OF TRANSFER FROM SECONDARY EDUCATION
(BY TYPE) TO HIGHER EDUCATION

Percentages

	1965	1970	1975	1976	1977	1978	1979
CANADA							
High School Total		51.7	54.5	52.4	52.6	51.3	51.4
- University		25.0	24.1	23.2	21.9	22.6	23.2
- Non-University		26.7	30.4	29.2	30.7	28.7	28.2
DENMARK	(1966)						
Universities and Centres	59.3	54.6	53.8				

SPAIN

Ratio of pupils enrolled for a pre-university or COU year and those who have taken a sixth general baccalaureate year or a 7th technical baccalaureate year in the preceding year.

	51.7	50.2	82.5				
UNITED STATES	(1966)						
"High School" U + NU	52.5	61.5		58.1		58.8	
FRANCE		(1973)					
Preparatory classes for Grandes Ecoles							
- General baccalaureate		12.1	12.1			12.9	
- Technician's baccalaureate		0.3	0.2			0.8	
Universities							
- General baccalaureate		53.3	54.7			55.5	
- Technician's baccalaureate		13.5	15.0			16.5	
IUT							
- General baccalaureate		6.4	6.9			7.3	
- Technician's baccalaureate		14.0	13.3			14.7	
Higher technician							
- General baccalaureate		6.4	7.7			8.9	
- Technician's baccalaureate		18.1	18.6			19.0	
Total							
- General baccalaureate		78.2	81.4			84.6	
- Technician's baccalaureate		45.9	47.1			51.0	

JAPAN

New entrants to the universities and junior colleges as a percentage of 1st cycle secondary school-leavers three years previously

	M F	M F	M F	M F	M F	M F	M F
	22.4 11.3	29.3 17.7	43.0 32.4	43.3 33.6	41.9 33.3	43.1 33.5	41.4 33.1

NETHERLANDS

First-year university students as a percentage of pre-university school-leavers
(1971)

	79.4 52.7	94.6 69.7	94.0 60.7	93.0 61.9	91.5 58.6	86.0 58.8	

UNITED KINGDOM

Destination of secondary school-leavers with the following passes:

Universities							
3 or more A-levels		68.2 57.6	66.9 55.2		66.0 54.9		
2 A-levels		20.9 11.3	21.7 14.8		18.7 13.7		
1 A-level		1.7 0.7	0.7 1.2		1.4 0.7		
5 or more O-levels		0.2 0.1	0.1 0.1		0.2 0.0		
1 to 4 O-levels		0.0 0.0	0.0 0.0		0.0 0.0		
Further Education							
3 or more A-levels		15.4 28.1	13.6 24.4		15.4 22.7		
2 A-levels		41.4 61.3	38.0 45.9		40.4 44.4		
1 A-level		41.7 61.0	35.6 46.3		36.8 42.8		
5 or more O-levels		26.5 42.2	27.7 40.2		24.0 38.1		
1 to 4 O-levels		16.6 25.8	14.7 27.3		13.3 28.4		
Total universities and further education							
3 or more A-levels		83.6 85.7	80.5 79.6		81.4 77.6		
2 A-levels		62.3 72.6	59.7 60.7		59.1 58.1		
1 A-level		42.8 61.7	36.3 47.5		38.2 43.5		
5 or more O-levels		26.7 42.3	27.8 40.3		24.2 38.1		
1 to 4 O-levels		16.6 25.8	14.7 27.3		13.3 28.4		

Source : Drawn from national statistics

Table 9

AGE DISTRIBUTION OF NEW ENTRANTS TO UNIVERSITY HIGHER EDUCATION

Percentages

	1965		1970		1975		1976		1977		1978	
	M	F	M	F	M	F	M	F	M	F	M	F
GERMANY	Tot. (1)		Tot.		Tot.							
17 and under	-	-	-	-	0.1	0.1			0.2	0.3	0.1	0.2
18	0.2	0.2	9.6	12.6	5.1	7.3			4.2	8.0	4.2	8.4
19	10.5	18.2	30.3	43.5	25.0	40.2			16.5	37.9	16.7	38.3
20-24	81.9	75.7	51.3	38.5	54.8	41.0			71.0	46.2	71.5	46.1
25 and over	7.4	5.7	8.7	5.5	14.9	11.3			8.1	7.6	7.4	7.5
AUSTRALIA(2) FT			1971									
17 and under			41.9	52.8	44.9	48.8	43.7	49.2	42.5	45.4	34.2	38.2
18			38.4	36.8	36.5	33.8	37.0	32.1	35.8	33.6	30.7	30.4
19			8.9	4.5	8.2	6.3	8.6	5.9	9.4	7.4	11.4	8.8
20-24			8.5	3.7	6.9	4.3	6.7	5.1	8.1	6.2	15.9	12.0
25 and over			2.4	2.1	3.5.	6.8	4.0	7.6	4.2	7.3	7.7	10.6
AUSTRALIA PT			1971									
17 and under			13.7	9.0	13.0	8.0	8.9	5.0	11.8	4.6	4.3	1.5
18			20.3	11.2	17.3	8.5	15.7	5.5	15.6	5.4	6.2	2.5
19			6.3	7.3	6.0	3.7	6.3	3.8	4.6	3.5	3.6	2.1
20-24			27.5	31.2	19.1	19.6	17.6	18.2	17.5	17.4	25.3	24.6
25 and over			32.1	41.2	44.5	60.3	51.5	67.5	50.6	69.1	60.6	69.2
AUSTRIA	1970		1972		1975							
17 and under	-	-	-	-	-	-					29.5	44.1
18	19.9	41.6	29.3	46.4	32.8	48.9					31.4	29.7
19	22.4	32.2	25.9	28.9	25.2	29.2					32.9	20.7
20-24	52.0	21.0	38.7	20.2	35.4	17.2					6.1	5.5
25 and over	5.7	5.1	6.1	4.5	6.6	4.8						
DENMARK												
under 21			48.8		44.5							
21 - 26			43.9		42.0							
27 and over			7.2		13.5							
SPAIN												
17 and under			13.9	15.3	28.2	21.7	34.2	39.5	34.6	37.5		
18			20.7	19.8	21.4	24.1	22.8	23.6	22.3	22.3		
19			16.5	17.2	14.8	15.0	14.2	12.4	12.2	10.7		
20-24			34.1	33.3	23.6	27.4	18.6	16.8	14.0	13.0		
25 and over			14.8	14.5	12.1	11.8	10.2	7.8	16.9	16.5		
FINLAND												
17 and under					-	-	-	-	-	-		
18					1.8	2.0	1.8	2.0	1.6	2.6	1.8	2.2
19					30.1	32.3	29.0	34.1	30.1	33.2	29.0	35.1
20-24					53.5	51.2	53.0	50.5	53.1	49.3	52.6	48.3
25 and over					14.6	14.5	16.1	13.3	15.1	14.8	16.5	14.3

1. Excluding foreign students.
2. Students starting a bachelor's degree at university.

FT = full-time   PT = part-time

Table 9 (contd.)

Percentages

	1965		1970		1975		1976		1977		1978	
	M	F	M	F	M	F	M	F	M	F	M	F
FRANCE			(3)									
17 and under	6.2	8.3			7.7		8.2		7.9		5.4	8.9
18	18.2	23.1			26.8		31.2		32.6		26.2	37.5
19	22.9	24.5			22.9		25.0		25.1		26.6	24.6
20-24	40.5	37.3			27.2(4)		24.3(4)		23.9(4)		28.6(4)	19.0(4)
25 and over	12.3	6.7			15.4(5)		11.3(5)		10.5(5)		13.1(5)	9.9(5)
GREECE (3)												
18 and under	28.3	43.6	24.4	37.2	31.5	46.5	42.8	60.5				
19	20.9	27.8	23.0	30.8	18.4	21.5	18.5	20.2				
20-24	31.6(4)	25.1(4)	32.7	25.9	25.9	20.1	22.0	12.9				
25 and over	19.2(5)	3.5(5)	20.0	6.1	24.1	11.9	16.7	6.4				
ITALY		1964		1967		1973						
18 and under	0.3	4.4	10.6	26.9	9.5	22.6						
19	14.2	27.3	31.3	36.5	36.8	43.5						
20-24	72.4	44.4	48.1	31.5	38.7	26.5						
25 and over	13.0	9.5	10.0	5.1	15.0	7.4						
NETHERLANDS				1971		1974						
under 18			8.9	8.1	0.6	0.7						
18			25.2	28.8	31.1	35.5						
19			21.1	25.0	25.6	26.4						
20-24			31.8	26.2	29.7	23.5						
25 and over			13.0	11.9	13.0	13.9						
UNITED KINGDOM (universities)												
18 and under	44.6	55.9	42.2	54.0	39.9	47.6			40.3	45.9	40.6	45.9
19	34.3	30.1	32.1	28.0	30.9	29.5			30.9	30.3	30.6	29.7
20	8.4	5.7	9.7	7.1	10.5	8.7			10.7	9.3	10.6	9.1
21-24	8.4	4.4	10.8	6.6	12.3	8.0			11.8	8.2	11.9	8.4
25 and over	4.2	3.9	5.2	4.3	6.3	6.2			6.3	6.2	6.2	6.9
UNITED KINGDOM (further education - advanced)												
18 and under			17.6	27.1								
19			24.2	25.8								
20			14.7	11.2								
21-24			25.2	16.1								
25 and over			18.2	19.7								
SWEDEN (6)				1971								
25 and over			35.0	33.3	48.6	51.4	46.8	52.7				
of which, covered by the 25/5 rule			8.8	9.7	24.1	24.9	22.7	25.3				

3. First-year students.
4. 20-23
5. 24 and over.
6. New entrants in the Philosophy faculties.

Source: National statistics.

Table 10

INTERVAL BETWEEN COMPLETION OF SECONDARY EDUCATION
AND ENTRY INTO HIGHER EDUCATION

Percentages

	1965 M	1965 F	1970 M	1970 F	1975 M	1975 F	1976 M	1976 F	1977 M	1977 F	1978 M	1978 F
GERMANY												
Same year									46.4	81.0	46.1	78.1
1 year later									34.9	11.0	34.1	12.0
4 years or more									18.7	8.0	19.8	9.9
AUSTRALIA - University FT												
Following calendar year					92.2	92.6	85.9	85.5	83.6	82.8	82.2	81.0
1 year later							7.4	7.2	8.1	8.0	8.1	7.7
More than 1 year later					4.5	4.4	3.8	3.7	4.8	4.7	4.3	3.9
Other (1)					3.3	3.0	2.9	3.6	3.5	4.5	5.3	7.3
CAE - FT												
Following calendar year					82.7				79.4	86.2	78.8	85.4
1 year later					7.8				10.8	7.1	10.0	7.0
More than 1 year later					9.5				9.8	6.7	11.2	7.6
Other					-				-	-	-	-
Universities PT												
Following calendar year					46.3	33.0	31.7	27.1	33.8	27.0	30.7	17.2
1 year later							8.4	7.3	7.2	7.8	7.6	8.3
More than 1 year later					28.5	37.6	29.6	33.8	30.7	30.8	20.4	22.2
Other (1)					25.3	29.4	30.3	31.8	28.3	34.4	41.3	52.3
CAE PT												
Following calendar year					48.0				45.3	45.5	40.4	38.3
1 year later					13.0				14.3	11.0	13.0	14.6
More than 1 year later					39.0				40.4	43.5	46.6	47.1
Other (1)					-				-	-	-	-
UNITED STATES												
Same year			65.4		55.7		54.8		54.1			
1 to 3 years			17.5		22.2		22.1		20.9			
4 years and more			17.1		22.1		23.1		24.9			
FRANCE												
Total university + IUT												
Same year					74.3						79.0	
1 year later					11.8						5.8	
2 years or more					12.7						12.3	
Indefinite					1.2						2.9	
IUT												
Same year					86.6						92.3	
1 year later					10.3						4.9	
2 years or more					3.0						2.2	
Indefinite					0.1						0.6	
NETHERLANDS												
University - Transfer rate and interval according to secondary school-leaving certificate												
Gymnasia			(1971)		(1974)							
Same year	75.5	63.4	85.8	68.3	79.6	56.9						
1 year later	13.9	12.7	..	..	..	..						
4 years or more	2.4	2.0	..	..	..	..						
Total	91.8	78.1	..	..	..	..						
HBS (Atheneum in 1974)												
Same year	44.2	21.1	53.4	29.3	69.4	39.3						
1 year later	11.7	6.2	..	..	..	..						
4 years or more	4.0	3.6	..	..	..	..						
Total	59.9	30.9	..	..	..	..						

1. Including qualifications obtained through adult or "concessional" education which are only classified in the "other" category by all universities for 1978.

FT = full-time   PT = part-time

Source: National statistics

The advantages and drawbacks of this type of strategy constituted a central topic of debate in the United States and elsewhere during the 1960s. Few would question the key role played by the American Community Colleges in enlarging educational opportunities for young people and adults, particularly from less privileged milieux. Although, however, the Community Colleges helped to provide all segments of the population with more formal schooling, certain groups, especially middle-class youth, still constituted the bulk of new entrants into the selective and more prestigious institutions. The risk in developing post-secondary systems with strong hierarchical differentiation among institutions is that they may succeed in having a more democratic recruitment without significantly reducing social inequalities. As will be discussed later, the changing employment situation and its consequences for individual demand, plus a variety of measures adopted in the 1970s in regard to both access and student aid, may have contributed to blurring hierarchical distinctions and to promoting a greater social mix of students within institutions.

In the United Kingdom, the expansion has been tackled by setting up a binary post-secondary system. The distinctive feature of this policy is the development of a non-university sector comprising all levels of education from sub-degree to doctorate. Whereas some people have viewed the development of a strong competitive sector primarily as a means of diversifying higher education provision, circumventing the universities to meet the needs of new student populations, others have seen it mainly as a means of protecting universities from the impact of massive demand. Whatever the case, the creation of the Polytechnics with quasi-university status - a cornerstone of the binary policy - has served to diversify degree-level studies and to maintain the high standards of British higher education. A consequence of this has been to discourage the enrolment of students in sub-degree level or part-time courses.

In many continental European countries, notably France, Italy, and Spain, the trend in the 1950s and 1960s to cope with demand largely through the university sector cannot be attributed to an explicit strategy but rather to the strong pressure on governments to maintain the long-standing right to a university education for all academically-oriented qualified school leavers. The prestige of the universities together with their open access policies made these institutions the obvious choice for the growing number of qualified young people in spite of government efforts aimed at diverting demand and expanding opportunities outside the university sector. At the same time, however, the existence of a highly developed post-secondary technical sector in a number of European countries (e.g. Belgium, Denmark, Netherlands, Norway) greatly contributed to coping with growing demand. Table 11 on the relative weight of the university and the non-university sectors in terms of actual intake, shows that in these countries the latter recruits a higher proportion of new entrants than the universities.

c) Reappraisal of the individual demand approach

Underlying the laissez-faire policies which guided the development of higher education in most Western industrialised countries was

Table 11

ANNUAL ENTRY TO HIGHER EDUCATION AS A PERCENTAGE OF THE RELEVANT AGE GROUP

1976

	Age spread encompassing at least 70 per cent of new entrants	University	Non-University	Total Higher Education
Australia	17-18	16.5	21.2	37.7
Austria	18-20	13.5	5.1	18.6
Belgium	18-20	13.0	20.8	33.9
Canada (1)	18	20.1	10.8	30.9
Denmark	19-21	16.6	20.2	36.8
Finland	19-21	15.9	10.1	26.0
France (2)	18-20	18.8	8.9	27.7
Germany	19-21	13.6	5.6	19.2
Italy (3)	19-21	29.5	1.1	30.6
Japan	18	27.3	11.9	39.2
Netherlands	18-20	8.7	16.8	25.5
Norway	19-21	16.2	-	-
Spain (3)	17-19	28.9	2.5	31.5
Sweden (3)	19-21	33.3	-	-
Switzerland	18-21	11.9	8.6	20.5
United Kingdom	18-19	19.6	14.0	33.2
United States (4)	18	26.2	16.5	42.8
Yugoslavia (3)	18-20	8.8	25.7	34.6

1. 1971. Data includes only those first-year students who were in secondary school the previous year.
2. Excludes new entrants to "Grandes Ecoles" and "Instituts d'Université".
3. First-year students.
4. Degree credit students only.

Source: Educational Statistics in OECD Countries, OECD, op.cit.

the generally accepted principle that provision at this level should be adapted to private demand, i.e. the number of people with recognised qualifications applying for entry. Tradition, the difficulties of applying other planning methods and especially the combined pressures in favour of expansion gave political support to this type of approach.

Other new interpretations were already being given to such a development strategy during the post-World War period (see following sections). However, it is only in recent years that the policy of merely adapting places at the tertiary level to the needs and wishes of qualified school leavers came to be more severely questioned, in particular in the European Member countries (10).

In the first place the expansion in the number of qualified secondary leavers from less than 10% to over 20% of the relevant age group has raised the political question of whether societies can or should afford to guarantee freedom of access and choice to a population which had already been the main beneficiary of expansion of opportunities at the secondary level.

Secondly, there is a widespread belief, supported by considerable evidence, that the expansion of higher education in response to demands of school leavers has not been particularly instrumental in reducing educational inequalities. OECD countries have varied considerably in their success in boosting access to higher education by working-class children, but none have come anywhere near the kind of equality of achievement which would make expenditure on higher education economically redistributive or even neutral.

Thirdly, the issue of graduate employment or under-employment further raised doubts about the value of basing growth of higher education on individual demand. In many OECD countries there has been a resurgence of interest in forecasts of qualified manpower requirements but mostly as a way of determining the main lines of higher education development. Recent reports in Sweden, Denmark, Federal Republic of Germany have proposed that far greater note be taken of the state of the labour market. However, the difficulty of making reliable long-term forecasts in the free labour market conditions pertaining in OECD countries has so far defeated any attempt at closely relating student numbers to estimated market needs, except in certain health and technical fields and the teacher training sector. Even in these areas, such attempts have by no means been uniformly successful and in view of persistent methodological problems as well as lack of consensus as to the assumptions on which they should be based, their exclusive use in determining the intake capacity of these sectors is a matter of strong controversy.

Fourthly, in practically all OECD countries the rate of expansion, even if inadequately financed, has led to conspicuous increases in the costs of higher education as a proportion of overall educational expenditures (11). The recent and continuing recession has undoubtedly

---

10. This section draws on G. Williams: "Planning the Size and Shape of Post-Secondary Systems during the 1980s", OECD, Paris, 1978 (mimeo).
11. See "Higher education expenditure in OECD countries", OECD document, Paris, 1981.

exacerbated the problem: increased expenditures are far more difficult to justify at a time of general retrenchment. As a result, financial considerations have acquired growing importance in shaping decisions on the organisation of provision at the higher levels.

Fifthly, changing attitudes and behaviour of the traditional higher education clientele - as witnessed by the recent sharp reduction in the demand for certain types of programmes in several countries - plus the trend to open up certain sectors to new groups with very diverse backgrounds and qualifications, are compounding the difficulty of maintaining a close adaptation of supply to demand.

While certain traditional planning principles are currently being seriously reappraised in the light of these factors, the majority of the OECD countries have up to now maintained one of the central commitments inherent to the individual demand approach, namely that all qualified school leavers claiming direct entry into post-secondary education should be able to find a place within the system.

There is however a significant and growing minority of countries which either do not adhere to this principle or openly declare that under certain circumstances total higher education provision cannot or should not be adjusted to private demand. In Greece and Turkey, for example, the number of qualified candidates applying for entry exceeds by far the total intake capacity of higher education, thus leaving a considerable proportion of young people with no possibility of pursuing further studies in their own country. In Finland a similar, though less acute, situation has emerged in recent years. In some countries, such as Denmark and Sweden, ceilings are being set for the total intake capacity of higher education; but in view of the fact that these ceilings are based on quite "generous" assumptions of private demand, it is claimed that expected student numbers continue to be of key importance for planning purposes.

It could therefore be argued that although individual demand still remains a primary criterion for planning total provision at the post-secondary level, a growing number of countries are inclined to set ceilings or targets in regard to intake. Restrictions at the system level will therefore most likely depend on the assumptions and criteria on which these targets are based as well as on the future evolution of private demand.

Within the OECD area, strong tensions due to an overall lack of places in higher education are only being experienced by a few Mediterranean countries. The majority of Member countries are facing a different problem, namely that of excess demand in certain parts of the system and insufficient demand in others.

This suggests that, in spite of uncertainties and likely differences in the evolution of global demand, Member countries will be confronted with a series of common problems when planning the shape of their post-secondary systems over the next few years, the structure of supply and the intake capacity of the different types of institutions or lines of study. It is precisely in this area where laissez-faire policies implying a rather passive adjustment to individual demand are being particularly called into doubt. Indeed, already in the 1970s the influence of demand in the allocation of students within the system was declining.

As decisions concerning rates of expansion or contraction of the different parts of the system, be it institutions or fields of study, are primarily based on financial, employment and social considerations, the tendency is to narrow applicants' choice of study programmes. In brief, then, in a growing number of countries the individual demand approach to planning higher education is still basically understood as a commitment to ensure a place within the system but not necessarily in the institution or field of study of the candidate's choice.

These statements need to be qualified in at least two respects. Firstly, several OECD countries, particularly those with mass comprehensive secondary schools (United States, Japan, Canada) or a selective university sector (United Kingdom, Australia) have for a long time interpreted the individual demand approach in this "restricted" sense. Secondly, even in countries where freedom of choice is a long-standing tradition, it has been applied only to the transition from academic secondary schools to universities.

It is important to stress this latter point since <u>a major characteristic of recent admission reforms in higher education has been the combination of restrictions on access for qualified school leavers from academic lines of study</u> (12) <u>with measures aimed at facilitating the entry of groups which hitherto had been excluded or had been only marginally represented</u> (e.g. adults, racial minorities, people without formal qualifications).

The different schemes developed by the various countries and the problems faced in implementing them are discussed elsewhere in the report. It should, however, be stressed here that since secondary school leavers still represented in the late 1970s the large majority of the pool of applicants and new entrants to higher education (see Table 12), the net effect has been that of a stronger and more explicit control over the inflow into this level. This control is manifest in policies aimed at the reallocation of students within the system as well as in the more stringent selection procedures applied to school leavers with the traditional qualifications for entry to higher education. Of special significance - particularly in the Western European context - are changes in policies vis-à-vis access of this group.

d) <u>The preferential link between academic secondary streams and universities</u>

It is not surprising that restricted entry into universities is a far more sensitive and controversal issue in continental Europe

---

12. Examples of qualified school leavers with traditional qualifications for entry or from academic streams are those with the baccalauréat in France, Abitur in Germany, Matura in Austria, Switzerland.

Table 12

EDUCATIONAL BACKGROUND OF NEW ENTRANTS TO UNIVERSITY (U)
AND NON-UNIVERSITY (NU) HIGHER EDUCATION

In percentages

	1965	1970	1975	1976	1977	1978
AUSTRIA						
- University						
General Secondary		84.6	83.7			77.4
Technical and vocational		15.4	16.3			22.6
DENMARK						
- Total U + NU						
Studentereksamen		77.1	68.6			
HF(1)		7.0	17.5			
Other		16.0	14.0			
- Faculties of Arts						
Studentereksamen		91.3	69.7			
HF		1.7	18.4			
Other		7.1	11.9			
- Faculties of Science						
Studentereksamen		92.6	77.4			
HF		0.7	11.6			
Other		6.6	11.0			
- Technical university						
Studentereksamen		87.4	85.7			
HF		-	1.7			
Other		12.6	12.6			
- Schools of economics and management						
Studentereksamen		68.5	76.8			
HF		-	3.8			
Other		31.5	19.5			
- NU teacher training colleges						
Studentereksamen		72.3	57.4			
HF		27.3	38.8			
		0.5	3.9			
- NU Teknika						
Studentereksamen		3.0	10.5			
HF		-	2.3			
Other		97.0	87.2			
SPAIN						
- Faculties						
- Pre-university - COU* (1)				85.4	86.8	73.6
- Technical education				6.1	4.7	12.3
- Students over 25				1.7	1.9	3.4
- Other				6.8	6.6	10.7
- Higher technical schools						
- Pre-university - COU* (1)				87.4	85.6	70.0
- Technical education				7.2	9.0	20.5
- Students over 25				0.4	0.4	0.9
- Other				5.0	5.0	8.6
- Architecture, technician-engineers						
- Pre-university - COU* (1)				70.7	74.5	63.8
- Technical education				6.6	6.2	11.4
- Students over 25				0.5	0.5	0.6
- Other				22.2	18.8	24.2
- Basic school teachers						
- Pre-university - COU* (1)				93.2	92.9	92.1
- Technical education				0.8	0.6	1.2
- Students over 25				0.5	0.7	0.8
- Other				5.5	5.8	5.9

* COU = University foundation course.

1. Preparatory examination for higher education intended mainly for people who have not completed secondary education and wish to resume their studies.

Table 12 (contd.)

	1965	1970	1975	1976	1977	1978
FRANCE						(1980)
- Universities + IUTs			(2)			
- BAC A, B, C, D			80.4	81.6	77.6	76.5
- BAC E, F, G, H			8.3	15.2	15.6	16.7
- Equivalent examinations			7.8	1.4	5.6	5.3
- Special entrance examinations			2.3	1.2	0.9	1.2
- Social advancement programme			1.2	0.6	0.3	0.2
- IUTs only						
- BAC A, B, C, D			50.1	49.4	47.2	51.4
- BAC E, F, G, H			43.1	46.9	47.8	44.8
- Equivalent examinations			2.5	1.1	2.7	2.2
- Special entrance examinations			2.0	2.3	2.0	1.4
- Social advancement programme			0.4	0.3	0.3	0.2
ITALY						
- University, total						
- Secondary, general	44.2	37.4	45.0	45.3		
- Secondary, teacher training	18.1	19.4	12.2	12.0		
- Secondary, technical	34.8	40.2	37.9	35.3		
- Secondary, vocational	-	-	-	4.0		
- Other	2.9	3.0	4.9	3.4		
- Faculty of Arts						
- Secondary, general	35.1	27.2	36.4	35.1		
- Secondary, teacher training	55.1	58.6	39.5	38.2		
- Secondary, technical	7.0	12.6	19.1	20.2		
- Secondary, vocational	-	-	-	3.7		
- Other	2.8	1.6	4.9	2.7		
- Technology						
- Secondary, general	58.8	40.9	41.2	42.7		
- Secondary, teacher training	-	0.4	0.6	0.6		
- Secondary, technical	37.4	54.5	51.9	47.4		
- Secondary, vocational	-	-	-	3.8		
- Other	3.8	4.3	6.3	5.6		
- Economics						
- Secondary, general	14.3	19.3	26.4	30.2		
- Secondary, teacher training	-	3.0	4.4	3.9		
- Secondary, technical	82.6	76.4	64.4	58.4		
- Secondary, vocational	-	-	-	4.4		
- Other	3.1	1.2	4.9	3.0		
SWEDEN						
- University						
- Gymnasium (3 or 4 years)	86.3		56.8	54.0		
- Other secondary school-leaving certificates	0.7		4.4	5.7		
- Priority students	-		11.9	12.6		
- 25/5, 25/4 (3)	-		18.3	18.1		
- Adults with no secondary school-leaving certificate	-		-	-		
- Other	13.0		8.6	9.7		
- Total higher education						
- Gymnasium (3 or 4 years)					54.9	57.4
- Other secondary school-leaving certificates					6.7	9.4
- Priority students					6.4	5.5
- 25/5, 25/4					13.5	11.2
- Adults with no secondary school-leaving certificate					4.7	4.3
- Other					14.5	12.2

2. Excluding IUTs.
3. People of 25 and over who have five or four years' work experience.

Source: National statistics

than in other OECD countries. The fact that most European universities have had a long tradition of unlimited access is of course an obvious, but only partial, explanation. Of crucial significance in this context is the particular status of final examinations and certificates awarded by academic secondary streams which historically have fulfilled the twofold function of certifying successful completion of studies and of entitling holders to direct entry into universities. In France, for example, the baccalauréat is formally considered as a higher education examination and thus can be said to fulfill in practice the role of a university entrance examination.

Thus, whereas in the non-European countries and the United Kingdom university entry is considered to be in a certain way a privilege, with the decision being basically left to the discretion of higher education institutions, in continental Europe it is understood as a basic right of qualified school leavers.

This constitutional or formal entitlement to proceed from secondary to higher education applies only to the transition from academic secondary streams to universities. At least in theory, this means firstly that, with the exception of the universities, any stream or institution, be it at the upper secondary or post-secondary level, may restrict entry when faced with excess demand. Secondly, secondary school leavers from academic lines of study may be subject to selection for entry into all types of post-secondary institutions (even into vocational secondary schools) except universities.

The alternative facing governments reluctant to expand universities at the same rate as secondary schools has been either to limit the output of qualified school leavers with guaranteed access to universities (partly by adopting a restricted definition of who qualifies) or to reduce the selective role of these streams and progressively abolish some of their traditional rights. During the 1970s certain countries (e.g. Switzerland, Austria)(13) appear to have favoured the first option, namely that of maintaining a relatively small academically-oriented pre-university sector with high transfer ratios to universities and maintaining students' rights to choose their study programmes and universities.

The majority of European countries have moved towards the second option, that is, they have expanded general and academic type streams while gradually imposing transfer restrictions. Few, however, have abolished the legal entitlement to university entry of academic type diplomas. In Finland, Greece, Portugal, Sweden and the United Kingdom, such formal entitlement never existed or has been abolished; but the preferential link between academic lines of study and universities is still largely maintained. In Belgium, Denmark, France, Federal Republic of Germany, Netherlands, Norway, Spain, etc., school leaving examinations (baccalauréat, Matura, etc.) continue to give formal right of entry into university. These diplomas have long been considered as one of the mainstays of a social selection process -

---

13. Educational Policy and Planning: Higher Education and Research in Austria, OECD, Paris, 1975.

based on merit or achievement rather that on inheritance and hence viewed as a symbol of social justice. There are many who claim that in spite of their drawbacks they are likely to be the last bastions of the educational system. Nevertheless, the conditions for their maintenance, reform or abolition continue to be central to the debate on selection and admission policies.

The changes which have taken place, both in terms of the economic and social value of these certificates and of their real value as qualifications for university entry, are mainly the result of growth in the number of holders and also of slow, frequently disguised but significant changes in the access policies of universities.

e) Towards restrictive university entry in continental Europe

With the rapid expansion in the pool of qualified applicants in the 1960s, some countries began to introduce more specific requirements for entry into the different faculties. These requirements were defined primarily in terms of lines of study, specialisation or subjects chosen at the upper secondary level. Although more upper secondary lines of study granted qualifications for university entry (i.e. a wider range of general streams and a growing number of technical streams), choice of stream tended to become increasingly important in determining subsequent choice of university studies. France provides a clear illustration of this trend. In 1977, 92% of students who obtained the Baccalauréat in the humanities enrolled in the law and humanities faculties, while 82% of those completing mathematics - the only line of study which qualifies for all higher education programmes - enrolled in sciences, medicine and pharmacy.

Another measure aimed at keeping closer control over student intake has been that of gradually assigning more weight to performance at the upper secondary level. Without going as far as allotting a fixed number of places, a growing number of traditionally open access faculties or departments confronted with 'excessive' demand started setting requirements in terms of marks obtained in the course of studies or in the final school leaving examination (see Chapter III).

Policies designed to ensure a more balanced geographical distribution of higher education provision, although formally intended to favour the participation of new groups, have also had the effect of narrowing university choices for some qualified candidates. For quite some time certain universities, generally those located in large urban centres or under strong demand because of their quality or prestige, have been able to apply entry restrictions, on the grounds that, in theory at least, students had the possibility of pursuing similar studies elsewhere.

Gradual restrictions at the level of access and, not least, the multiplication of informal selection procedures operating after entry, especially during the first year of studies, represented last-ditch attempts at coping with increased student demand without having to tackle head-on the sensitive issue of numerus clausus. But it is evident that such measures paved the way towards the ultimate adoption of policies aimed at introducing numerical limitations at the national level within certain sectors of the university system, or in some cases within the university system as a whole.

Some of the advantages and drawbacks of restricting entry or choice for certain categories of secondary school leavers have been discussed above and are also dealt with in Chapter III. The point which could be made at this stage is that selective university admission tends to be a typical feature of education systems which have reduced selection at the secondary level and postponed it to a later stage. Indeed, countries with quasi universal secondary education (Canada, United States, Japan, USSR) have had selective universities for a long time whereas many of the European countries started or accelerated the introduction of restricted entry after a period of massive growth of qualified school leavers.

Thus, contrary to what is often claimed, support for free university access may, and sometimes does, indicate explicit or implicit support for maintaining the selective role of secondary education, especially when there is a simultaneous refusal to accept large numbers of drop-outs in the course of higher education. For, if it is accepted that post-compulsory education has a selective function, it follows that maintaining open access at entry necessarily implies imposing greater restrictions before and/or after entry.(14)

The controversy could be further heightened by arguing that certain forms of restricted access to universities may in fact prove to be an effective strategy for accelerating the expansion and democratisation of secondary schools. Governments may be more willing to adopt the relevant policy measures if it is clearly understood that final secondary school qualifications will not automatically entitle or guarantee leavers direct entrance to universities.

The consequence of limiting entry or imposing closer government control on access into certain university fields of study depends to a large extent on the rules and criteria being adopted.

f) Admission policies: variations within countries

A review of trends and international comparisons in this area is hampered by the fact that in recent years access policies and admission procedures have been subject to rapid and sometimes drastic changes in most Member countries.

Most countries have by now some fields of study where numerical limitations are applied throughout the country on a more or less permanent basis. Medical faculties have been among the first to introduce and maintain such a policy. At present, with the exception

---

14. Ladislav Cerych: <u>Access and Structures</u>, Institute of Education of the European Cultural Foundation, Paris, 1975.

of Italy, Austria and Switzerland, medical studies are subject to a numerus clausus policy in all OECD countries. Other health-related fields, e.g. pharmacy, dentistry, biology, affected by the overflow of rejected applicants to medicine, have been quick to adopt similar restrictive measures.

However, in addition to a quasi-permanent selective sector, many countries have a range of programmes where access policies may vary from stringent selection to free entry depending on whether or not demand exceeds the supply of places. Indeed, maintaining a degree of flexibility is often considered an essential element of admission policies aimed at avoiding the establishment of a clearly defined selective sector.

Also, policies vis-à-vis numerus clausus have changed quite substantially over a rather short time span as in Sweden and Germany. In Germany before 1977 the Federal as well as many Länder governments supported rather strongly the introduction and generalisation of numerus clausus within universities. As a result, the number of fields of study with restricted entry, or subject to a centralised placement procedure grew constantly from 10 in the summer semester of 1974, to 26 in 1976 and an estimated 43 subjects in the winter semester of 1976/77. Inability to establish selection devices which complied with the court ruling on the legal rights of Abiturienten, increased bureaucratisation and the trend among a growing number of unsuccessful university candidates to take jobs or enrol in school/ training schemes designed for young people with lower levels of qualifications were among the factors which led to a drastic reversal of government policy. By the end of the decade, as a result of the policy of opening up and of overcrowding universities and of a certain slackening in the demand for university education, the number of numerus clausus subjects was reduced to 10.

In Sweden the change of government in 1976 led to the rejection of the U-68 Commission proposals of applying restricted entry to all university lines of study. The principle of applying selection for the majority of university programmes was kept but certain lines determined by the central authorities remained open. The debate on whether or not to maintain open-access lines of study continued and in June 1979 the Parliament decided that numerus clausus could be introduced in all sectors and programmes of higher education when demand exceeded the number of places available.

g) Admission Policies; variations between countries

Despite the many common problems faced by OECD countries the picture emerging in the early 1980s continues to be one of considerable contrasts, not only in history and traditions, and in priorities and viewpoints on the functions of higher education, but also in political climate and governments' freedom of action in introducing and carrying through highly controversal reforms.

Even within continental Europe the policy of setting restrictions to the demand for university education cannot be said to have been generally applied. Over the 1970s Italy, Switzerland and Austria largely maintained "open access" policy within their universities. Given the fundamental differences between the Swiss and Austrian education systems and the Italian one, such a policy had of course radically different features and implications. In Italy, it reflected implicit or explicit support for opening up the universities to mass education, a particularly drastic step in view of the fact that this country did not have nor did it develop a non-university sector and that only a very small percentage of the student body enrolled in short-cycle programmes within universities. By 1976 37% of the relevant age group qualified for university entry and new entrants to Italian universities represented 31% of the 19-21 age group. In Switzerland, on the other hand, such a policy implied primarily the preservation of the traditional entitlement to free access and choice for a minority of academic school leavers (8.4% of the relevant age group) rigorously selected at an earlier stage and trained almost exclusively with a view to pursuing university studies.

At the other extreme are countries like Greece, Turkey and Finland where demand by far exceeds the total capacity of their higher education systems, and more recently Sweden and Denmark with a more balanced relationship between supply and demand but nonetheless moving in the direction of planning or actually introducing entry restrictions within all segments of the post-secondary system.

In Greece, for example, in spite of the fact that the number of places almost doubled from 1968 to 1977, (Greece had the highest growth rate of all OECD countries during the early 1970s) the proportion of candidates admitted throughout the system remained at around 25%. The chances of entering the university sector, however, have narrowed considerably from 29% of successful applicants in 1968 to 18.2% in 1977 with considerable variations in admission rates among fields of study. Reforms introduced at the secondary level have focused on reducing overall demand for post-secondary education and enhancing participation in short-cycle technical education.

In recent years the Greek government eliminated the general university entrance examination and introduced instead two successive national examinations to be taken during and at the end of upper secondary education. These examinations, together with average school grades, are taken into account in calculating a composite selection index for entry into higher education (15). The dangers of selection formula in which crucial and irreversible decisions are taken at an early stage cannot be sufficiently emphasised and are at the centre of the debate on education policy in Greece.

In Finland numerus clausus is now current practice in all institutions and fields of study. The number of students seeking admission to higher education far exceeds the number of those that can be accepted. By the late 1970s, the ratio of applicants to admissions was between 4:1 and 3:1 with variations according to field of study (theology 1.5:1, technology 12:1).

---

15. Educational Policy and Planning: Educational Reforms in Greece, OECD, Paris, 1980.

The situation is far less dramatic in Sweden and Denmark particularly in view of the waning demand for full-time studies. However, it is interesting to note that these Scandinavian countries share many viewpoints on the issue of access. They have all taken the political decision to curb the expansion of educational provision at the post-secondary level and it is now argued that a key objective should be to reduce the prevailing inequalities in participation; this can only be achieved by broadening the definition of demand and exercising much tighter control over the student intake so that groups with different social and educational backgrounds are given a greater chance of competing for entry.

In Finland, on the basis of a 1978 Act, the Ministry of Education has prepared a plan aimed at increasing the proportion of students coming from vocational education. By the end of the century 20% of the annual openings in higher education will be reserved for school leavers from vocational streams.

Another objective, particularly stressed in Sweden during the early 1970s and more recently in Denmark, is that of increasing adult participation, thereby shifting the balance between the initial and recurrent education functions of post-secondary education. One of the differences between these countries and others showing a similar concern for decreasing group disparities is that they openly admit that in higher education programmes with strong demand, the acceptance of adults with work experience may imply excluding school leavers from academic secondary streams with very good grades. Sweden is currently facing the opposite problem, namely that of having to design an admission system which at least partially redresses the balance in favour of young qualified school leavers.

A third consideration is that greater uniformity in entry conditions and regulations across the total system of higher education may be one way of avoiding strong hierarchical differentiation between the various types of institution or fields of study. This argument was used by the U-68 Commission in Sweden in advocating a policy of restricted entry for the entire post-secondary system rather than closing only certain lines of study.

Whatever the advantages of maintaining a relatively closed post-secondary system, it is clear that the success, or even the viability, of such a policy in liberal societies will depend on the following conditions:

i) that the curricula and organisation of studies at the upper secondary level, in particular in the pre-university streams, take account of increased entry restrictions in higher education and equip students for other training or employment options;

ii) that these other opportunities, whether in education/training or in employment, be made available to young people - an obvious minimum requirement but which present societies seem increasingly unable to fulfill;

iii) that these options be perceived as meaningful alternatives to initial higher education; this is more likely to be the case in countries where, for a variety of economic and social reasons, higher education has become a less attractive option than in the past;

iv) that the advantages of recurrent education over initial training also be made apparent - a rather difficult proposition to accept so long as the more privileged groups in terms of talent and social origin choose to take the latter option. Even in cases where secondary school leavers represent a smaller fraction of the student intake, the fact that in the competition for entry it is those who perform best who are "rewarded" with direct access implies recognition that initial education still represents a privileged option. A reduction in the number of places made available to these groups without due consideration of these factors risks enhancing the attraction of initial education - not least because of its scarcity - and correspondingly exacerbating tensions due to unsatisfied demand.

As with most reforms designed to limit access to young school leavers, much of the hope for their success is based on future demographic trends. Indeed the decrease in the college age cohorts may well represent the single most important factor in easing the strains inherent to measures of positive discrimination.

With the exception of Italy on the one hand and Greece, Finland, Sweden and Turkey on the other, OECD countries can be expected to enter the 1980s with post-secondary systems which still comprise a combination of relatively open and restricted entry sectors. Reforms within individual countries as well as differences among countries essentially relate to changes in the mix and balance between sectors but have not resulted in totally "closed" or "open" post-secondary systems.

In the non-European countries as well as in the United Kingdom the traditional binary distinction between a selective university sector and a less selective or open access non-university sector has not been substantially altered during the last decade. But at least in the United States, Canada and Japan, faster growth of the non-university sector seems to indicate a move towards <u>greater openness of the overall system</u>.

In continental Europe some countries - Switzerland and Austria for example - have largely maintained the binary distinction between, on the one hand, a university sector with free access and choice for qualified school leavers and a non-university sector with restricted entry for a larger pool of candidates on the other. The majority of European countries which are in the process of introducing numerical limitations within certain university fields of study have <u>in fact extended the coverage of the selective sector</u> (16).

---

16. Lévy-Garboua, in a synthesis of recent statistical research, has shown how coverage has extended in France: in 1951/52 25% of students were enrolled in the higher education sectors with restricted entry; in 1971/72 the proportion was 30% and in 1975/76 39%.

This does not necessarily mean that in these countries entry into higher education has been rendered more difficult. The existence of a free sector, the expansion of provision within the restricted entry sector, aided in some cases by the recent stabilisation in demand, have obviated a serious imbalance between supply and demand.

However, one consequence of having a wider spectrum of university programmes with restricted entry has been a narrowing of choices open to young secondary school graduates and less chances for candidates with average scores in secondary schools to enrol in programmes of their first choice or ranking high in demand.

Another consequence, already discussed in Chapter I, is the development of a new pecking order, sometimes a clear split, between programmes or institutions with restricted entry - whether university or non-university type - and those with open access. The introduction of restricted entry within a relatively wide range of university options is having the quite natural effect of raising the prestige of those programmes with restricted entry while decreasing the relative attraction of those options where access remains open. These hierarchical differences become stronger when, in a tight labour market situation, the restrictions applied are justified or are being perceived in terms of availability of jobs: whereas access to the selective sector is seen as a guarantee of employment, access to the open sector is at best a way of increasing one's chances in the competition for the better jobs, at worst a way of avoiding immediate unemployment.

Without attempting to establish a strict causal relationship, one could interpret recent trends in demand in the light of the fading attraction and prestige of certain university programmes. In countries where the total number of new entrants to post-secondary education has increased only slightly or remained stagnant, this may be due to the fact that candidates who are actually rejected in the competition for entry or, even more, those who see their chances of entering selective programmes as very dim, choose to abstain from pursuing post-secondary studies rather than enrolling in the open access sector.

Such an hypothesis could be substantial only through surveys of school leavers or data on the actual destination of rejected candidates. In the absence of individualised data, however, there are some trends which point to a growing disaffection with certain types of university studies and the emergence of a "pecking order" which cuts across the traditional university/non-university type distinctions.

In the first place there is evidence of increased "self-selection" in countries where transfer rates have declined (see Table 8). Secondly, the decrease in transfer rates to universities acquires particular significance in countries where the slowdown in demand for university places coexists with a tightening in the competition for entry into selective programmes, in particular within the short-cycle or non-university sector. This appears to be the case in

France (17), Sweden and Denmark. It would be interesting to know whether the non-university sector is attracting a clientele of academic secondary school leavers which a few years ago would have opted for long-cycle or academic-type studies. The "cascade effect" could be to provoke a narrowing of opportunities for candidates from secondary level technical streams, i.e. less privileged groups for whom these options represented the natural follow-up and sometimes the only possibility of pursuing post-secondary studies. Also significant is the coexistence of lower transfer rates with growing demand on the part of qualified school leavers for short vocational courses or training schemes outside the formal sector or offered by a growing number of vocational secondary schools.

Finally, student behaviour after entry can also be taken as a significant indicator of the relative attraction and prestige of different university programmes as well as their vulnerability in the light of expected trends in demand during the 1980s.

3. SELECTION AFTER ENTRY

As mentioned in Chapter I, the fact that a relatively high proportion of new entrants to higher education institutions never obtain a degree or diploma, or do so with considerable delay, is a matter of major concern in many Member countries. At the same time, there is growing controversy over the use of such terms as "drop-outs", "wastage" or "inefficiency" in referring to this phenomenon. It is clear that with the greater heterogeneity of the student population and with more diverse modes of attendance, the definition, measurement and analysis of the implications of departures in the course of higher education studies pose extremely complex problems both of a technical and a conceptual nature. Among the difficult questions raised are: how to distinguish between students who quit the system, those who interrupt their studies, those who transfer to another programme or institution, etc.; under what conditions are departures without a degree to be considered as "wastage" or "failure"; and if the concept of failure is introduced does it apply to the individuals or the institutions ?

It is not possible to engage here in a detailed discussion of these questions. The aim of this brief section is merely to give some illustrative examples of how selection and self-selection operate in the course of higher education studies, relating the analysis whenever possible to points raised in the previous sections.

Evidently, systems, programmes or institutions with unrestricted access - usually also associated with high teacher/student ratios and long duration of studies - tend to have a higher proportion of students who leave without obtaining a final qualification. Tables

---

17. See B. Girod de l'Ain, "Où va l'enseignement supérieur ?", in Le Monde, 15 and 19 November 1978.

13 and 14 give very rough indications on this relationship. As is well known, the high graduate output in the United Kingdom in relation to enrolments is linked to the relatively small proportion of the age group enrolling in higher education but, above all, to the short duration of degree courses and the high teacher/student ratio which has so far prevailed. On the other hand, Italy, France and Spain - countries where in the early 1970s most or all university faculties had free access - have also the lowest percentage of graduates. Low graduation rates for Sweden are mainly due to the high proportion of mature students enrolled in single courses.

Table 15 shows the increase in the number of drop-outs in Italian universities during the years in which access was liberalised. In 1960, the last year with restricted entry, one student in eight dropped out during the first year of study, whereas the figure rose to more than 25% in 1973. Moreover, "the years in which the drop-out rate increased more rapidly - 1965 and 1969 - were the years in which the liberalisation measures came into effect and there was the greatest increase in new entrants. Faced by a sharp increase in the number of new entrants and at the same time by a change in their composition (increase in the proportion of new entrants coming from schools other than the classical and scientific), the institution's reaction was a marked increase in the drop-out rate"(18).

In France, the period of rapid expansion was also accompanied by an increase in the number of dropouts: "whereas in 1964, 47% to 60% of new entrants completed the first two years of university studies, in 1975 only one out of three or four new entrants attained this level"(19). Regional surveys of institutions show that faculties with open access, e.g. law, humanities, pure and natural sciences, have consistently higher dropout rates than institutions with restricted entry such as the Grandes Ecoles, faculties of medicine or the IUTs. Departures tend to be concentrated in the first year or cycle of university studies. In the mid-1970s the proportion of first-year university students in France who did not even present themselves for their examinations was 41% in letters, 43% in economics and 32% in law (20). The official figures are given in Table 16.

Of particular interest is a French study which shows that, contrary to general belief, faculties of medicine and of dentistry which have strict numerus clausus are globally less selective than the faculties of science and as selective as law faculties, both of which have open access policies (21). It is furthermore noted that the severe screening which takes place in the science faculties

---

18. C. da Francesco and P. Trivellato: Drop-Outs from Italian Universities: 1960-1975; in Paedagogica Europea, Vol. XII, 1973, p.88.
19. Lévy-Garboua, "Les demandes de l'étudiant ou les contradictions de l'université de masse", Revue Française de Sociologie, Vol. XVII, 1976, p. 62.
20. G. Lassibille, L. Lévy-Garboua et al. : De l'inefficacité du système français d'enseignement supérieur, CREDOC-IREDU, Paris, December 1980.
21. L. Lévy-Garboua, ibid.

Table 13

TOTAL ENROLMENT AND GRADUATES IN HIGHER EDUCATION

		Enrolment (thousands)	Graduates (thousands)	Percentage of Graduates
GERMANY	1972 (1)	533.5	70.1	13.1
AUSTRALIA	1970	111.1	32.8	29.5
	1974	158.1	46.5	29.4
AUSTRIA	1965 (1)	48.9	5.2	16.6
	1973 (1)	73.6	6.3	8.6
BELGIUM	1965 (1)	48.8	7.2	14.8
	1970 (1)	75.1	10.8	14.4
	1973 (1)	79.5	12.9	16.2
CANADA	1965 (1)	206.2	43.2	21.0
	1970 (1)	356.7	79.3	22.2
	1974 (1)	417.2	91.2	21.9
DENMARK	1965	48.1	6.9	14.3
	1970	69.4	10.4	15.0
	1973	89.5	13.6	15.2
SPAIN	1965	274.1	8.6	3.1
	1969	320.4	12.8	4.0
	1974	484.8	41.1	8.5
UNITED STATES	1965	5,526.3	821.4	14.9
	1970	7,920.2	1,331.2	16.8
	1973	8,519.7	1,409.4	16.5
FINLAND	1965	56.2	6.3	11.2
	1970	75.2	9.2	12.2
	1974	86.4	10.9	12.6
FRANCE	1966 (1)	477.3	56.0	11.7
	1972 (1)	791.3	105.5	13.3
GREECE	1965	64.3	6.6	10.3
	1968	84.0	9.7	11.5
	1974	(112.0)	17.0	(15.2)
IRELAND	1965	20.7	5.0	24.2
	1974 (1)	20.8	7.1	34.1
ITALY	1968	574.6	47.9	8.3
	1973	879.3	74.2	8.4
JAPAN	1966	1,232.1	247.1	20.1
	1970	1,665.4	378.2	22.7
	1973	1,899.9	448.9	23.6
NORWAY	1965 (1)	19.1	2.0	10.5
	1970 (1)	28.7	3.7	12.9
	1973	67.7	14.6	21.6
NEW ZEALAND	1965	22.1	3.2	14.5
	1969	23.5	5.2	22.1
	1973	29.0	7.1	24.5
NETHERLANDS	1965	119.9	26.2	21.9
	1969	164.8	35.6	21.2
	1973	202.5	35.8	17.7
PORTUGAL	1965	34.9	2.7	7.7
	1973	65.4	7.6	11.6
UNITED KINGDOM	1966	213.8	56.6	26.5
	1970	277.5	78.7	28.4
	1973	307.1	80.4	26.2
SWEDEN	1966	99.3	13.5	13.6
	1972	138.6	29.3	21.1
TURKEY	1965	97.3	10.6	10.9
YUGOSLAVIA	1965	185.0	29.3	15.8
	1970	261.2	32.8	12.6
	1973	328.5	43.7	13.3

1. University-type only.

Sources: Enrolment: OECD data file. Graduates: based on UNESCO Statistical Yearbooks.

Table 14

ADMISSION RATES IN 1970/71 AND 1975/76 AND GRADUATION RATES IN 1977/1978

	Ratio of new entrants to university-type higher education in relation to relevant age group (1)		Ratio of first degrees awarded in relation to relevant age group (2)
	1970/71	1975/76	1977/78
Australia (3)	12.1	16.8	12.9
Austria	8.8	8.6	4.9 (4)
Canada	19.2	19.9	19.1
Denmark	11.8	17.5	9.6 (4)
France	...	21.8	7.5 (4)
Germany	11.6	14.4	9.0
Italy	25.6	31.1	9.9
Japan	17.6	27.6	22.2
Netherlands	8.3	8.5	9.1
Spain	14.5	19.8	7.6
United Kingdom	...	19.5 (5)	14.5 (6)
United States	30.9	27.9	23.2
Yugoslavia	15.9	19.5	6.5 (4)

(1) For definition of relevant age group see Table 11.

(2) Average age corresponding to new entrants plus formal duration of studies in each country.

(3) New entrants to universities.

(4) 1976/77.

(5) New entrants to university-type higher education.

(6) First degrees awarded by universities, CNAA and the Open University. Sources : new entrants : Educational Statistics in OECD Countries, op. cit. : for degrees awarded : M. Shattock, "Demography and Social Class : The Fluctuating Demand for Higher Education in Britain" in European Journal of Education, Vol. 16 No.3-4.

Source : OECD Data File.

Table 15

EVOLUTION OF NEW ENTRANTS AND DROPOUTS IN ITALIAN UNIVERSITIES

Academic year of matriculation	New entrants in year A	Enrolments for the second year of course in year t+1 B	Dropouts during the first year of course (A-B)	$\frac{(A-B)}{A}$ 100	Enrolments for the third year in year t+2 C	Dropouts during the first and the second year (A-C)	$\frac{(A-C)}{A}$ 100	Enrolments for the fourth year in the year t+3 D	Dropouts during the first, second and third year (A-D)	$\frac{(A-D)}{A}$ 100
1960/61	59 708	51 606	8 102	13.6	44 812	14 896	24.9	42 716	14 732	25.
1961/62	65 214	55 439	9 775	15.0	46 974	18 240	28.0	44 622	18 357	29.
1962/63	75 058	61 994	13 064	17.4	53 381	21 677	28.9	50 515	21 915	30.
1963/64	77 227	63 560	13 667	17.7	56 704	20 523	26.6	53 791	20 736	27.
1964/65	86 397	73 304	13 093	15.2	65 551	20 846	24.1	61 702	21 706	26.
1965/66	105 480	86 009	19 471	18.4	73 227	32 253	30.6	69 891	33 035	32.
1966/67	119 480	94 402	25 438	21.2	85 528	34 312	28.6	81 452	35 030	30.
1967/68	125 265	102 999	24 266	19.1	94 631	32 634	25.6	93 946	30 175	24.
1968/69	142 653	118 156	24 497	17.2	107 907	34 746	24.4	104 915	34 207	24.
1969/70	175 249	137 720	37 529	21.4	125 811	49 438	28.2	114 794	57 010	33.
1970/71	194 280	154 591	39 689	20.4	133 460	60 820	31.3	121 749	69 298	36.
1971/72	214 417	160 808	53 609	25.0	141 641	72 776	33.9	130 804	80 374	38.
1972/73	213 226	159 228	53 998	25.3	140 598	72 628	34.1	129 090	81 102	38.
1973/74	213 619	158 031	55 588	26.0	141 052	72 567	34.0			
1974/75	231 075	166 625	64 450	27.9						

Notes: whereas in the other columns also diploma course students were considered, the figures in the last and penultimate columns were calculated considering only the relevant new entrants in degree courses. We did so because the length of a diploma course is never of four years (minimum length of a degree course).

Source: Table extracted from C. de Francesco and P. Trivellato, "Drop-outs from Italian Universities: 1960-1975" in Paedagogica Europaea, Vol. 12, 1977-3, p. 89.

Table 16

COMPARISON OF ENROLMENTS DURING THE FIRST TWO YEARS OF STUDY AND OF EXAMINATION RESULTS OR DIPLOMAS, BY DISCIPLINES

Year 1976-1977	Law	Economics	Letters	Pure sciences	Medicine	Dentistry	IUT
First year students No. passing examinations %	37 042	13 862	66 020	29 128	PCEMI 40 950 10 811 26.4		28 001
Second year students as a % of first year students	17 502 47	7 187 52	32 424 49	13 809 47	9 744	2 904	18 492(2) 70
Students successfully completing second year % (1)	9 117 52.1	4 530 63.2	15 946 49.2	7 466 54.1	9 288 95.3	1 803 82.1	16 153 87.4

1. Calculated by relating the number of students who succeeded in the examinations in relation to the number of second year students.
2. Including special year.

Source: Etudes et Documents, L'Enseignement supérieur en France: Etude statistique et évolution de 59/60 à 77/78, ministère de l'Education et ministère des Universités, 80.2, p. 32.

Table 17*

NEW ENTRANTS TO UNIVERSITY IN 1973/74 BY SUBJECT:
DROPOUT RATES DURING THE FIRST YEAR AND CHARACTERISTICS OF NEW ENTRANTS

(Percentages)

	Dropout rate[1]	General secondary school graduates[2]	Sons of university or secondary school graduates[3]	Do not work or seek job[4]
Mathematics	29.5	58.9	27.7	56.6
Physics	41.0	36.3	24.4	36.0
Chemistry	26.5	55.5	31.1	53.2
Geology	40.0	29.4	24.8	36.5
Computer Studies	42.8	38.8	21.0	45.6
Natural Science	35.7	46.3	28.5	50.4
Biology	26.0	58.5	28.5	54.4
Pharmacy	12.4	56.1	34.5	55.2
Medicine	7.6	81.0	42.1	66.1
Engineering	25.6	39.2	27.2	50.4
Architecture	22.8	28.9	31.6	38.5
Agronomy	30.1	31.3	25.2	39.8
Veterinary Medicine	18.5	49.2	32.7	48.7
Economics and Commerce	43.5	20.0	23.7	29.8
Politics	38.4	27.8	23.8	22.3
Sociology	39.7	19.2	21.5	22.4
Law	27.3	48.8	36.0	37.2
Letters	12.7	71.5	42.4	48.1
Literary Subjects	33.7	3.2	18.8	45.1
Philosophy	12.3	68.7	34.8	40.7
Pedagogics	33.7	3.0	16.5	42.0
Modern Foreign Languages	21.1	52.6	34.9	44.4
Foreign Languages	30.6	15.4	25.3	46.2
Psychology	31.1	26.9	30.4	33.1
Total (All Subjects)	26.0	43.0	30.6	44.4

1. "Dropout rate" is the proportion of 1973/74 new entrants who dropped out during their first year of university.
2. "General secondary school graduates" is the proportion of 1973/74 new entrants who come from general secondary schools (licei).
3. "Sons of university or secondary school graduates" is the proportion of 1973/74 new entrants who are sons of secondary school or university graduates: because of the lack of other indicators I consider this level of educational attainment as an indicator of upper-middle or upper social origin.
4. "Do not work or seek job" is the proportion of 1973/74 new entrants who declared they did not work and did not intend to seek work.

Sources: for the dropout rate: ISTAT, Annuario Statistico Italiano 1975 and 1976.
For the characteristics of new entrants: ISTAT, Indagine speciale sulle caratteristiche degli studenti universitari iscritti al I anno di corso, Rome, 1977.

* Table taken from: C. de Francesco "The Growth and Crisis of Italian Higher Education during the 1960s and 1970s in Higher Education, Vol. 7, n° 2, Elsevier, May 1978.

cannot be linked to student aptitudes since these faculties recruit 90% of their students from the more "noble" or selective lines of study in secondary schools. The point made is that, having accepted the existence of an inverse correlation between the degree of selectivity at entry and that which occurs after entry, differences in dropout rates between programmes cannot be accounted for only, or even primarily, by variations in admission policies. In addition to length of studies one factor which is considered crucial in determining students' propensity to complete a degree course successfully is the perceived economic and/or social value of the degree awarded.

Table 17 on dropouts in Italian universities shows that in a country where all disciplines have open access, medicine is the subject with the lowest dropout rates. It is of interest to note that medicine also has the highest percentage of traditional students, that is, students coming from academic-type secondary schools, from families with relatively high levels of educational attainment and who attend courses on a full-time basis. At the other extreme are subjects such as pedagogics, literary subjects or sociology with the highest dropouts and at the same time the highest proportion of "non-traditional" students.

In other countries also, there is evidence that in recent years, with the deterioration in employment prospects for graduates, there has been a change in student behaviour both in regard to the options they choose and how they participate in higher education. On the one hand, there seems to be a levelling off, and even a growing proportion of the traditional type of student (male, middle-class origin, high achievers) in higher education institutions or programmes more likely to guarantee high economic and social rewards. In these elite options, most with restricted entry and with few possibilities of studying part-time, students' chances of success are relatively high, even though it is claimed that performance is not always very satisfactory, considering the fierce competition for entry and the grades of those admitted. On the other hand there are other disciplines or institutions which, because they are in the open access sector and/or their graduates face difficulties in a depressed labour market, recruit a far wider range of students who attend higher education for very diverse reasons. They represent the more inefficient options in terms of the number of entrants not obtaining final qualifications. Their case calls for more sophisticated measurement of wastage or inefficiency and for more ingenuity in the interpretation of selection or self-selection after entry. The following factors need to be borne in mind in any such discussion.

Firstly, as already mentioned, many of these programmes have the explicit or implicit function of selecting after entry; whatever the economic and social disadvantages of this policy, it is clear that delayed selection gives chances to many students who on the basis of limited entry would be excluded. Secondly, students frequently use these options as a means of circumventing programmes with selective entry and enrolling at a more advanced stage through special transfer schemes. Thirdly, there is the phenomenon of multiple enrolment and the use of these subjects or institutions as reserve or "fall-back" options by students competing for entry elsewhere. Fourthly, these options tend to have a more flexible organisation of studies and therefore attract mature students many of whom attend without the intention of completing a programme or obtaining a final qualification.

There is considerable debate as to the impact on the behaviour of students in their initial education of a depressed labour market situation or a decrease in private returns on certain types of higher education studies. The French study referred to above claims that, under these conditions, students tend to devote less time and effort to completing their studies and prefer either to take a job or spend more time in leisure activities. What has been called the "penalty effect" is however also in operation: students are aware that although university credentials do not guarantee high level jobs they are nonetheless essential in the competition for these jobs and in maintaining or increasing their social status. In other words, the penalty for non-graduation tends to increase (22) so that students are under stronger pressure to complete their studies.

One conclusion which could be drawn from this discussion is that, precisely as some type of academic qualifications cease to ensure access to higher positions in society and pursuit of higher education studies becomes more of a "gamble", there are wide differences in students' behaviour depending on their chances of winning and, even more, on the risks involved in losing in such a gamble. It is the social and economic implications of this type of development which will need close monitoring by institutional leaders and governments in the years ahead.

---

22. R. Geiger: "The Limits of Higher Education: A Comparative Analysis of Factors affecting Enrolment Levels in Belgium, France, Japan and the United States", Yale Higher Education Research Group, Working Paper YHERG No. 41.

GERMANY

DISTRIBUTION OF STUDENTS BY SOCIO-ECONOMIC ORIGIN

	Independent workers	Civil servants	White collar workers	Blue collar workers	Others	Total = 100.0	Total (thousands)
I. University Sector (1)							
1966 (2)	30.9	28.6	31.8	6.5	2.2	100.0	40.7
1970	26.5	25.2	34.0	12.0	2.3	100.0	66.1
1975	22.8	22.6	36.7	15.0	2.9	100.0	91.5
1977 (3)	21.3	21.8	37.1	14.8	5.0	100.0	95.2
II. Non-University Sector							
Fine Arts Schools							
1966	26.7	28.5	31.5	7.4	5.9	100.0	0.8
1970	24.1	24.4	35.9	9.2	6.4	100.0	1.3
1975	22.0	24.6	39.1	10.6	3.7	100.0	1.6
Higher Technical Schools							
1966	25.3	20.4	33.3	17.5	3.5	100.0	21.9
1975	21.8	14.4	32.8	27.6	3.4	100.0	32.1
1977	21.5	14.3	33.5	26.7	4.0	100.0	35.4
III. Total Higher Education							
1966	28.9	25.8	32.3	10.3	2.7	100.0	63.5 (2)
1970 (4)	26.5	25.2	34.0	11.9	2.4	100.0	67.4 (4)
1975	22.5	20.5	35.7	18.2	3.1	100.0	125.3
1977	21.4	19.8	36.1	18.0	4.7	100.0	130.6

1. Universities, teacher training schools, "Gesamthochschulen".
2. Teacher training schools excluded.
3. Fine Arts schools included.
4. Higher technical schools excluded.

Source: Grund und Struktur data, 1977, p. 90 et 1979, p. 140.

FRANCE

SOCIAL ORIGIN(1) OF UNIVERSITY STUDENTS

	1965/66	1970/71	1975/76	1976/77	1977/78	1978/79
Farmers	5.8		5.6	5.5	5.4	5.2
Farm workers	0.6		0.5	0.4	0.4	0.5
Industrialists and tradesmen	14.9		11.4	11.2	10.9	10.5
Professionals and higher level executives	29.0		33.3	33.6	33.7	30.7
Middle level executives	16.7		17.0	17.1	17.5	15.6
Clerks	8.7		3.3	2.3	0.1	8.2
Blue collar workers	9.5		12.4	12.6	12.9	11.0
Service workers	1.1		0.8	0.9	0.9	0.9
Other categories	4.7		6.9	6.7	6.4	6.1
Not in work-force	9.0		2.8	2.7	2.8	3.0
No answer						8.3
Total	100.0		100.0	100.0	100.0	100.0
(French and non-French) Total	413.756		811.258	821.591	837.776	-

1. By socio-economic status of head of household.

Sources: - Statistiques de l'enseignement (since 1975-76, including la Réunion and les Antilles, as well as the Institut des langues orientales and l'Institut d'études pédagogiques de Paris).
- Etudes et documents "L'enseignement supérieur".
- Jarousse, Evolution du comportement des étudiants, CREDOC, Paris, December 1981, p. 8.

143

Chapter III

SELECTION METHODS AND CRITERIA

There is an observed trend in a growing number of OECD countries to limit the intake of certain university fields of study and to set greater restrictions on choice, often on entry, to secondary school leavers from academic streams. This has brought to the forefront issues relating to methods and criteria for selection among young people coming directly from secondary education. For a number of reasons, these issues have become highly sensitive politically. Firstly, there is, in most countries, an important problem of sheer numbers as this group still represents the large majority of new entrants. Secondly, attempts to decrease prevailing inequalities in participation at the tertiary level inevitably imply the elimination of a number of long established privileges and acquired rights which this group, as a whole, has traditionally enjoyed and to which naturally there are strong reactions. Moreover, in view of their social status, these students, and their parents, are in a privileged position to exert pressure on policy makers, resort to legal measures or articulate their claims through the mass media. Thirdly, difficulties are compounded by the fact that, practically everywhere, academic secondary streams continue to be organised as pre-university courses; this precludes any other options for these candidates who see their disappointment and frustration increased when thus rejected by the institutions or programmes on which they place their expectations and for which they are primarily trained. A vicious circle tends to develop as increased competition for entry into selective options renders even more difficult the task of reorganising and diversifying upper secondary academic streams: schools and teachers tend to stress the academic orientation of programmes in accordance with university requirements in order to increase the chances of their students in the competition for entry. This is also a means of preserving or increasing the prestige of schools and their staff whose status depends to a large extent on the number or proportion of their pupils who succeed in entering the more prestigious options of higher education (their "transfer potential").

Whatever scenario is envisaged for the future, the question of selection methods and criteria will undoubtedly remain a central issue. For, even assuming that there will be a fall in demand for higher education and growing numbers of empty places in some institutions, certain sectors of higher education will continue to witness strong and possibly increased, competition for entry. Indeed, as discussed in Chapter II, this is already the case in a number of countries.

While many aspects of these problems are common to the majority of Member countries, approaches proposed or adopted are known to vary considerably from country to country and within countries over time, particularly in those where restricted university entry is a relatively new phenomenon. Solutions are necessarily experimental and constantly revised in the light of the results achieved; they must also be meshed in with reforms in other related educational areas and to the changing socio-economic circumstances. Finally, experience has shown that changes in political leadership may also exert quite a strong influence on the type and direction of reform in this area.

It may be useful at this point to briefly review the admission procedures currently operating in different Member countries. These schemes will not be discussed in detail since this information is readily available in the contributions by national authorities and experts and in official national papers. The purpose of this section is merely to analyse the more significant trends and new ideas, in particular in relation to selection procedures, and to highlight some of the problems and issues.

A number of basic criteria usually guide the choice of admission schemes and commonly serve in assessing selection procedures. A recent American report on selective admissions in higher education (1) identifies four criteria, defined as follows:

"Validity is often considered the most important basis for evaluators. It refers to the reasonableness of the measure as well as its effectiveness in differentiating among students who are and are not likely to succeed. Fairness refers especially to whether students have a reasonable opportunity to meet a particular admission standard and whether imposition of the standard has an adverse impact on some students that is unrelated to the demands of the educational programme. Feasibility refers to whether reliable measurement is a practical possibility, whether the cost of such assessment is within reason, and so on. Secondary effects refers to the positive or negative effect the use of an admission standard has upon the health of the educational institution, upon its feeder schools, or upon professions for which it serves as the principal or only mode of entry."

A fifth criterion which is related to, but not explicitly mentioned under fairness, could be added, namely that of social equity.

The ensuing analysis of the advantages and drawbacks of the various selection procedures in terms of these criteria is primarily concerned with their use in regard to the traditional clientele of qualified school leavers whose proportion in relation to the total number of new entrants may be declining more rapidly in some countries than others. Indeed, in some cases - the best known example being Sweden - a key feature of the recent reforms is that, to enhance diversity and avoid unfair competition for entry, candidates are

---

1. Willingham et al. "The status of selective admissions" in Selective Admissions in Higher Education, Jossey-Bass, San Francisco, 1977

divided into groups according to background characteristics (age, level and type of education), each subject to a different quota (i.e. competing among themselves). This means that in measuring the extent to which the equity objective is being achieved, account must be taken of the results obtained <u>within</u> each group as well as those emerging from comparisons in participation rates <u>between</u> the groups.

1. SECONDARY SCHOOL MARKS

In practically all Member countries access of secondary school leavers proceeding directly to higher education is primarily, if not exclusively, determined on the basis of <u>secondary school records</u>. For entry into open access institutions the <u>successful completion of</u> secondary school studies is usually the sole requirement. When additional requirements are set these tend to be typically expressed in terms of school background (type of school, of streams, of subjects taken) and/or school performance (grades or marks, ranking order in classroom). Similarly, measures of previous academic performance or of cognitive achievement, in particular, school marks, constitute in most countries the main basis for formal selection at entry. In this respect it should be noted that in spite of growing criticisms and the recognised drawbacks <u>of using school marks for selection purposes, no country seriously envisages abolishing their use, at least not in the near future</u> and their maintenance is advocated by people with quite diverse ideological viewpoints.

Tradition and public confidence in "objective" indicators of school achievement as well as academic pressures undeniably account for much of the support for grades; other arguments contribute to strengthen the case. First and most important, studies conducted in many countries have shown a correlation between grade point average or marks obtained in final secondary school examinations and performance at the higher levels. And although in most cases this correlation is not sufficiently high to justify the exclusive use of grades, even on efficiency grounds, no other assessment method has been found to have a stronger predictive validity.

Another frequent claim is that school marks play a useful role in the sense that they both reflect and influence pupils' motivation for pursuing further studies. Thus, failure to give adequate recognition to high marks would have adverse effects on pupils' morale, performance and interest in academic achievement. Without going into the serious pedagogical implications of this type of argument, it is important to note that, whereas wide consensus exists as to the advantages of assigning a greater role to motivation in the selection process, it is far from being generally accepted that marks should be used as an indicator of this dimension or should have even greater influence than is the case at present on pupils' attitudes and motivation vis-à-vis higher education studies.

No doubt the difficulties in developing other acceptable measures of cognitive achievement or of motivation explains to a large extent the dominant role of marks in the selection process.

Concern for legitimacy and the need to account for the decisions taken, in particular in the case of rejected candidates, constitute a real and understandable barrier to change and diversity.

More recently, however, undue reliance on marks has been questioned on other than the typical meritocratic and egalitarian grounds which have usually dominated the debate on selection procedures. There is indeed a growing concern for the secondary school in particular on feeder institutions (i.e. secondary schools), of assigning increased importance to indicators of secondary school performance. These, which have been observed for quite some time in Japan, are now found in most Member countries where selection among academically-oriented school leavers has been introduced or reinforced. In Germany, for exemple, when rapid growth in the early 1970s in demand coincided with the adoption of a numerus clausus, secondary schools were strongly affected. The following observations on the German scene could equally well apply to other national contexts:

- The great importance of the average Abitur mark in the award procedure under the Länder Agreement has had extremely deleterious effects on schools in general and on teacher-pupil relations and pupils' attitudes to one another in particular.
- Pupils feel compelled to concentrate almost exclusively on getting high marks and distinguishing themselves from their fellow pupils.
- Teachers are subject to heavy pressure to award higher marks. They cannot therefore be asked to set standards to ensure comparability of marks.
- After years of effort the schools achieved a basis for internal reform in the Länder Agreement of July 1972 on the reform of upper classes in secondary stage II. They now find that the pressure for higher marks is undermining the pedagogical objectives of the new course system.
- A few remarks on teachers' marking and on pupil attitudes may serve to highlight the problem.
- As the ZVS tables (2) reveal, applications from candidates of German matriculation standard reveals a clear upward trend in marks. In the summer semester of 1974 only 2 per cent had obtained certificates with an average mark of 1.7 or higher, whereas one year later the same qualifications had been reached by 3.3 per cent. There is a similar upgrading apparent from 2.5 upward: in 1974 20 per cent of candidates scored this or a higher mark, while in 1975 28 per cent did so(*). These are signs of inflation in the marking system, originating in the teachers' understandable inclination, given the numerus clausus, to give candidates the benefit of the doubt more often than before.
- Conversely, a recent poll of 241 pupils in the three senior classes of the Gymnasium showed them to be subject to growing stress as the Abitur approaches. "Submissive behaviour" increases. The atmosphere of the classroom suffers: 60 per cent agreed that anxiety

---

* According to the German marking system: 1=very good, 6=fail.

2. Zentralstelle für die Vergabe von Studienplätzen.

about obtaining a university place made everyone "look out for himself". One of the most disquieting features is that the performance motivation of the large group of middling and weaker candidates declined steeply with the approach of the examination, because they felt incapable, even with the utmost application, of meeting the high demands of "numerus clausus" subjects.

The importance attached to secondary school options and marks by selective higher education institutions has a strong effect too on students' behaviour and choices both at secondary and post-secondary level. Individual choices tend to be made on the basis of strategies designed to increase chances or minimise risks rather than on genuine vocation, aptitudes or preferences.

When the type of stream chosen at the upper secondary level constitutes a key criterion in determining entry, as is the case in France, choices made at the age of 15 or 16 are not only crucial but often irreversible. In France, young students, especially those from middle class families, are under strong pressure to enrol in the mathematics stream at the upper secondary level since this is the only line of study which guarantees access to all options in higher education and is required by the majority of the selective institutions. This trend is reinforced by the fact that the growing number of university faculties or departments introducing selection also favour the Baccalauréat in mathematics, not necessarily because it is relevant to future studies but because of its screening role in secondary education.

In countries such as Sweden and the Netherlands, where entry requirements are primarily determined on the basis of marks obtained in the course of secondary schooling or in the final matriculation examination without assigning great value to the type of subjects taken, different problems arise. In order to improve their chances in the competition for entry into universities, pupils favour choices in the humanities and social sciences, considered to grant them a stronger possibility of obtaining high marks. In Sweden such a trend has been considered as one of the explanatory factors in the lack of demand for scientific and technological university studies; in the Netherlands it is claimed that it has fostered the need for remedial courses within the scientific faculties so as to bring new entrants up to the required level.

Marks can also play a significant role in the process of self-selection (3): pupils, aware of the significance that is assigned to marks and accepting them as measures of predictive validity, tend to base decisions and future educational plans on the results they have obtained. The importance assigned to marks is likewise conducive to the phenomenon of "artificial demand" which is manifested in a variety of ways. For example, pupils with high marks or having succeeded in the "noble" subjects tend to choose restricted sectors, not necessarily because they are interested in or have a vocation for the studies or professions to which they lead but because they perceive

---

3. For a more detailed discussion see K. Härnqvist: Individual Demand for Education, op. cit.

them - and rightly so - as a guarantee of higher educational standards, better employment prospects and higher financial rewards. The clearest example of this trend is the high proportion of young people talented in mathematics and other basic sciences (commonly used entry criteria) seeking to enter medical studies though they are not necessarily motivated or particularly qualified for the practice of the profession.

It is not possible to undertake, in this report, a thorough review of the many problems posed by the exclusive use of indicators of school performance for selection among the pool of qualified school leavers. There is however one general point which merits special consideration, namely, that reforms concerning assessment and marking procedures at the secondary level and the role they are assigned by higher education institutions reflect a basic inherent tension between the needs and requirements of secondary education and those of higher education. This tension, scarcely noticeable when practically the sole function of academic secondary streams was selection and preparation for higher education studies, has definitely heightened in recent years; given the general lines of secondary school reform, it can be expected to become even more acute in the future. Indeed, the trend to broaden the aims and functions of upper secondary education and to develop polyvalent streams may well contribute to strengthening the conflict of interests between the two levels. Groups primarily committed to these secondary school reforms are likely to advocate changes in curricula and assessment schemes considered to be ill-suited to the needs of higher education institutions, in particular the more selective ones. On the other hand, groups within the academic world will no doubt strive to maintain or develop indicators of secondary level performance which correspond to their own definition of standards and quality.

The debate in the mid-1970s in the United Kingdom on the reform of the "A" level courses, which are roughly equivalent to academic upper secondary streams and constitute the basic university entrance qualification, provides a good illustration of this growing tension between the requirements of schools and universities. The proposal of the Schools Council to introduce instead the so-called "N" and "F" scheme (4), basically implying a broadening of the curriculum so as to correspond better to the needs and aptitudes of a larger and more heterogeneous student body, has met with widespread opposition from the university world. Their main arguments do not relate so much to the intrinsic merits or drawbacks of such a scheme, but far more to whether the "N" and "F" curricula will enable school leavers to meet the standards set by the universities. Since university teachers considered that the proposals did not meet this requirement and that such a scheme would require the lengthening of most first degree programmes by one year - which in itself implies a corresponding increase in resources, difficult to accept under present economic conditions - it is not surprising that the scheme was finally not adopted. In Germany a similar debate took place in recent years with respect to the admission of graduates from comprehensive secondary schools (Gesamtschulabsolventen).

---

4. Schools Council: "Examinations at 18+", Examinations Bulletin 38, Great Britain, 1978.

The trend in many countries, including the United Kingdom, is towards a greater adaptation of higher education institutions to reforms at the lower levels. However, there are equally important countertrends, particularly in view of the growing concern for maintaining minimum tertiary level entry standards in order to prevent higher education institutions from becoming too heavily involved in compensatory or remedial education. The experience of the United States with the open access system is not likely to encourage Europeans to take this path.

Thus, growing awareness of potential conflict of interests and objectives between the two levels reinforces the need, on the one hand, to reform assessment procedures at the secondary level to take better account of these conflicting requirements, and on the other, to design admission schemes which decrease the overriding role played by school marks.

This type of concern is clearly reflected in current discussions on the choice of more appropriate assessment and certification procedures at the secondary level. Among the central issues being discussed are: whether cumulative evaluation can or should replace final examinations; whether internal school assessment should replace external public examinations; whether there should be a clearer separation between assessment designed to certify completion of secondary studies and that measuring ability to pursue tertiary level studies; whether a cumulative type of assessment should be complemented by tests or other measures ensuring comparability of grading procedures and standards among schools, etc.

While in a number of countries the official policy is in favour of replacing final, often externally set, examinations by successive school assessments - generally advocated on pedagogical and social grounds - such a move is often resisted by parents and public opinion in general. In Australia where very different assessment schemes are used in the various states, the quite clearly conflicting viewpoints on admission policies are: following the abolition of external examinations at the and of year 12 in Australian Capital Territory, Queensland and Western Australia and the introduction of moderated school assessment, the report points to a renewed emphasis on publicly accepted qualifications and a move in favour of reinforcing the place of the final year examination.

Policies aimed at limiting the weight assigned to school marks in admission or selection into higher education institutions are not necessarily of recent date. For quite some time, many OECD countries have used other assessment methods, although also largely based on cognitive criteria or indicators of academic talent and scholastic ability. Entrance examinations and objective tests have been, and are, among the more commonly used procedures, intended either as means of reinforcing selection (especially in the case of countries with a large pool of qualified candidates) or as tools to enhance the predictive validity of selection schemes.

2. ENTRANCE EXAMINATIONS AND STANDARDISED TESTS

In a number of Member countries, e.g. Greece, Japan, Portugal, Spain, Turkey, Yugoslavia, selection is based on the results of special entrance examinations used exclusively (Portugal, Turkey) or more often in combination with school marks. In some cases (Spain, Portugal) these examinations can be taken only after a one-year preparatory course; in others they are taken before or immediately after completion of secondary studies. Examinations may be organised by each single institution (Yugoslavia) more commonly at national level or, as in Japan, through a combination of both.

At least in principle, entrance examinations have the advantage of marking more clearly the difference between the standards required for completion of secondary education and specific aptitudes and qualifications for different types of higher education studies. Thus, they could help relieve, at least partially, the selective role of secondary schools and also increase the chances of pupils who, for a variety of reasons, did not perform well at school but have the interest and potential to pursue tertiary education. In practice, entrance examinations generally do not seem to offer these additional opportunities. They are mostly used to assess past knowledge and cognitive achievement and tend to reinforce selection on the basis of the same criteria as school marks.

In the majority of countries where entrance examinations are currently used, they have become the subject of much controversy and criticism: in Japan, the system of entrance examinations which for many years has been a key aspect of education, has been considerably overhauled; in Spain and Portugal reorganisation is being seriously envisaged; in Greece the plan is to abolish entrance exams as from 1981. Some of the problems they give rise to are similar to those posed by the use of school marks, others are inherent in the use of examinations for selection purposes.

A major source of concern in a number of countries, e.g. Finland, Greece, Portugal, Japan, is the importance acquired by individual tutoring and/or private schools exclusively devoted to preparing and coaching students for these exams. There is above all the major social bias introduced by the fact that these are fee paying services or institutions, a bias which is further enhanced with the lengthening of the period between completion of secondary school studies and the time the examination is taken. Indeed, added to an increase in the direct costs of attendance are the indirect costs resulting from a prolonged non-active status (i.e. income foregone).

Family background tends to play an even greater role when competition for entry is particularly strong. It largely accounts for the differences in attitudes or strategies vis-à-vis "high risk" options and also determines the extent to which candidates who have been rejected once can or will persevere in seeking entry into the institutions of their choice.

In Greece other undesirable effects resulting from the proliferation of private cramming schools have been identified. In 1974, 84 per cent of those enrolling for the competitive entrance examination had attended one of these schools; this high participation rate, also applicable for more recent years, represents a significant financial burden for many families and adds considerably to the overall social costs of education. Secondly, candidates having attended these schools had only a slightly higher success rate in the competitive entrance examinations (44 per cent) than the minority who did not enrol (38 per cent). Thirdly, evidence of a widening gap in performance in the entrance examinations shows that these schools tend to favour the best pupils (i.e. those with higher secondary school marks) rather than increasing the chances of the weaker ones. It is further claimed that the presence of these schools has served to expose the flaws of the public education system and undermine confidence in the selection process.

In Japan, cramming schools pose very similar problems; though the variety of issues raised in relation to the university entrance examinations can only be understood with reference to the central role these examinations play in Japanese society. In the words of an observer "there can be no other industrialised country in the world where the success in life of an individual hinges so dramatically on the results of such a short performance"(5). Given the formidable tensions and pressures surrounding the "examination", it is obvious that the social problems posed are acute, not least those pertaining to the secondary effects on the lower levels of education. The fierce competition in Japan is due not so much to a shortage in the overall capacity of the higher education system, but far more to its hierarchical nature and the overriding dominance of a few elite institutions. It is very common for secondary school leavers, unable to meet the standards of the institutions of their choice, to make repeated attempts to enter in the following years. The presence of these "ronin" students who in 1976 represented 24 per cent of the total number of applicants to universities and junior colleges obviously accentuates the competition.

In the Japanese case a strong competitive situation, entrance examinations can have a feedback effect on secondary schools similar to or even more pronounced than school marks. With reference to scholastic ability tests as the main selection procedure, it is stated that questions of a nature too advanced to be answered by those students who have done normal upper secondary studies or odd questions deviating from the aim of the entrants' selection test have come to be set. In these circumstances, upper secondary school students have come to spend much more time and energy on preparatory study for university entrance examinations than on ordinary study in upper secondary schools, and upper secondary school education has come to adapt itself to such study practices. Moreover, the number of students attending special private cramming schools preparing them for university entrance examinations is also growing.

---

5. U. Teichler, "Some Aspects of Higher Education in Japan" in <u>KBS Bulletin on Japanese Culture</u>, June -July 1972, p. 9.

After long debate and research a new selection scheme was introduced in Japan in 1979. So far the so-called Joint Achievement Test is applied only in national and public universities, excluding the private sector and all national and public junior colleges. The main lines of this two-stage test are as follows:

Applicants for national and public universities are required to undergo a first stage examination around the end of December simultaneously throughout the nation. This multiple-choice test, designed to assess applicants' level of general and basic scholastic attainment is imposed in five subject areas - the national language, social studies, mathematics, science and a foreign language - within the academic scope defined as compulsory under the curriculum of upper secondary schools.

They then undergo the second stage examination, held around early March, in each university. This test, designed to assess applicants' ability and aptitude for the chosen undergraduate course, is given in such forms as a written scholastic ability test, practical skill test, interview and small thesis-type test. Since all national universities and most public universities are expected to hold this second stage examination on the same date, each applicant will now only be able to take an examination in the one national or public university he prefers most.

Each university decides whether or not the candidate is rated as successful after examining his results in the joint achievement test and the separate second stage test as well as his credential and other relevant data. The joint achievement test is not therefore designed to function as a determining factor, but is delivered to each university concerned for use in the overall decision-making process.

In addition, even under the new selection formula, each university still has the right to admit without examination some applicants on the recommendation of the principal of their upper secondary school.

This scheme is intended to assign more weight to performance at the upper secondary level, and more especially to prevent candidates from taking several entrance examinations at a time.

Among OECD countries it is mainly in the United States and Japan that special standardised objective tests have been developed for admission and selection among qualified school leavers. Although in the United States school marks are considered to be the more valid criterion for recruitment, the majority of colleges and universities use them in combination with the results of national standardised tests set up and administered by a central non-governmental agency, such as the Educational Testing Service (ETS) and the American College Test (ACT). The well-known SAT (Scholastic Aptitude Test), taken by school leavers seeking entry into higher education, enables institutions to compare the performance of candidates coming from a highly decentralised and diversified school network. Although tests have been shown to improve the predictive validity of the selection process, in recent years their use for admission or assessment purposes in higher education has come under strong attack in the United States.

While in the United States, and also to some extent in Japan, tests have long played a major role in education as well as in other social sectors, in the majority of European countries more confidence has been placed on essay-type examinations more closely linked to the teaching process. In Europe, attitudes vis-à-vis the use of objective aptitude tests for individual assessment and selection purposes have in general ranged from scepticism to outright rejection. This marked contrast in attitudes cannot be explained merely by technical or organisational factors and no doubt has its roots in the different psychological and learning theories which have prevailed in the two continents.

In practice, the differences between examinations and standardised ability or aptitude tests may be less marked than is sometimes assumed and there are some signs of a narrowing of the traditional gap in the approach to assessment. In the United States, in view of the present concern over standards of high school leavers, particularly in the field of written and oral communication, there is growing interest in assignments tools - whether they are called tests or examinations - which include written essays, analysis of tests or other assessments typically corresponding to the more "discursive" or "holistic" approach of traditional examinations. On the other hand, European countries which are now facing problems of selection among a considerably enlarged pool of qualified candidates and are developing centralised admission systems, are also beginning to experience the need for easily administered national norm-referenced assessment procedures, particularly in countries where secondary school final examinations have ceased to guarantee access or have ceased to exist altogether. Up to now efforts have been mainly focused on achieving maximum comparability between school marks, whether these are based on final examinations or cumulative evaluation. Sometimes this may imply introducing assessment techniques typically associated with standardised tests, e.g. multiple choice, closed questions, etc. More often, perhaps, the policy has been to devise systems whereby the secondary school marks can be adjusted to national norms.

Growing awareness of the advantages of using complementary or, in the long run, alternative selection procedures, rather than endlessly refining and adjusting school marks to higher education requirements, has induced some OECD countries, e.g. Australia, Sweden and Germany, to assign considerable resources to the development of tests specifically designed for admission purposes.

In Australia developmental work started in 1968, financed by the Commonwealth Government. The programme, initially designated the Tertiary Entrance Examination Project (TEEP), was aimed at "determining whether such tests could improve tertiary entrance selection and reduce wastage in tertiary institutions when used in conjunction with matriculation examination results". In 1970 the Australian Scholastic Aptitude Test (ASAT) was developed from the TEEP tests and was designed to measure general verbal, numerical and related skills and to be independent of knowledge gained by studying specific subjects. Studies have shown that test results were considerably less successful than traditional public examinations in predicting tertiary performance, although for certain academic courses it has proved possible to achieve superior prediction using a combination of TEEP or ASAT results and public examination subjects. The ASAT test is now being used in the Australian Capital Territory, with student scores being used to scale teacher assessed scores to produce the tertiary entrance score.

In the other two countries, it is claimed that developmental work in this area has been slow and not always satisfactory. In Sweden, the original idea was to develop an aptitude test as a means of selection among all applicants, even if taken only on a voluntary basis. However, after heated public debate, the Parliamentary decision of 1975 stated that the aptitude tests would not be applied to qualified school leavers, would be taken only by candidates without the traditional qualifications and remain voluntary. It is likely that a substantial proportion of those who apply on the basis of work experience (25/4 schemes) will take this test since it grants the opportunity of gaining additional credits.

In Germany, the Federal Government University Enabling Act of 1976 makes provision in the case of special selection for an assessment procedure designed to give candidates an opportunity of showing abilities and knowledge likely to be of importance to success in the course but not revealed by previous school leaving examinations.

Since 1975, the federal government and Länder authorities have been sponsoring the development of models of university entrance tests for a number of fields, e.g. medicine, dentistry, sciences, psychology, technology, law, economics. Of great significance in accelerating work in this area was the fact that public opinion polls and surveys among students and teachers revealed that the use of tests in combination with marks was regarded as one of the fairest solutions to the problem of selection (6). More recently, the enthusiasm seems to have declined, partly because of the prevailing scepticism vis-à-vis some of the tests which were developed. The latest decision has been to start introducing sample tests in 1980/81 for a 3-year trial period and only in the fields of medicine, veterinary studies and dentistry. It is clear that far more time and experimentation will be needed before the future of university entrance tests in Germany will be more permanently settled. It should be underlined, however, that the main reason for developing tests in Germany was not to replace marks but to complement them so as to give added legitimacy to the selection process. A crucial consideration in this context was the decision of the Federal Court that whenever selection among academic secondary school leavers (Abiturienten) was necessary, the procedures used had to measure other criteria than those taken into account by the Abitur examination.

---

6. Fifty six per cent of the public favoured this scheme while 80 per cent rejected a lottery system. In 1975, 44 per cent of teachers and 46 per cent of students opted for tests and Abitur marks while 5 per cent favoured the lottery.

At present, the key question is not so much one of school marks versus tests, but rather the extent to which complementary procedures should take additional account of academic talent or ability, or whether more importance should be assigned to non-cognitive criteria as a way of decreasing bias resulting from an exclusively meritocratic-based scheme. Thus, in many OECD countries various other methods are being proposed as means of mitigating the problems posed by too narrowly-based selection schemes.

In discussing these alternative methods, it is perhaps important to distinguish between selection procedures which can be roughly characterised as having a _positive_ orientation and those which imply a more "resigned" or negative approach. In the case of the former there is an attempt to introduce, identify or access other criteria considered to be relevant to the objectives pursued, e.g. motivation, personal characteristics of candidates, social background, etc.; interviews, measures of positive discrimination, recognition of work experience are examples of this type of positive-oriented or affirmative action schemes. The second category, although often pursuing similar objectives, focuses exclusively or primarily on decreasing the weight of the traditional indicators of merit or talent but without otherwise attempting to pursue these objectives in a more explicit way. Lottery systems, waiting periods are more closely associated with this type of approach.

Although the adoption of non-cognitive criteria is most commonly associated with egalitarian objectives, a number of other arguments, often based on efficiency considerations, are also being advanced in support of more diverse entry or selection criteria, such as how to better identify motivation or vocation for specific studies; enrich the educational experience through greater diversity of the student body; assign greater value to personal characteristics relevant to the exercise of certain professions; contribute to a more varied membership within professions known to have specialisations requiring different profiles and types of competences.

3. INTERVIEWS

In quite a number of OECD countries, especially those with an Anglo-Saxon tradition and lengthy experience with selective entry, many institutions have for a long time used interviews (often combined with letters of reference and school reports) for admission purposes.

The main problem posed by the generalised use of interviews to determine entry - and certainly not at all a negligible one in mass higher education systems - is that of the time and resources which this type of assessment procedure requires. A second type of major obstacle relate to their informal and subjective nature, and on difficulties in comparing candidates, of accounting for decisions taken, as well as the risk that results be more linked to the personality and experience of the interviewer than that of the candidates. However, even in countries where there is no established tradition of informal selection techniques there is growing interest in interviews, often seen as more acceptable than objective tests.

Proposals for using interviews on a wider basis are more frequent in fields of study where motivational and certain personal characteristics of students are considered to be highly relevant for training and the subsequent practice of the profession. This is especially the case with certain service professions, e.g. health professions, teachers, social workers, etc. An OECD survey on the teaching profession shows that where personal characteristics and aptitude for teaching are taken into account, there is a marked preference for interviews over testing. Special aptitude tests have been tried but are now seldom used and in some countries (e.g. Sweden) they have been recently abandoned. However, the conclusions also indicate that, given the difficulties of specifying and identifying the relevant personal characteristics, interviews tend to have a negative screening role, that is, they serve primarily to eliminate candidates considered to be clearly ill-suited for teaching. This example may be indicative of a more general trend, namely that interviewing techniques are likely to gain in importance as a supplementary criterion in the case of borderline candidates or where school marks or other indicators have failed to provide a clear assessment.

The future of interviews is also linked to progress in developing special aptitude tests to discriminate among a pool of applicants with very similar formal qualifications as well as to policies concerning the type of information schools are to provide to higher education institutions. Where letters of recommendation and/or detailed school records exist, these may be considered as providing sufficient evidence. However, in countries where serious consideration is being given to the protection of individuals' files, or where there is an explicit policy not to transmit subjective information with regard to behaviour, attitudes and motivation, especially if these are likely to handicap pupils in the competition for entry, the urgency of developing interviewing techniques suited to the purposes of different institutions and programmes is likely to be stronger. Whether interviews will fulfil these requirements and gain legitimacy as a selection instrument will of course largely depend on the knowledge and acceptance of their terms of reference and, perhaps even more than with other procedures, on the professional quality of those responsible for the assessment.

4. MEASURES OF PREFERENTIAL TREATMENT

At least for analytical purposes it is important to distinguish between special schemes designed to facilitate the access of groups which do not meet the formal entry requirements (see Chapter IV) and the use of preferential treatment measures for selection among the pool of qualified applicants. It is the latter type of measure, discussed in the present section, which is now posing very sensitive social and legal issues.

In the first place, discrimination on the basis of socio-demographic characteristics tends to be more visible and difficult to accept when applied to a group of candidates who meet the minimum requirements and are expected to compete primarily on the basis of merit. Secondly, while special schemes for non-qualified candidates are more commonly found in relatively free access institutions or programmes, preferential treatment measures among qualified applicants are mainly used as selection tools, often in highly competitive institutions. They are therefore far more carefully scrutinised, and more vulnerable to criticisms and legal action on the part of those who consider themselves as having been unfairly rejected.

Even if one of the major underlying objectives pursued through measures of preferential treatment is that of increasing the participation of qualified candidates from disadvantaged groups, <u>indicators of socio-economic status are very seldom considered as relevant criteria for selection purposes</u> (7). Some countries or institutions have small quotas or specific regulations in favour of special hardship cases, but unlike some of the Eastern European countries no global policies exist to take explicitly into account the social origin of candidates. It is mainly through student-aid schemes that family background and income are taken into consideration, the purpose being to dissociate these variables from the actual decisions concerning access or selection; while at the same time providing incentives for demand and ensuring that once candidates have been granted admission they are not prevented from enrolling or pursuing their studies because of financial constraints (8).

A number of OECD countries are attempting to cope with the problem of access of the socially disadvantaged in an indirect way, for example, through preferential treatment measures for specific minority groups and more recently for immigrants. With rising overall levels of educational attainment, problems related to these groups which were mostly restricted to the lower levels of education have become a matter of growing concern at the post-secondary level. Australia, Germany and Sweden are among the countries which explicitly mention the rising political commitment to cater for the specific needs of these groups, but it is in the United States where this problem has in recent years become a major social and educational issue debated outside academic and educational policy circles.

The proceedings and final decision of the Supreme Court of the United States on the Bakke versus University of California case revealed a wide range of sensitive issues posed by the implementation of "affirmative action" schemes and the lack of consensus in respect both to the objectives pursued and to the means through which these can be attained. Indeed, many of the groups which are in agreement with the University's decision to admit black students with lower entry scores than white candidates who had been rejected, were highly critical of the method which was applied, namely the setting of a

---

7. In some universities such as Cosenza in Italy, Paris X, and Dauphine in France, income or SES is being taken into consideration.
8. For a more detailed discussion on the relationship between the extent of selectivity in admission and the degree of selectivity in student aid schemes see Chapter V.

predetermined strict numerical quota for black applicants. The trend in the United States seems now to be in favour of less formalised measures applied on an individual basis but the debate on this issue is far from being closed. The rather inconclusive decision by the Supreme Court has given rise to a variety of interpretations as to the actual legal boundaries within which institutions can manoeuvre; and in view of the complexity of the legal and social problems involved, affirmative action measures have been going through a critical period.

However, it is still too early to know whether, as many observers in the United States fear, universities and in particular the highly competitive professional schools, e.g. medicine and law, will back away from their commitment to minority groups. Although the meritocratic/equity dilemma is central to all debates on preferential treatment measures, the Bakke case has brought to the fore the key question of to what extent policies designed to favour certain target groups can result in greater social injustice vis-à-vis other equally less privileged sections of the population. The claim in the United States is that the concern for black students has led to other minority groups, e.g. Spanish speaking groups, being ignored as well as various categories within the majority population, in particular white people from lower socio-economic backgrounds, and women.

As mentioned in the previous chapter, another indirect way in which countries have been trying to cope with the problem of achieving a more balanced social mix of the student body has been through a broader definition of the formal qualifications required for entry. A relatively recent trend is the policy of setting goals or quotas for those school leavers from upper secondary streams who in the past were scarcely, if at all, represented in the more prestigious and selective higher education institutions. Positive discrimination in favour of candidates from technical and vocationally-oriented streams, often accompanied by special training schemes have been introduced or are planned in a number of highly selective institutions, e.g. in France (Grandes Ecoles), Sweden, Finland, Denmark, etc.(9).

Whereas practically all Member countries are attempting to tackle the social equity issue through indirect measures - i.e. focusing on changes in supply, affirmative action measures which take direct account of the sex and age of candidates at the access stage are somewhat more frequent and better accepted.

While the general and quasi universal increase in the participation of women in tertiary education responds primarily to global educational and social trends, explicit measures are being taken in quite a number of Member countries to redress the balance in certain programmes with either a predominantly female or male population. Responses to the OECD survey on admission policies in teacher training institutions show, for example, that Finland, New Zealand and Sweden use quotas or less formal procedures as a means of increasing the proportion of male students. Similarly, it is claimed that highly

---

9. For more details, see Chapter IV.

selective or prestigious institutions, in particular those training for the medical, engineering and management professions with a dominant male recruitment, have been tending to favour applications from women candidates in recent years. The success of these measures is difficult to assess; at least up to quite recently it could only be marginal since the bias in the sex distribution of applicants is to a large extent out of the control of higher education institutions. Furthermore, where positive discrimination is applied to qualified school leavers - whether in favour of minority groups, men or women - a virtually universal condition is that applicants meet the minimum requirements set by selective institutions.

Age

Age has always been a key criterion in determining access to post-secondary education. The strong bias in recruitment, typically in favour of young school leavers, is the result of the traditional "front end" or sequential pattern of education as well as of the established practice of student-aid schemes and of many institutions - in particular the highly selective ones or those training for the professions - to set eligibility criteria designed to exclude candidates above a certain age limit.

Although age restrictions of this type continue to be very frequent, data on the age composition of new entrants (10) show that in a number of countries there were some significant policy changes, ranging from a more favourable response to the demands of mature candidates to explicit positive discrimination and outreach activities in favour of different groups of adults (see Chapter IV).

Of special interest in the context of this discussion are the admission/selection measures aimed at encouraging, or at accepting far more than in the past, qualified school leavers who take time off between completion of secondary school and entry into higher education. Of course, deferred entry has become a more established pattern in countries where national policies have favoured such practice (e.g. some of the Scandinavian countries) or where universities or selective institutions enjoying a certain degree of autonomy and having more flexible selection procedures have taken a positive stance, e.g. Australia, the United Kingdom, Canada, the United States. Selection procedures in favour of older qualified candidates range from greater responsiveness to their demands to more explicit affirmative action, e.g. a place to school leavers who apply one or two years before they actually enter the institution; awarding additional credits for work or learning experience gained outside formal education, etc.

Among the Member countries with decentralised systems, the United States is the one to have moved furthest in this direction. The practice in this country of assessing relevant competences and skills acquired outside formal education and of recognising them as part of the first degree programme has also been an incentive towards postponing entry.

---

10. See Statistical Annex, Table A-12.

Among the countries where admission and selection procedures are decided centrally, Sweden has been the first to introduce a special quota for qualified leavers with work experience. Older candidates have indeed benefited from this scheme during the first years of implementation.

However, as shown in the first evaluations of this scheme (11) one of the problems is that a substantial proportion of those admitted on the basis of educational qualifications plus work experience came from relatively privileged groups, many had pursued other post-secondary studies and some had already earned other academic qualifications.

It is difficult to anticipate at this stage to what extent current and foreseen problems of youth unemployement will affect both demand patterns and institutional practices. The Swedish experience has already revealed some of the unforeseen consequences of favouring older qualified candidates; serious tensions will be created if such a policy leads to the rejection of a substantial number of young school leavers, often from less privileged groups, who may find it increasingly difficult to gain the work experience required by selective institutions.

As discussed in greater detail in the following two chapters, the extent to which a recurrent pattern of attendance will become a more established practice will also be heavily dependent on policies vis-à-vis the financial support of older students. Special ingenuity and foresight will be needed in order to avoid the risk that the more privileged categories of adults, both in terms of level of educational attainment and social status, become the sole or primary beneficiaries of preferential treatment measures, as this would result in a more socially biased recruitment than in the past.

5. WAITING PERIODS

Among OECD countries it is mainly in Germany where waiting time has been systematically used in recent years as a major criterion for selection into higher education. In the early 1970s, 30 to 40 per cent of the places made available in subjects with numerus clausus have been allocated on the basis of this seniority principle. One of the main reasons for setting up this type of scheme has been that the courts ruled as unconstitutional a situation in which secondary school leavers completing the Abitur with low marks were effectively excluded from restricted branches of study.

The extraordinary growth in demand for some of these closed programmes led to such long waiting lists that waiting periods

---

11. K. Abrahamsson, L. Kim and K. Rubenson: The Value of Work Experience in Higher Education, Institute of Education, Stockholm, 1980.

extended easily up to five or six years. Under these circumstances the current practice among these candidates has been to register in other open access courses without any intention of completing their second choice studies. According to estimates for the winter semester of 1975/76 there were 50,000 "parked" students enrolled just to mark time. The educational, social and economic consequences of this distortion in demand led the German authorities to modify the selection rules. The Federal Frame Law of Higher Education (1976) retained the principle of waiting time for selection purposes but to be applied in a far more limited number of cases, a condition made easier by the radical change of policy in 1977 which led to a strong reduction in the number of subjects with numerus clausus. One major modification has been introduced, namely that time spent by students in other tertiary courses is no longer considered as part of the waiting period. The proposal of taking into account only waiting time spent at work was debated but this principle was not retained.

6. DRAWING LOTS

Although lottery as a selection procedure in higher education made the headlines in the international field some years ago, its use by individual institutions, in particular as a final screening device among tied candidates, is not so recent or infrequent. In Denmark and Norway the claim is that lottery is used less frequently than in the past; in other countries it continues to be used sporadically by individual universities or departments. In yet others, where concern for selection is of more recent date, the debate is only now beginning to take shape. Only in the Netherlands and in Germany has a more generalised use of lottery been considered at the highest political level.

In the Netherlands, the Parliament approved in 1974 the introduction on a temporary basis of a lottery system to be used in combination with school-leaving grades as a means of selecting candidates for entry into restricted faculties. This type of weighted lottery, which is currently still in operation in a small number of programmes, is organised in such a way that, for example, in 1976-77 applicants to medical faculties who had an average grade of 8.5 or above (out of a total maximum of 10) were granted automatic entry, whereas among all others who took part in the lottery those with an average grade between 8.0 and 8.5 were given three times more chances of being selected than those with a 6.5 average grade. From its inception the weighted lottery in Holland has been the target of strong criticisms mainly because it represented a compromise solution which left unsatisfied those advocating a uniform lottery for all candidates - a position adopted by the Ministry of Education in 1975 - and those in favour of a more meritocratic selection scheme, a position now favoured by the present government which has made public its intentions to revert to selection on the basis of formal indicators of ability.

The idea of using a weighted lottery system on a more systematic basis has also been discussed at length by the German Federal and Länder authorities who viewed this procedure as another way of meeting the conditions set by the courts that all qualified candidates should be given a chance to enter numerus clausus courses. The Federal Frame Law of Higher Education of 1976 made provision for its use not only in deciding between applicants of equal qualifications according to the "General Selection Procedure" but also as an active element in the new "Special Selection Procedure" envisaged for admission into courses in which demand most markedly outweighs supply.

It should be noted that it is mainly in countries which stress the objective and formal methods of assessment that a lottery system seems to have greater chances of being adopted. When confidence in the validity of school marks or tests decreases and other informal methods such as interviews or preferential treatment measures are not considered feasible or desirable, the idea of having a formal and explicit screening technique such as the lottery gains ground; all the more so when it can be defended on equity grounds and as a means of halting the escalation in the entry qualifications of highly selective institutions. However, it is quite obvious that proposals which use the luck of the draw as a criterion for determining entry are considered by a large majority of people as unacceptable, if not outright sacrilege. Even among those who openly recognise the arbitrary element in most selection procedures, there are many who reject the idea of a lottery, considering it to be a proof of failure and consequently detrimental to the internal ethos and external image of higher education institutions.

Chapter IV

NEW GROUPS IN HIGHER EDUCATION[*]

In the last decade, there has been a considerable growth of interest in OECD countries in what have been described variously as "new groups", "non-traditional students" or a "new clientele" in higher education. The purpose of this chapter is to review such developments, drawing where possible and appropriate on examples from Member countries, and to discuss both the short-term problems and long-term issues entailed. In so doing, the chapter addresses four main questions, which dictate the four main sections of the paper:

- what are these new groups?
- where are they studying?
- what special admission policies are involved?
- what long-term issues do the new groups raise?

It will not be possible to answer these questions without some reference to the traditional intake of students. What is traditional varies from country to country, and reflects among other things the overall size of the higher education system, as measured by the percentage of the relevant age group admitted to higher education, percentage which varied in 1975/76 from under 15 per cent in some countries to over 40 per cent in others. Thus women might be considered a new group in some countries, a well-established though minority group in the majority and an incipient traditional group in a few others.

There is another aspect to the relationship between new and traditional students, which is that in some countries the increased interest in new groups reflects a declining intake of traditional students, a decline due to a combination of demographic factors and demand. In such cases, new groups might be more accurately described as alternative groups.

Before embarking on an analysis of new groups, a note of statistical caution should be entered, for two reasons. First, the figures

---

[*] The Secretariat wishes to acknowledge its indebtedness to Geoffrey Squires for the authorship of this chapter.

on new groups often do not go back very far, reflecting the comparatively recent interest in these categories; it can hence be difficult to obtain an adequate time series, and establish trends. Secondly, the statistics on certain types of new groups, notably part-timers, are not always reliable, since such students sometimes live, perhaps deliberately, on the fringes of the system, maintaining a shadowy existence both in educational and employment terms.

1. WHAT ARE THE NEW GROUPS ?

As noted in one of the Conference discussion notes, "the terms 'adults', 'new groups' or 'non-traditional students' encompass a large, vague and diverse universe; a more precise categorisation is needed to facilitate policy discussion" (see p. 29). The discussion note goes on to identify four groups:

- young entrants from upper secondary vocational streams mainly in European countries;
- unqualified mature entrants;
- young qualified entrants, who nevertheless choose to combine work and study in various ways i.e. alternating work and study, combining the two, or postponing entry until after a period of employment;
- qualified or partly qualified adults who wish to pursue post-secondary education a few, or many years after completing their secondary education.

In addition to these four groups, the literature on new groups (as they shall henceforth be called) frequently refers to other categories of students: women; students of low socio-economic status; ethnic minority students; students who are updating professional knowledge and skills; students studying at a distance. Given the difficulties of arriving at a more precise categorisation, it may be helpful to classify new groups of students in terms of a typology of age and qualifications, as follows:

Age	Qualified	Unqualified
Young	A	B
Older	C	D

The traditional intake of higher education - young qualified school-leavers - is represented by category A. However, some new groups also come into category A since while women, students of low SES, ethnic and regional minorities may all be young and qualified, they do not belong to the traditional intake of male, white, middle-class students. Category B comprises students who though young have not qualified in the usual way, i.e. do not come from the academic streams of upper-secondary schools; hence category B covers those who enter higher education from vocational and technical streams in secondary education, sometimes referred to as "second route" students. This category applies mainly to European countries with streamed secondary systems. Category C covers students who, though qualified, either spin out their attendance over a longer period than normal, through alternating or combining work and study, or defer it until adult life, for reasons of employment or family. Category D represents adult students who have not qualified in the normal way, and thus enter under special admission policies: three years "clear" of secondary education is the usual requirement, though it may be more. This four-part categorisation is not wholly satisfactory, but it is hoped that the analysis in the next section of the paper will complement it, giving an overall set of categories which is clear enough to be useful, yet accurately reflecting the complexities of the situation across a wider range of countries.

It was noted that category A represents the traditional intake of higher education - the young, qualified student - but also includes groups which have traditionally been under-represented within this intake. One of the most obvious of such groups is women. Table 18 gives the percentages of female enrolments in higher education for both the university and non-university sectors between 1965 and 1975. With the exception of Finland where females already account for over half total enrolments, the percentage of women enrolling in higher education has increased in every country for which figures are available. In 1975, the proportion of women was higher in the non-university sector than the university sector in all but three countries: Germany, Ireland, and Portugal. Where more recent figures are available, they tend to confirm the rising trend in female enrolments. In Canada women accounted for 48.3 per cent of all full-time and part-time university enrolments in 1978/79, and, interestingly, 34.4 per cent of post-graduate students, as against only 18 per cent in 1965/66 (1). In the United States, the female percentage for the whole of higher education had risen to 49.8 per cent in 1978/79 (2). In France, female enrolments in universities (including IUTs) had reached 48 per cent in 1977/78 (3). In Sweden, the figure for university type enrolments had risen from 41.2 per cent in 1976/77 (4). The historical under-representation of women in higher education thus seems to be being steadily corrected in most countries, within several cases the figures approaching their proportion in the population at large.

Another historically under-represented group has been students of low socio-economic status. Indeed one of the driving forces or legitimating arguments behind the massive expansion of higher

---

1. Universities: Enrolments and Degrees, Statistics Canada, 1978, Cat. 81-204.
2. Digest of Educational Statistics, 1979 (provisional figures).
3. L'Enseignement supérieur en France: Etude statistique et évolution de 1959/60-1977/78, Etudes et Documents.
4. Arsbole 79, Table 8 A11. Includes universities and specialised colleges.

Table 18
PERCENTAGE OF FEMALE ENROLMENTS IN HIGHER EDUCATION

	University			Non-university			Total		
	1965	1970	1975	1965	1970	1975	1965	1970	1975
Australia	...	29.7	37.3	...	64.0	54.0	...	39.6	44.6
Austria	23.9	25.0	32.1a)	33.3	57.1	60.0a)	24.2	28.9	35.6
Belgium	24.0	28.6	33.3	44.9	49.5	50.5	32.7	38.2	41.5
Canada	31.5	35.9	38.4b)	59.5	49.9	49.9b)	38.4	39.2	41.3b)
Denmark	30.2	31.7	28.5b)	41.0	49.6	65.0b)	34.3	37.8	41.1b)
Finland	49.3	47.6	48.8	55.3	51.7	55.7	50.9	48.5	50.3
France	41.4	...	...	35.1	...	42.4a)	40.3	...	...
Germany	22.5	30.6	35.8	6.5	12.8	24.7	18.8	26.1	33.7
Greece	30.4	31.0	34.9b)	28.7	33.1	35.6	30.2	31.3	35.0b)
Iceland	...	...	...	...	...	...	...	...	...
Ireland	28.1	33.5	41.8	34.0	85.6	32.8	29.5	34.0	38.6
Italy	32.5	37.0	38.4b)	46.0	46.0	47.7b)	32.9	37.2	38.5b)
Japan	16.1	17.9	19.7b)	72.6	78.5	80.0b)	24.2	28.0	30.1b)
Luxembourg	...	...	...	...	...	...	...	...	...
Netherlands	18.0	19.6	23.1	33.5	35.5	39.2	25.2	26.3	30.5
New Zealand	...	27.4	31.1	...	75.9	74.4	...	38.8	39.8
Norway	24.1	26.8	32.8a)	54.9	50.6	50.0a)	38.7	37.7	40.9a)
Portugal	40.2	46.6	43.0	29.5	33.6	40.4	37.5	43.8	42.6
Spain	21.1	26.2	33.1	34.1	31.4	44.1	28.1	28.3	36.4
Sweden	36.1c)	38.1	37.6b)	...	72.7	82.5a)	...	44.6	45.3b)
Switzerland	24.7	...	...	15.1	...	...	21.0	...	...
Turkey	...	28.3	32.9	...	58.2	58.9a)	...	40.0	41.7a)
United Kingdom	39.1	41.5	44.1	38.0	41.5	47.3	38.9	41.5	44.8
United States	32.6	38.4	40.1a)	35.1	41.7	42.8a)	33.5	39.4	40.9
Yugoslavia									

a) 1974   b) 1973   c) 1966
Source : Based on <u>Educational Statistics in OECD Countries</u>, OECD, Paris 1981.

education over the period 1960-1975 was the idea that expansion would lead to a more balanced participation: an egalitarian rationale. Low working-class achievement rates in compulsory education translate into low participation rates in post-compulsory education. The whole issue of social class and educational achievement is a major and complex one, on which there is a massive literature, and comments here can only be tangential.

First, it is not possible to generalise about students of low SES status in higher education in the way that one can about women. This is partly because the category is itself less well-defined, partly because the available figures are patchy, and partly because such evidence as there is, is ambiguous. In addition, type of institution and mode of attendance represent important variables. Farrant (5), analysing trends in the United Kingdom, notes that the social composition of university intake has hardly changed in twenty-five years, and that recent figures suggest that the proportion of students from the professional classes is increasing. Other data on the social origins of university students also show no marked changes in distribution between the mid-1960s and mid-1970s (6). However, there is evidence in some countries of increased working-class participation in the "less élitist" institutions or faculties in higher education, (non-university institutions, community colleges, colleges of advanced education, open faculties, etc.) especially among part-time students (7). These are, however, the parts of the system with typically the highest failure and drop-out rates, so the notion of "participation" needs to be qualified by reference to "completion".

Ethnic minority students are another traditionally under-represented group in certain countries and this problem is perhaps associated above all with the United States. In the period 1974-78, the enrolment of ethnic minority students in the United States grew by 27.2 per cent, the fastest rate of increase of any identifiable group (female enrolments grew by 24.9 per cent)(8). How far this rapid growth was due to special admissions policies for blacks and other races, and how far it was due to general expansion is difficult to say. Whatever the explanation, it is the view of one writer at least that the United States' higher education system has in recent times become a central vehicle for social mobility and social integration (9).

---

5. Farrant, J., Trends in Admissions to Higher Education in England and Wales, Leverhulme/Society for Research into Higher Education (forthcoming).
6. See Chapter II.
7. Towards Mass Higher Education: Issues and Dilemmas; OECD, Paris, 1974; Corrado de Francesco, "The growth and crisis of Italian higher education during the 60s and 70s, Higher Education, Vol. 7(2), May 1978; Farrant, op. cit.
8. NCES, Digest of Education Statistics, 1980, p. 99.
9. Trow, M., "Comparative Perspectives on Access to higher Education", paper prepared for the Leverhulme/Seminar on Demand and Access, Edinburgh, June 1981.

So far the discussion has focused briefly on some groups of students - women, students of low SES, ethnic minorities - who although traditional students in the sense of being both young and qualified, are nevertheless non-traditional in the sense that they have historically been under-represented in higher education. What of the other three categories of students ? Category B referred to young students who were not qualified in the normal way, i.e. students from technical and vocational streams in secondary education who are given a "second route" into higher education, by-passing the normal academic route. This category is relevant to European countries such as Austria, Denmark, France, Germany where upper-secondary education is either formally or effectively streamed. It is also relevant, to a lesser extent, to the United Kingdom, where students may enter higher education via non-advanced further education, i.e. with technical and commercial qualifications rather than the more academic "A" levels. The proportion of such "second route" students in most of these countries was rather low in 1970 (10) but since then changes in admissions - e.g. in France, Italy and Germany - have opened the door to a higher percentage. Such developments point to an increasing permeability of higher education boundaries, and an increasingly flexible system of entry.

Category C students are normally qualified, but somewhat older than the traditional intake because they did not take up the option of higher education on leaving school (for vocational or family reasons) and are thus returning to study after some, perhaps many years. Women in their late twenties or thirties often fall into this category. Or they may become older because they alternate or combine work and study, thus taking much longer to complete their course than the traditional full-time student. In some countries, this second group seems to have grown rapidly and spontaneously in recent years, and one suggestion is that students are deliberately "hedging their bets" on higher education, partly because of the uncertain value of degrees and diplomas, and partly because of the need to maintain a foothold in the job market (11). Such students will aim only to get by in their courses, and will spend the minimum possible amount of time and effort on their course work. Nevertheless, they do not drop out altogether, because although the relative value of a degree may have declined, it is still better than not having one. The percentage of French students who admit to being employed at least part-time, from time to time, has risen from 32 per cent in 1973 to 49.5 per cent in 1979 (12). In fact, the growth of part-time study is one of the most marked features of higher education in recent years in a number of countries. More than 50 per cent of new entrants

---

10. Pellegrin, J.P., "Admission Policies in Post-Secondary Education" in Towards Mass Higher Education, OECD, 1974, p. 40.
11. Geiger, Roger, "The changing demand for higher education in the 70S; Adaptations within three national systems", Higher Education, Vol. 9 (3), May 1980.
12. Jarousse, Evolution du comportement des étudiants, CREDOC, 1981, p. 9. These figures should be interpreted with some caution, for the reasons stated earlier.

in some Italian faculties attend part-time or plan to attend on a part-time basis (13). In the United States, part-time students constituted 35.5 per cent of the total student body in 1978, against 33.4 per cent in 1974 (14). In Canada, the percentage of part-time university enrolments grew from 26.3 per cent in 1965/66 to 37.3 per cent in 1978/79 (15). Increases in part-time study have also been reported in Australia, Sweden and the United Kingdom (advanced further education and the Open University). Such increases appear to be sharper in the non-university sectors of higher education, but they are sufficiently widespread and cross-national to warrant a general explanation.

Category D students are also older and most of them do not have the normal qualifications for entry. Evidence for increases in this "new" group is mixed, though there has been substantial growth in a few countries. In the United States, from 1974 to 1978, enrolments in the 25-34-year age group increased by 16.7 per cent and by over 27 per cent for those aged 34 and more. The larger increase in the latter group can be accounted for by woment enrolling in college (thus two of our "new groups" overlap) (16). In the United Kingdom the increase has been much sharper in polytechnics and colleges than in the universities; students over 21 now account for 37 per cent of all full-time public sector entrants (excluding overseas students) (17). While it is impossible at present to generalise across all OECD countries, it seems that there is enough evidence to justify considering category D students as a major new group.

When reviewing evidence on the increased participation in some countries of new groups - women, students of low SES, ethnic minorities, students from non-academic secondary streams, part-time students, and adult students- it is clear that some of these categories overlap; a 30-year-old part-time woman student would fall into three of them. However, it is useful to maintain the distinctions in analysing possible reasons for the increases, four of which are cited below.

The first and most obvious reason is the general expansion of higher education which, though now halted in many countries, has been reversed in one or two. To explain the new groups in these terms is to posit a general order of arrival of types of students, with the relatively privileged arriving first, and the most disadvantaged arriving last. Therefore, as the system expands, more and more of the historically under-privileged groups get drawn into it, accounting for an increasing proportion of enrolments. To maintain their relative advantages, the privileged groups concentrate more in the elite parts of the system, or else find ways of maintaining their position outside the system altogether. Inherent in this explanation is a view of education as a positional good. Participation by the newer groups only rises as participation by established groups reaches near-saturation, the growth rate for each group taking the form of an elongated

---

13. See Chapter I.
14. NCES, Digest of Education Statistics, 1980, p. 9.
15. Universities: Enrolment and Degrees, Statistics Canada, 1978.
16. NCES, op. cit.
17. Squires, G., "Mature Entry to Higher Education", Leverhulme Seminar on Demand and Access, Edinburgh, 1981.

S-curve (18). this model implies that the order of arrival can only be altered (or the curve sharpened) by special admissions policies targeted at the group in question.

A second reason for the growth of new groups may be in the decline of traditional groups. In some countries demographic trends have led to, or will lead to, a decline in the intake from secondary schools. In some countries too, demand for higher education is either static or declining, among qualified, young school-leavers. In such circumstances, institutions can only maintain their size and staffing levels if they actively go out and attract new groups of students to compensate for the actual or impending fall-off. Whether national governments allow them to tap new markets in this way is another matter.

Thirdly, new groups may be generated by broad social movements and/or social policies: women and ethnic minorities come to mind as examples. The relationship between movement and policies is complex, and one can perhaps distinguish between movement-led increases (women ?) and policy-led increases (ethnic minorities ?). However, it seems clear that a policy must have the backing of a broad social movement to be successful, and the relative failure of policies to increase participation among students of low SES can be perhaps partly explained by the absence of a major social egalitarian movement in the 1960s and 1970s comparable to the movements for women's and ethnic rights.

The fourth type of explanation for increased participation by new groups relates specifically, or perhaps only to part-time and occasional students. It has been suggested that such students are hedging their bets as between education and employment (and leisure). In a quasi-rational calculation they perceive that the benefits of higher education (as a positional good) are no longer clear, and accordingly they modify their commitment to it. Thus, paradoxically, while the expansion of higher education may have led more people to participate in it, that same expansion is a reason for not participating fully. With the rise in unemployment in many OECD countries, this approach must make sense to many young adults since there is no guarantee that they will get back into the job market if they once commit themselves exclusively to higher education. Thus the trend towards recurrent education may result more from uncertainty (both about higher education and the labour market) than from the more "positive" reasons advanced by protagonists of the recurrent model.

The comparative weighting of these four explanations - general expansion, demographic decline, specific policies, and uncertainty - will vary from country to country not only because of the different state of its higher education system, but because of differences in the labour market and in social ethos. For those who work in higher education, however, two implications seem fairly clear. First, the intake of students is already, and is likely to become, much more mixed than before, in terms of background knowledge, age, and

---

18. Halsey, A.H., et al. Origins and Destinations: Family, Class and Education in Modern Britain, Clarendon Press, Oxford, 1980.

expectations. This possibility has already been discussed widely, and is fairly familiar. The second implication is less familiar. In the past, higher education has been seen as a <u>total</u> activity in the sense that it was the exclusive preoccupation of its students. Henceforth, staff may now have to come to terms with students for whom their studies are only a part of their lives.

2. WHERE ARE THEY STUDYING ?

If the notion of an "order of arrival" is correct, it implies that new groups of students enter higher education in its least prestigious sectors, institutions and faculties, while the privileged traditional groups retreat to the higher ground of the "noble" institutions. The "order of arrival" would thus be complemented by an "order of access", in which the most open institutions rank lowest in academic prestige, and the most selective institutions highest. This section therefore, takes this notion of an order of access as a hypothesis, and reviews the evidence for and against it. Are the new groups in fact to be found in the less prestigious institutions ?

The question is complicated by the fact that academic prestige and employment value may or may not coincide. Indeed, the University of Aston which has one of the best graduate employment records in the United Kingdom, has recently received one of the largest cuts from the University Grants Committee. Whereas in the period 1960-75, the distinction between "noble" and "less noble" institutions may have been fairly clear and useful, since then the growing emphasis on vocational relevance is leading to a different type of hierarchy based on academic prestige and employment value.

		employment value	
		High	Low
Academic	High	I	II
Standing	Low	III	IV

Where then do the new groups appear, in terms of these four quadrants ? Following the above line of argument it could be expected that they do not appear in I - the quadrant of high prestige, and employment value (professional subjects such as medicine, law and perhaps engineering). An analysis of the social origin of Italian university entrants (19) provides some support for this, although one notes the very high proportion of "traditional" students in

---

19. See Chapter I.

other subjects as well, notably letters, philosophy, modern languages and chemistry. The fact that quadrant I includes several traditionally male-dominated professions might serve to reduce the proportion of women students, and even of older students since the professional career-path typically necessitates early entry. In France, the percentages of traditional students are correspondingly high in medicine, chemistry, engineering and the écoles normales supérieures, but much lower in law (20). In Canada, women seem to have made some inroads in enrolments in medicine, but much less so in law or engineering (21). In general, what evidence is available from a number of countries suggests that of all the new groups, women are the most likely to have penetrated quadrant I but that even they are still a small minority in some professional fields of study.

Quadrant II is more complex, for two reasons: first the evidence is more mixed, and secondly, there are strong variations among countries, depending on how selective the subjects are and/or on the particular employment situation for graduates. In the United Kingdom in particular, a good degree in classics, English, philosophy or history is taken as evidence of a high all-around intellectual ability, which will benefit the possessor in the non-specialist graduate market (e.g. Civil Service entry). Quadrant II also includes many subjects appropriate to the teaching profession, and would thus attract students looking to such a career; on the other hand, school populations and therefore teaching opportunities have been declining in a number of countries. The impression from the figures available is that while quadrant II may include a substantial proportion of women students, and some mature students, the proportion of students of low SES, or from vocational secondary streams are unlikely to find their way into the rather "pure" academic subjects that characterise this quadrant. And although such subjects can lend themselves to part-time study, the selectivity associated with their academic prestige implies that even if part-time students are admitted, attrition rates may be high.

Quadrant III includes subjects which are vocationally marketable, but not particularly prestigious in academic terms: the links of technical and commercial subjects taught in many of the short-cycle, non-university institutions which grew up in OECD countries in the last twenty years, as part of the attempt to diversify higher education. There is a good deal of evidence from the United Kingdom polytechnics and colleges, the United States community colleges, the French IUTs (Instituts universitaires de technologie), the Australian CAEs (Colleges of Advanced Education), and the Canadian CAATS (Colleges of Applied Arts and Technology) and CEGEPs (Colleges d'enseignement général et professionnel) that such institutions attract new groups in substantial numbers, in particular students of low SES, from ethnic minorities, and from vocational secondary streams. Such students presumably view higher education primarily as a means towards employment, or better employment, and for them

---

20. L'Enseignement supérieur en France: Etude statistique et évolution de 1959/60 à 1977/78, p. 63.
21. Education in Canada, op. cit.

the positional value of a qualification is paramount. And since these types of institutions often permit and encourage part-time study, the proportion of part-timers enrolled is often very high indeed. Where older students are involved, they will often be upgrading an existing vocational qualification.

Quadrant IV is low in both academic prestige and vocational relevance. It includes some social sciences, some non-traditional arts subjects, and some subjects difficult to classify, e.g. life skills, independent study projects, ethnic studies. Quadrant IV seems to attract fairly large numbers of non-traditional students, and it is this fact that raises some difficult questions about the orerall expansion of higher education. Is quadrant IV simply acting as a cheap safety valve for the new groups? Are such students being deluded into thinking that such an education will give them a relative advantage in the job market, when it may not? Are standards generally lower in quadrant IV? Are attrition rates higher? As against these problems, one must set the fact that quadrant IV does reach out to groups of students who have not been reached before and in so doing, often displays considerable ingenuity and innovation in marketing, curricula and teaching.

3. SPECIAL ADMISSIONS POLICIES AND PROCEDURES

Not all new groups of students enter higher education through special admissions policies. Insofar as the growth of new groups is due to the general expansion of higher education, such students are likely to enter under the normal admissions regulations, and their identity as a group is something that is perceived after, rather than before admission. However, special admissions policies have also played a key role in facilitating the access of some new groups, in particular adult and ethnic minority students, and the aim in this section is to review examples of such policies in a number of countries. It is important to emphasize that the special policies must always be seen in relation to the traditional policies of the country concerned.

Many Australian universities now make some provision for the special admission of "non-standard" (e.g. unqualified) or mature students [22]. In most cases, the number involved seems to be relatively small, although some institutions consider each case on its individual merits rather than abiding by a pre-set quota. Control over such special admissions is often left to individual faculties and departments. The requirements and procedures vary fairly widely, as will be seen from the following examples of special admissions schemes in Australian universities:

---

22. Australian Vice-Chancellors Committee, Special Admissions, Canberra, 1975.

"Some mature age applicants satisfy admission requirements by gaining an aggregate of marks on three subjects (rather than the standard five) in the New South Wales Higher School Certificate. The University specifies the aggregate required which is normally approximately 3/5 of the aggregate required for standard admission. Other 'non-standard' candidates are not given any kind of score and are not ranked. The decision on whether to admit or not to admit is made on the basis of the individual merits of each case." (ANU)

" Candidates must have suffered from 'educational disadvantage' as defined by the Committee on Special Admissions, a joint Council/Professional Board Committee which controls our Special Entry Scheme, and must not have the necessary minimum entrance requirements. They are ranked for admissions purposes by means of an ASAT test provided by the Australian Council for Educational Research. Control data supplied by our Faculty of Education in conjunction with our Higher Education Advisory Research Unit is used to relate the scores obtained by candidates in this test to the normal entrance requirement." (Monash)

"The University operates a scheme specially designed to cater for persons whose study may have been interrupted in earlier years or who may have been educationally disadvantaged, for whatever reason. This applies to persons over the age of 25 on 1st March of the year in which they intend to enrol and such applicants who do not meet our ordinary, special or adult matriculation requirements are invited to write a letter to the University indicating their reasons for believing that they are capable of successfully undertaking university study." (New England)

"In 1975, the University admitted about fifty people of mature age who had no academic qualifications on which matriculation could be given. These people were admitted on a committe's assessment of their clarity of purpose, motivation, and capacity. The University had decided to continue this scheme for 1976 in an amended form and it is likely that about fifty places will again be made available, most in courses that do not require mathematics or science prerequisites." (New South Wales)

These examples give some idea of the variation in special admissions schemes in Australian universities. However, it should be remembered that many, perhaps most, mature students enter with conventional qualifications, which they return to school to obtain. By contrast, a national scheme of quota-based admissions has recently been introduced in Danish universities (23). This scheme has been prompted by two problems: first, the massive increase in the proportion of nineteen-year-olds qualifying for entry to higher studies (now approaching 30 per cent of the age group); and secondly the high wastage rates in certain branches (approximately 70 per cent in the humanities and 50 per cent in the social sciences). The new admissions

---

23. *Times Higher Education Supplement*, 25 March 1977.

scheme is part of an attempt to control and plan overall access to higher education; medical faculties have already imposed a numerus clausus.

The new Danish quota scheme applies to all faculties except psychology and teacher training. There are three quotas: one for students coming directly from the academic streams in upper-secondary education (based on marks); one for students who combine some secondary qualifications with some work experience; and one for mature students (25 or older), foreigners and students with special qualifications.

Both school marks and work experience are translated into a common system of admission "points". The student's school-leaving marks are averaged on a 1 - 13 scale. For nine months' work, 1.09 points are given, plus 0.01 points for every subsequent month up to a maximum of 1.18 points. These work-points can then be added to the school-leaving mark. A unique feature of the Danish scheme is that the proportion of students entering under each quota varies from faculty to faculty, thus reflecting different emphases on academic qualifications and work experience. The proposed ratios for 1976 were as follows:

	Marks only	Marks and Work Experience	Mature Students and others
Natural Sciences	70	20	10
Humanities/ Social Sciences	60	20	20
Medicine/Dentistry	50	40	10

In the technology faculties, the work experience must be relevant to future studies, and have lasted for at least eighteen months. The quotas for all faculties may be altered from year to year, as may the total number of new entrants. It is too early to say how the Danish scheme will work in practice, but in theory at least, it solves two problems. The first is that of the student who is neither adequately qualified nor adequately mature - for example the 22-year-old who has some work experience and moderately good school marks. In other countries, such students can fall between two stools, while "ordinary" students enter under a special policy. The Danish scheme allows for their case; and it is worth remembering that such students are often more able to take up the offer of a place (because they face fewer situational barriers such as lack of funds or time, family responsibilities, etc.) than the 25-year-old.

Secondly, the Danish scheme recognises explicitly the varying degrees of relevance which work and life experience may have to different branches of study. The difficulties experienced by mature students on science and mathematics courses has already been mentioned, and it is precisely here that the Danish quota for "marks only", i.e. direct admission from upper-secondary schools, is highest. Conversely, the value of experience, allied to some academic prowess, is recognised in the corresponding 40 per cent quota in medicine and dentistry. The fierce competition for entry to medical faculties in other countries, which reinforces the academic emphasis, may not be entirely beneficial for the training of general medical practitioners.

There is no national policy in Germany aimed at facilitating the entry of mature or unqualified students to degree courses. The upgrading of degrees and examinations taken at technical colleges (Fachhochschulen) has meant easier access to universities for students with technical/vocational qualifications. However, for the aspiring German student, entry to degree-level courses still lies mainly in the possession of the Abitur, the academic upper-secondary school-leaving certificate. The working adult student usually has to go to evening school to prepare for this examination in order to gain entry, although a third educational route has been opened up by the "examination for talented study applicants". The regulations for this vary to some extent from Land to Land, but applicants must normally be aged 25 or over.

There are a few local exceptions to this rule (which does not apply to non-degree courses). In the Land (region) of North Rhine-Westphalia, the Law on the Establishment and Development of Comprehensive Higher Education Institutions (Gesetz über die Errichtung von Gestamthochschulen im Land Nordrhein-Westfalen) states that exceptions to the general admissions requirements can be made for the purpose of testing new types of courses or institutions. The Fernuniversität Hagen (an experimental remote-study university in the region) is planning a special admissions scheme for unqualified students. The Fernuniversität constitutes the main effort to facilitate the entry of adults with work experience into post-secondary education. Nearly 74 per cent of students are over 25 years old, and nearly 50 per cent are studying part-time; 73 per cent of the students had previously completed some limited professional training.

In the above law, another clause allows for the admission to certain university-type streams of students whose previous schooling entitled them to admission to technical colleges only. A subject-oriented qualification for university admission can be given to those students who successfully complete the common, initial two-year period of study, together with bridging courses in English, mathematics and German. Beginners with lower qualifications can thus complete university studies without delay. This scheme has been in operation since 1973/74 and its popularity is steadily growing.

The comparative lack of special admissions policies in German universities must be weighed against the widespread opportunities for continuing vocational education which do not require possession of the Abitur, and which were reinforced by the Labour Promotion Act of 1969. This Act provided institutions with subsidies to expand their capacity for further vocational training, and subsistence payments to students, with reimbursement of fees under certain conditions. Some early evidence on the workings of the Act suggested that the opportunities were being taken up by employees under rather than over 35, skilled rather than unskilled workers, and that people without the primary school final certificate were scarcely represented. These findings, admittedly based on a survey conducted when the Act had only been in force for one year, are nevertheless similar to those cited by Besnard and Liétard in a study of the French schemes for subsidised continuing education (24). Besnard and Liétard also suggest that such subsidies are likely to be taken up by larger, rather than smaller companies, and by men rather than women.

A major reform of Swedish higher education affecting organisation, administration, planning, curricula and admissions was launched in 1977. Most of the changes involved were the final outcome of a process of innovation initiated by the 1963 University Planning Committee (U-68), although some of the changes stem from subsequent government commissions. These reforms have been examined in some detail by Dahllöf (25). The main thrust of the reform has been:

a) to create a more unified or comprehensive system of higher education, including universities and non-university institutions;
b) to organise this comprehensive system by regions;
c) to adopt a long-term, national planning strategy which controls overall demand and allocates resources;
d) to emphasize the vocational relevance of degree courses; and
e) to introduce a new national admissions scheme.

It is still too early to gauge the individual effect of these measures.

A second major source of changes in Sweden has been the fluctuations in demand experienced in recent years. These changes have mainly affected the open sector of higher education - the faculties of humanities, social sciences, law and theology, and to a certain extent the natural sciences. The closed sector grew steadily during the 1960s, and has since levelled out. Certain changes in the composition and distribution of the student body have also taken place, again mainly in the open faculties. Among these have been:

a) an increased number of students not completing their full degree and not aiming at so doing;
b) an increased number of adult students (over 25 years of age);
c) an increased number of students in first-year courses and a decrease at subsequent and post-graduate levels, and
d) a steady decline in the numbers studying the natural sciences.

The new admissions policy should be seen in the light of an experimental scheme which has been in operation since 1969. This has

---

24. Besnard, P., and Liétard, B., La formation continue, Presses Universitaires de France, Paris, 1976.
25. Dahllöf, U., Reforming Higher Education and External Studies in Sweden and Australia, Almqvist and Wiskell International, Uppsala, 1977. Lillemor, Kim: "Widened Admission to Higher Education in Sweden", European Journal of Education, Vol. 14, No. 2, June 1979.

allowed adults over 25 years of age, and with at least four years' work experience, to enter certain courses in the open faculties. This was only the general admissions requirement; the institutions and courses normally added special requirements, typically the achievement of a level equivalent to the 11th year of schooling in the relevant subject(s). Despite these special requirements, the percentage of students entering faculties of liberal arts and sciences under the 25:4 scheme rose steadily from 4.8 per cent in 1969-1970 to 22.5 per cent in 1975-1976. (The corresponding percentages for the "normal" entry from academic secondary education dropped from 85.1 per cent to 63.9 per cent over the same period).

Under the new admissions policy, there are four main categories of entrant:

i) those with three years' upper-secondary schooling (academic streams);
ii) those with two years' upper-secondary schooling (vocational/technical streams);
iii) those with a certificate from a "people's high-school";
iv) 25-year-olds and over, with at least four years of work experience.

Where places are limited, the number of students accepted from each of these groups is proportional to the number of applicants in each category (with the exception of foreign students who are allotted up to 10 per cent of available places). Applicants in the first two groups may add work experience to their school marks according to a credit-points system. There is also a rule stating that at least 20 per cent of the places on each course will be reserved for applicants with school marks alone. Applicants in the third group may also add work-experience as a credit point in the same way. Adult students in the fourth group require entrance points corresponding to school marks by taking a test of general study ability. They may also add "bonus" working experience (exceeding the four-year requirement). In all four groups the applicants are ranked according to their credit points, and selection is made according to their total. The whole scheme applies to full degree programmes; entry to single courses is decided locally and the requirements are less stringent.

The most obvious case of a special admissions policy in the United Kingdom is the Open University, which admits only adult students (over 21) on a first-come, first-served basis, subject to certain quotas. Part of the importance of the O.U. has been its demonstration that such a radical departure from conventional admissions policies is compatible with university-level education. However, all United Kingdom universities, polytechnics and colleges have special admissions policies, though, as in Australia, these are not centralised, and vary from institution to institution. In general, not much use is made of them in the universities, the vast majority of mature students, for example, being admitted on the strength of the conventional two "A" levels. However, the universities are beginning to develop part-time degrees, partly as a response to the impending fall in the relative number of 18-year-olds, and more "special case" admissions are therefore likely. In the public sector polytechnics and colleges the situation is much more complex. What can be said is that the proportion of mature and part-time students there has been rising substantially and steadily for some years, and this indicates a greater flexibility in admissions policies. Moreover, the public sector institutions also draw on "second route" students via the vocational qualifications of the Technician Education Council (TEC) and Business Education Council (BEC).

There is a great variety of special admissions policies for new groups of students in the United States. This reflects not only the size of the country and the diversity of its institutions, but also a concern for adult and unqualified students unparalleled in any other Member country. This is probably due to a number of factors: the early diversification of American post-secondary education; the flexibility and universality of secondary education; the high enrolment ratio at post-secondary level; the general ideology of "opportunity"; the concern in recent decades with minority or disadvantaged groups, whether in terms of colour, sex, or age; and the rise in the median age of the population. One might also add, in recent years, the fall-off in "normal" entrants due to the curve of the birth rate.

It is impossible here to give anything like a complete account of special admissions policies in the United States. (It should also be noted that the role of open admissions policies is central in some institutions, particularly the Community/Junior Colleges). Reference is made to three developments which may be of more general interest. They are the work of CASE/OEC (Commission on Accreditation of Service Experience/Office of Educational Credit); the College Level Examinations Program (CLEP); and the research carried out by CAEL (Co-operative Assessment of Experimental Learning).

The use of transferable academic credit is well established in the United States, though less familiar in Europe. Transferred credit may be used either to grant admission to an institution, or to grant admission and advanced standing (exemptions from certain course requirements)(26). This system operates to the peculiar advantage of adult students, who may well have interrupted their studies at one time or another, or have moved from place to place. The availability of advanced standing might persuade some adults that it is worthwhile completing their degree or continuing their studies, since they do not have to start again at square one.

The granting of credit for prior study at another college or university presents certain problems. On the practical level it takes time to evaluate a student's transcript, and to dovetail the courses he has taken with these he intends to take. Vast differences in standards also exist between institutions in the United States. Nevertheless, the system of inter-institutional credit transfer is widespread, effective, and accepted.

---

26. See Burn, B., "The American Academic Credit System" in Structure of Studies and Place of Research in Mass Higher Education, OECD, Paris, 1974.

The accreditation of prior learning in non-collegiate institutions is more difficult, and it is here that the work of the Commission on Accreditation of Service Experience (CASE) is relevant. For many years, CASE has evaluated training and education within the armed forces for transfer to educational institutions. This has enabled servicemen to move much more easily into post-secondary education than would otherwise have been possible. CASE periodically publishes Guides which list service courses and recommend credit equivalents, and to which admissions offices can refer quickly and easily. Each service course is evaluated by a three-member, subject-matter specialist team. The members of this team are nominated by regional accrediting associations, professional and faculty bodies, educational associations and institutions. Only service courses which are approved by a central authority within each service are considered. Provided that certain conditions are met, one semester credit hour is awarded for every 15 hours of classroom contact plus 30 hours of laboratory work, or for not less than 45 hours of shop instruction. However, the final decision on whether or not to award credit rests with the "recipient" institution (27).

Following recommendations by the Commission on Non-Traditional Study, CASE has been succeeded by the Office of Educational Credit (OEC) which extended its work to cover courses organised by businesses, unions, professional associations, as well as industrial and government training programmes. The consequence of this is that a much wider range of non-collegiate courses will now be "plugged in" to collegiate degree or credential programmes. There are problems, of course: courses on economics sponsored by businesses or unions may not necessarily be as objective as college-run courses. The logistical problem of properly evaluating the enormous numbers of available courses is daunting, as are the financial implications. Nevertheless, the work of OEC seems to take its place in a logical historical development which began with one university (Harvard), spread to other universities and colleges, grew to include the armed forces, and is now spreading into civilian life.

Another means whereby new groups of students can bypass the normal admissions procedures is the standardized non-taught examination, that is to say, an examination which is not prepared for by formal courses, but which has a relatively wide use and acceptability. The College Level Examinations Program in the United States is such an examination. The CLEP program was started in 1965 and introduced into colleges and universities in 1966. By the early 1970s, over 1,500 institutions in the United States granted credit on the basis of CLEP scores. Although the original purpose of CLEP was to open up channels to students who had acquired their knowledge non-formally, "conventional" students are now making increasing use of it to gain up to a whole year's credit before they start college: Trivette reports that in 1973, at least 40 per cent of all CLEP candidates were under 19 years of age (28).

---

27. Trivett, D.A., *Academic Credit for Prior Off-Campus Learning*, American Association for Higher Education, Washington, 1975, p. 42.
28. *Ibid*, p. 23.

CLEP is divided into two parts: general examinations and subject examinations. The General Examinations test basic knowledge in each of five main areas (English composition, humanities, mathematics, natural science and social sciences/history) through the use of a 60-minute multiple-choice test. The Subject Examinations test knowledge in particular subjects, with special emphasis on concepts, principles and relationships. They usually consist of a 90-minute essay. The scores in all examinations are norm-referenced so that the "cutting scores" (i.e. pass marks) can vary from one year to another. The "receiving" institution is also at liberty to decide at what score they will begin to award credit. Relatively small changes in the "cutting score" can alter the number of passes substantially. CLEP is not the only agency in the United States that grants credit by examination. A survey in 1973 showed that among institutions granting credit in this way, 78.4 per cent used CLEP, 8.4 per cent used the American College Testing Program, and 4.3 per cent used the New York Regents College Proficiency Examination Program.

Credit by examination appears to be well-established in the United States. There are certain criticisms, however: the fact that some conventional students take advantage of CLEP whereas many non-traditional students do not; the problem of fixing appropriate cutting scores, and "doubts about whether an examination can measure what one receives in a course"(29). The dissociation between a taught course and examinations has a precedent in the External Degree Examinations of the University of London, which date from the last century; a reminder that what is non-traditional in one country may be quite traditional in another.

One of the most recent and controversial ways in which normal admissions requirements in the United States have been modified is the accreditation of prior non-formal "learning experiences". Since adults have usually had many opportunities for such learning experiences or "experimental learning" during their adult, working lives, this innovation is of special significance to them. In the past, a certain amount of working experience in a particular field has sometimes been one of the requirements for admission to a master's degree programme. In-service or post-graduate courses have demanded a first degree plus x years' working experience in the field. And some degree courses have contained a practical "sandwich" element in which the student goes and works in a real-life situation (as an engineer in a factory, or a teacher in a school) for anything between three weeks and a year. "Experiential learning" is different from any of these; it entails the granting of academic credit for things which were learned quite outside any educational or instructional framework. Academic credit for experiential learning has been awarded by some institutions in the United States for several years now, and detailed research has been carried out by the Co-operative Assessment of Experiential Learning (CAEL) organisation (30). In particular, this body has the following four areas:

---

29. Ibid, p. 33.
30. Current Practices in the Assessment of Experiential Learning, CAEL Working Paper No. 1, Princetown, 1974.

- the awarding of credit for interpersonal skills;
- the use of portfolios in presenting evidence;
- the accreditation of work experience;
- the use of experts in assessing learning outcomes.

The potential advantage to non-traditional or adult students of this kind of development is obvious. Alan Tough's work has shown the extent to which adults habitually engage in "learning projects" in the course of normal life, spending anything from ten to several hundred hours learning about particular problems or areas which are of current interest or use to them (31). Non-formal learning seems to cluster naturally around themes; it is not random. Nor does it remain wholly unconceptualised, in a raw experiential state: sense and meaning are made out of it.

There are both practical and theoretical problems in the evaluation of experiential learning. To begin with, it is time-consuming; individual consideration has to be given to each candidate, and no two candidates are alike. Evaluation typically involves not one, but several members of staff. Experiential learning may remain largely pre-theoretical whereas formal knowledge is typically organised and structured with reference to concepts, theories and disciplines. However, one of the most interesting aspects of CAEL's work is that it inevitably raises questions about the evaluation of formal learning, as well as of experiential learning, and may lead eventually to a better understanding of conventional modes of assessment and evaluation.

The work of CASE, CLEP and CAEL represent only three examples of a wide range of developments which affect new students in the United States. The implications of such developments for educational standards will be discussed briefly below: the possibilities and problems of transferable credit have been explored further in the United States than in any other country.

In this section, examples of special admissions policies have been reviewed for six countries: Australia, Denmark, the Federal German Republic, Sweden, the United Kingdom, the United States. Many more examples, in these and other countries, have necessarily been omitted. It is very difficult to give any overview of these trends: the variety of developments defeats generalisation. On the other hand, precisely because of this variety, countries and institutions stand to learn much from one another. In any case, it is possible to identify a number of basic dimensions, notably those concerned with centralisation and decentralisation. A number of countries, among them Sweden and Denmark, have adopted centralised admissions schemes with uniform criteria and a common "points" system applying throughout the country. Others, such as Australia and the United Kingdom, have left control of admissions very much in the hands of individual institutions and even academic departments. There is

---

31. Tough, A., The Adult's Learning Projects, Ontario Institute for Studies in Education, 1971.

something to be said for both approaches: national schemes are complex and difficult to agree on, but they are likely to be nationally known and understood; local schemes are easier to set up, and potentially more responsive to individual cases, but they are unlikely to attract as much publicity, and are at the mercy of local academic interests which may fluctuate over time. The centralist/decentralist choice no doubt reflects the nature of the educational system as a whole in each country. It would thus be more useful to compare likes rather than unlikes, and comparative studies of schemes in Sweden and Denmark or Australia and the United Kingdom could well prove fruitful.

There is also a quantitative/qualitative dimension in special admissions schemes. This can be seen, for example, in the varying emphasis which Australian universities place on formal quantifiable measures (such as aptitude tests or examinations) or on less formal, qualitative measures, such as essays, statements of intent, or interviews. The admission of new students raises the same selection and assessment problems that exist with all students but these are perhaps made more acute by the attempt to measure "potential", or "motivation" in addition to, or in lieu of, achievement.

There is clearly also a legal and constitutional dimension to admissions. This has become most sharply apparent in the United States, with the Bakke case, in which a white student challenged the constitutionality of preferential quotas for disadvantaged ethnic minorities. The case involved complex questions about the balance between individual and group equity, and about the "natural relevance" of admissions criteria.

In general, it can be said that admissions policies in post-secondary education are becoming more complex, both in their criteria and in the procedures used. This complexity derives from the increasingly complex nature of higher education as a whole, and from its relationship with academic upper-secondary studies which, once unique, has now been relegated to a special relationship with many other factors and needs now being taken into account.

Finally a note of caution should be introduced. It is not enough for new groups of students to be admitted to higher education in general: they should be admitted to courses appropriate to their needs, interests and abilities. This implies a process of counselling before admission, a process which cannot be carried out by any one institution, since matters of choice may be involved. There is therefore a need for "neutral" counselling, particularly for adults, which can help to diagnose the individual's needs, and advise him or her on the appropriate alternatives. Such services have recently grown up rapidly and spontaneously in several countries: there are some 40 in the United Kingdom now, often operating on a quasi-voluntary basis. Greater support for such services would help ensure that new groups of students found the subjects, levels and modes of study most appropriate to them.

4. LONG-TERM ISSUES AND POLICIES

As seen above, substantial numbers of "new groups" of students are now entering higher education in a number of countries: women, ethnic minorities, students of low SES, part-timers, mature students. It has also been suggested that such students tend to concentrate in the less prestigious and/or more vocational sectors of higher education. We have reviewed some examples of the wide range of special admissions policies involved, and have argued that more comprehensive counselling services are needed. There are, no doubt, immediate and short-term problems associated with the admission of new groups, but what of the longer term? What does the advent of such groups imply for higher education as a whole, and for higher education policies?

It is worth pointing out that the intake of new groups is in itself the fulfilment, at least in part, of an earlier aspiration to make higher education more diverse, more flexible, and more open. The last two decades have witnessed an attempt not only to expand higher education, but to diversify it, and it can generally be said that, in terms of students, range of courses, structures of courses and qualifications, as well as types of institutions, there has been a considerable measure of success.

Much depends on whether one views higher education as an intrinsic, absolute good, or as a relative, positional good. In the first case, access to any kind of higher education is worthwhile and valuable. In the second case, one needs to examine the relative worth or value of the higher education received, and it is this consideration which gives rise to disquiet in the case of new groups. If some new groups are concentrated in the less prestigious parts of the expanded higher education system, has their relative position changed at all? In other words, is the transition from an elite to mass system merely a transition from an externally maintained stratification to an internally maintained one? Where previously the crucial distinction was between those who received higher education and those who did not, are the key distinctions now ones between different sectors, institutions or faculties? If they are, how much sense does it make to continue to speak of higher education as a whole?

A related question is that of standards. A good deal of concern has recently been voiced in the United States about the decline of higher education standards as measured by the Scholastic Aptitude Test verbal and math scores. Similar concern has been expressed in the United Kingdom, though without the same evidence. It is a short step from this to argue that the decline in standards has been brought about by the expansion of higher education, and _ergo_ by the admission of new groups of students. This _may_ be true: many non-traditional students _enter_ higher education with lower standards than traditional students, though whether they emerge with lower standards is another question.

However, the question of standards raises a more fundamental question: standards of what? Insofar as there is a general academic consensus about the criteria used for measuring students' performance, the answer is fairly straighforward. However, such criteria may themselves be open to question. Should everybody prefer the theoretical to the practical, the analytic to the intuitive, the specialised to the general? Are there perhaps educational and social costs involved in these preferences?

A more pluralistic student intake may thus lead to more pluralistic criteria for measuring achievement in higher education. The greater the number of independent dimensions of ability involved, the greater the statistical chance of any one student achieving above average on one of them (32). There may currently be a mismatch between the heterogeneity of student abilities, and the homogeneity of assessment criteria. If expansion means simply that more people are expected to fit into the same traditional mould, it would be hardly surprising if this leads to lowered standards or higher attrition rates.

Finally, the growth of part-time study, not as a planned move towards recurrent education, but as a market response to uncertainty, may have important implications for higher education. In many countries and institutions, the full-time student is seen as the norm, and part-timers have to do their best to fit in with arrangements which are essentially designed for full-timers. If the trend to part-time study continues, then the reverse may have to become the case: full-timers will have to receive most of their tuition in the evenings, or at weekends or during vacations, in order to accommodate the needs of the part-time majority.

Beyond such practical alterations, a more subtle shift in attitudes is implied. The trend is to think of "student" as a largely exclusive and sufficient role for someone to adopt for several years of his or her life, usually in late adolescence or early adulthood. If study becomes more diffused through adult life, and less exclusive as an occupation, the boundary between students and non-students will become much less clear. There are potential advantages to this, which advocates of recurrent education have not been slow to spell out: relatedness of study to work and life, a comprehensive view of lifespan development, perhaps more equal opportunities. However, it is worth remembering that certain forms and phases of higher education demand the contrary: concentration, consecutiveness, even isolation. Rather than polarising higher education into a small, young, elite, full-time sector, and a large, mass, older, part-time sector, one should perhaps be looking into ways in which full-time and part-time study can be sensibly combined, e.g. with students beginning and ending a course with a period of full-time study. This has implications not only for student support policies, but for developments in paid educational leave.

---

32. Cross, K.P., <u>Accent on Learning</u>, Jossey-Bass, San Francisco, 1976, p. 11.

A final general point may be made. It is useful, in considering new groups of students, to analyse to what extent the students have to adapt to the institutions, and to what extent the institutions have to adapt to the students. Much of this institutional adaptation is of a fairly practical and pragmatic kind: changing timetables, altering library opening hours, providing crèche facilities, and so on. But in some respects, the advent of non-traditional groups means that higher education has to take more account of, and is indeed more at the mercy of, market forces, than it has been in most countries up to now. The traditional school-leaving intake is now only a proportion of the total intake; and even that proportion is sometimes opting for a partial commitment to higher education, on a part-time or recurrent basis. In short, higher education appears to be becoming progressively detached from its traditional source - academic, upper-secondary education. If this is in fact the case, higher education will have to be viewed less as the apex of a system of consecutive schooling and selection, and more as an arena in which a plurality of groups, values and functions compete permanently for attention and resources.

Chapter V

THE LINKS BETWEEN FINANCE AND ADMISSION POLICIES
IN HIGHER EDUCATION *

The trends in admission policies for post-secondary education discussed in the earlier chapters have many cost and resource implications. As shown in one of the Secretariat reports (1), the rising levels of participation in higher education in the 1960s led to an increase in the proportion of education expenditure allocated for higher education between 1965 and 1970, followed by a more modest rise between 1970 and 1975 and a reduction thereafter. In some countries, concern about the rising costs of higher education, together with the economic recession and attempts to curb the growth of public expenditure has had a direct influence on admission policies, but, as Chapters II and III make clear, the development of admission policies for post-secondary education, and changes in selection procedures in upper secondary education reflect many different educational and socio-economic pressures, as well as financial constraints. Nevertheless, although it is true that the changes in admission policies cannot be explained purely in terms of economic and financial factors, recent trends in admission policy will clearly affect future levels of expenditure on higher education.

It is impossible to forecast the precise effect of these trends on expenditure because, as the Secretariat report mentioned (2), any change in higher education expenditure is the combined result of changes in enrolment and costs. In some cases admission policies are likely to lead to a reduction in expenditure, for example where the introduction of numerus clausus leads to a decline in post-secondary enrolments, or where the growth of short-cycle higher education leads to a fall in unit costs. On the other hand, policies designed to increase access for minorities, for adults or other "non-traditional students" may have the opposite effect. The impact of changes in admission policies on the overall level of expenditure is thus

---

* The Secretariat wishes to acknowledge its indebtedness to Maureen Woodhall for the authorship of this chapter.

1. "Higher education expenditure in OECD countries", OECD document, Paris, 1981.
2. Ibid.

difficult to predict, although it is probable that the combined effects of more selective university admission and general demographic trends will lead to a continuation of the decline in resources for higher education observed from 1975 on.

This in turn raises many questions about the implications of a declining share of educational expenditure, questions about the allocation of resources between different types of institutions and about the impact of declining resources on the structure of institutions. However, it is not the purpose of this paper to examine the wider implications of changing expenditure and resource patterns, but to look at a more limited but important question, namely the relationship between admissions policies and methods of financing post-secondary education, inasmuch as both admissions policies and methods of financing education determine the "price" of entry for the individual student and hence the demand for post-secondary education. The price that the student must pay includes not only the direct costs of study, i.e. tuition fees, where these are charged (as in Canada, Japan, the United States and the United Kingdom) and expenses on books or travel, but also indirect costs, i.e. the costs of maintenance or earnings foregone which, as shown on the report on Higher Education Expenditure (3), may account for as much as half the total cost of higher education in many countries. If access to post-secondary education were completely open, then the "price" of entry would consist of the direct and indirect costs of study. The student must normally be able to satisfy other conditions too, relating to age, ability, or entrance qualifications, in order to enrol in a particular school or college. These other conditions may, in fact, be more difficult to fulfil than the mere "ability to pay". Therefore, the "price" of education for the would-be student consists in satisfying all the conditions of entry, and not simply in finding the funds to finance his post-secondary education.

Governments and institutions therefore determine the demand for education both by their policies on selection, entrance requirements and admission procedures and by their financial policies which determine how the direct and indirect costs of education are shared between students or their families and the community. The purpose of this chapter is to examine the links between admission policies and methods of financing post-secondary education in OECD countries, to see the extent to which they interact to determine demand, and to see whether government and institutional policies on admission and selection are directed towards the same objectives and are consistent with their policies on the financing of education, and resource allocation. For the last decade has seen not only the changes in methods of selection for post-compulsory education which have been discussed in Chapter III, but at the same time changes in methods of financing tuition and student aid. However, there has been little discussion of the relationship between these two policy areas and of the extent to which admission and financing policies are interrelated, and mutually consistent; more detailed consideration needs to be given to the extent of coordination between the selection criteria determining access to post-secondary education and those determining eligibility for financial aid.

---

3. *Ibid.*, Table 5-1.

For a variety of reasons, the situation has begun to change. After a period of rapid growth in the 1960s, expansion of higher education slowed down markedly in most OECD countries during the 1970s, reflecting static, or declining demand for higher education in some countries, as well as demographic trends (4). These demographic trends are likely to lead to a continuing decline in student numbers in the 1980s or early 1990s in a number of countries, unless there is a fairly dramatic increase in demand from previously under-represented groups.

Thus, institutions of higher education will have a powerful incentive to re-examine both their admission policies and their financing, in order to stem the decline in numbers and resources. At the same time, social and political pressures, as well as the economic pressures of continuing recession and high unemployment, are forcing governments to reconsider the supply of post-secondary education and the distribution of resources.

Governments, as well as institutions, however, have a variety of objectives which determine admission and financing policies. In many cases, the objectives are not clearly defined, and the twin objectives of efficiency and equity may often conflict. Thus, government policies on admissions and financing may conflict, or at least, be badly co-ordinated. Governments may be attempting to limit public expenditure on economic grounds, while trying to broaden access to higher education on social grounds. Chapters I and II have shown that certain levels or types of education are becoming more selective while selection or streaming is being abandoned at other levels of education and similarly, student aid systems may become more selective while institutions are becoming committed to policies of open access.

All this means that the question of the links and interaction between financing and selection procedures is likely to receive more attention in the next few years than in the past. Governments are beginning to look more closely at the way in which decisions about the supply of places in higher education, and changes in the rules for determining entry admission affect their financial policies - decisions which determine the methods of subsidising institutions and students and the amount of such subsidies - influence who is admitted. More attention is now being paid in many countries to the influence of financial factors on the demand for education, and to the effect of financial barriers and assistance for pupils at the post-compulsory secondary education, as well as to the impact of financial aid to students at the point of entry. In other words it is increasingly recognised that the relationship between financing and admission policies is a two-way one, and that questions of who should be admitted to higher education and how the direct and indirect costs of that education are financed must be treated in conjunction. This raises a number of issues:

a) Does the way institutions are financed determine their selection and admission procedures ?

---

4. See Statistical Annex.

b) Are admission policies influenced by direct financial factors, such as students' ability to pay tuition fees, or to meet the indirect costs of education (maintenance costs and earnings foregone) or does financial aid to students succeed in eliminating such financial barriers ?
c) Are financial factors indirectly associated with selection criteria, for example in determining who stays on in post-compulsory education, and thus who gains the qualifications for entry to post-secondary education ?

The remainder of this chapter studies these issues, looking separately at methods of financing tuition and financial aid for students to cover their maintenance.

1. FINANCING TUITION COSTS

At present all OECD governments subsidise the costs of tuition in higher education, but there are important differences, both in the level of subsidy and the form it takes. On average, students, or their families, receive a smaller subsidy from public funds in the United States, Canada, or Japan, than in European countries. This is because fees are charged in North America and Japan, whereas fees have been largely abolished in Europe. The fact that fees are charged does not automatically mean that the individual student, or his family, bears a large proportion of the cost of tuition, since students may receive government aid towards tuition fees. Two quite separate issues are involved:

a) What should be the level of government subsidy for higher education ?
b) Should this subsidy be given in the form of grants to institutions, to allow the provision of free or low-cost tuition, or to students, to enable them to pay tuition fees ?

At present, fees are charged in higher education institutions in Canada, Japan, the United Kingdom, the United States, but are mostly non-existent in continental Europe and in Australia although the latter government has just announced its intention to introduce fees for post-graduate study. The proportion of income derived from fees and private donations varies considerably between countries and institutions. In Canada, for example, fees provide about 9 per cent of the income of all post-secondary institutions (5). In Japan and the United States the situation differs markedly between public and private universities or colleges, though fees are charged in both sectors. In Japan, fees and donations account for over 90 per cent of the current income of private universities, but less than 5 per cent that of public universities. In the United States 37 per cent of the current income of private universities is derived from fees,

---

5. Report of the Federal-Provincial Task Force on Student Assistance. Ottawa, Council of Ministers and Secretary of State, 1980, p. 108.

compared with 13 per cent in public institutions (6). In the United Kingdom, the pattern has recently changed. In 1974-75, fees amounted to only 4.5 per cent of all university income, but in 1977-78 fees were substantially increased, both for British and overseas students, and for the first time postgraduate fees were higher than undergraduate fees. The result of these increases was that the proportion of university income derived from fees rose to 18 per cent in 1977-78.

However, this did not mean that the burden of financing higher education shifted from the public to the private purse, for the majority of British students have their fees paid in full by Local Education Authorities. The increased fees meant that a larger part of the subsidy for higher education was channelled through individuals, rather than through institutions.

There had been many proposals for a shift in policy ever since the Robbins Committee pointed out that fees as a proportion of university income had fallen from 33 per cent in 1939 to 15 per cent in 1951, and advocated a reversal of this trend. In fact, income from university fees continued to fall providing less than 5 per cent of total income by 1974-75. The arguments for channelling a larger share of government subsidies through individual students, rather than through institutional grants, were that:

a) it would give universities a greater degree of autonomy;
b) it would encourage universities to be more responsive to student choice since their income would depend on their ability to attract students;
c) it would make the true costs of higher education - and the size of government subsidies - more apparent to students and to taxpayers, and explicit subsidies are more efficient than "hidden" subsidies;
d) it would encourage greater diversity of institutions, in terms of type and quality of courses offered.

All these arguments have implications for admissions policy. If universities derive their income from a variety of sources, including private as well as public funds, they are less likely to be subject to detailed government control on admissions policy and selection criteria than if the bulk of their income comes directly from government grants, as in most European countries. Moreover, if institutions depend for their income on their ability to attract students, and directly on the fees they pay, then they have a greater incentive to compete with each other in terms of the type of courses offered. This may lead to greater diversity of institutions in terms of admissions standards, as well as curriculum and type of course. There is no reason to believe that institutions would necessarily compete with each other by relaxing admission standards. On the contrary, student demand is often greatest for institutions with the most stringent entry standards. Institutions which charge fees are no more likely to seek to attract students by lowering entry requirements than colleges receiving direct government grants. However, if the supply

---

6. C. Finn, Scholars, Dollars and Bureaucrats: The Brookings Institution, Washington, 1978, p. 48.

of places exceeds student demand, then colleges will have to pay far more attention to the factors influencing student choice, including both admissions policies and the level of fees. There has recently been some research in both the United States and the United Kingdom on the responsiveness of student demand to price changes (7), but the question still has not been fully answered.

In the United States, the question of whether government funds should be channelled through students (by means of student aid which enables students to pay tuition fees), or through institutions (by means of grants which enable colleges or universities to charge low or even zero fees) is highly controversial, raising a number of issues including not only the question of efficiency and equity but also the legality of government subsidies to institutions, given that many institutions have religious affiliations and that the American Constitution requires the clear separation of Church and State. Because of the wide variety of public and private institutions, with very different levels of fees, and because of the great differences between the financing policies in the individual states, there are considerable disparities in the opportunities available to citizens of different states. For example, tuition fees in public institutions in California represent only 8 per cent of the actual average expenditure per student, whereas in Pennsylvania they are equivalent to 55 per cent and in Vermont to over 90 per cent (8). In addition, most states charge higher fees to students in public institutions who are not resident in the state. This additional geographical criterion, combined with the considerable variations in availability of student aid in different states, results in considerable disparities in the costs of attending college faced by different students. For example in 1977-78 tuition fees in two-year public institutions averaged $389, compared with $1,812 in two-year private colleges, and in four-year public universities they were $621, compared with $2,476 in private four-year institutions.

According to one recent American study, this makes for a "warped market place" for higher education in which two institutions offering much the same education end up charging widely differing prices for it. This condition does not enhance equality of opportunity, nor does it foster educationally motivated choices on the part of the college-bound student, and in a time of declining enrolments it compounds the difficulties faced by some colleges and universities (9).

If demographic and economic changes force institutions to compete more directly for students, then the level of fees and admissions standards represent policy variables which could be used by institutions to influence student demand. In the conditions of excess student demand in the 1960s mechanisms for influencing demand

---

7. See, for example, M.S. McPherson, "The Demand for Higher Education" in D. Breneman and C. Finn, Public Policy and Private Higher Education, The Brookings Institution, Washington, 1978, pp. 146-196.
8. C. Finn, op. cit. p. 50.
9. C. Finn, op. cit. p. 51.

and regulating admissions to higher education were seen largely in terms of discouraging surplus students. This role is beginning to change, and demographic trends in the 1980s and 1990s may well lead to a more marked change in emphasis, as institutions seek to use these variables as a means of attracting students, rather than limiting entry.

This raises the important question of fee differentials between different courses, different levels or different students. In the United States and Japan, considerable variations exist between fees at public and private colleges, between undergraduate and postgraduate fees and in some cases between fees charged for different subjects. In the United States, as mentioned above, there are differentials in public institutions between in-state residents and students from other states. In the United Kingdom, since 1967, overseas students have been charged higher fees than British students, but since 1980 the fees charged to foreign students are supposed to cover the full cost of tuition, and for the first time there are marked differences in the fees charged for different subjects. In 1980-81 overseas students taking a university degree in the arts or humanities paid £2,000 a year, students taking science or technology courses paid £3,000 and those taking medicine or veterinary science paid £5,000 (10).

The purpose of these dramatic increases in fees was to reduce the costs of the government subsidy to overseas students as part of the general policy of cutting public expenditure. However, the policy of charging full-cost fees has a number of implications for admissions policies in the future. It could mean, for example, that only overseas students with generous scholarships or other forms of financial aid, or those from the highest income groups will be able to afford to enter British higher education, particularly to study the more expensive subjects. It will mean that institutions will apply different selection criteria for British and foreign students. It is likely not only to reduce demand for higher education in the United Kingdom, but to change the composition of overseas students, with particularly adverse effects on students from the poorest developing countries. On the other hand, if linked with a policy of selective scholarships a policy of full-cost fees means that government subsidies could be concentrated on students judged to be of the highest priority, either in terms of academic standards, the needs of particular countries, or other criteria. A policy of selective aid, rather than one of indiscriminate subsidy in the form of low or zero tuition fees, as is the pattern in most European countries, focuses attention on the criteria for student assistance. Many people argue that this policy is more efficient than one of general subsidies for all students, particularly at a time of growing financial constraints when the alternative to a policy of full-cost fees may well be the imposition of quotas for foreign students, such as were introduced in a number of European countries in the 1970s.

---

10. For a full discussion of the policy of full-cost fees for overseas students see P. Williams (Editor) The Overseas Student Question: Studies for a Policy, Heinemann, London, 1981, for the Overseas Student's Trust.

The idea of numerical quotas is anathema to many, while others find the idea of students paying different fees for identical courses of study equally unacceptable and oppose all attempts to apply the rules of the market to academic institutions. In fact the choice of whether to subsidise institutions or students reflects many historical and political factors as well as differences in educational and financial policies but it does have some interesting implications for admissions policy. For example, it is significant that the countries where fees are substantial, notably the United States, Canada, Japan and the United Kingdom, are those where selection for higher education takes place at the point of entry, rather than in secondary schooling. Differentiation between types of secondary school, or streams, is much less in the United States for example, than traditionally in Europe, and the proportion of secondary school pupils gaining a school-leaving certificate is much higher (about 75 per cent) than in most European countries (where it averages 20 to 35 per cent). Accordingly, there is no assumption that a school-leaving certificate "guarantees" the right to higher education, as it has traditionally done in France or Germany; a policy of charging fees is hence perfectly consistent with an admissions policy that confers no automatic rights. Given the great diversity of admissions standards in the United States and the marked differences in the level of fees, there has been considerable debate about the need for financial assistance to students to guarantee choice of institution as well as access for students from all socio-economic backgrounds, including those from the lowest income groups. Both federal and state governments now provide considerable financial aid to students in the form of grants, highly subsidised loans and subsidised work-study programmes, and this student aid is used to finance tuition fees as well as living expenses. But the debate continues as to whether this financial aid is sufficient to ensure choice as well as access.

There is plenty of evidence that American students' choice of institution is related to their family income level. Table 19 shows the percentage distribution of undergraduate students by type of institution and family income in 1976. Low income students are more likely to go to public universities or colleges, where fees are, on average, lower and those from the highest income category are more likely to go to private institutions where average tuition fees are more than four times as high as in public institutions. Nevertheless, the existence of financial aid for students does ensure that some students from the lowest income category are able to afford the more expensive institutions. However, those who advocate a policy of highly subsidised tuition argue that such a policy whould help low income students even more than student aid which enables them to pay fees. On the other hand attempts to analyse exactly how responsive demand for higher education in the United States is to changes in fee levels suggest that "cutting tuition (fees) in half... would only raise enrolment by about 15 per cent... A major implication of the low rate of price response is that attaining high enrolments through keeping tuition rates low across the board is a very expensive way to achieve access goals. Since most of the foregone tuition revenue resulting from a price cut would accrue to students who would attend college anyway, it apparently costs more than $4,000 in foregone tuition (fees) for each additional student attracted into college via a general price reduction(11)."

In other words, it is not possible to justify a policy of free or highly subsidised tuition, simply on grounds of equity or equality of opportunity. Such a policy in fact involves considerable transfers of funds from the general taxpayer to the higher income groups who generally benefit most from higher education. Even if the aim of the policy is to ensure that all students have freedom of choice of institution, and that low income students are not discouraged from high-cost colleges or universities, it is by no means obvious that a policy of low or zero fees necessarily achieves this objective.

Table 19

PERCENTAGE DISTRIBUTION OF UNDERGRADUATE STUDENTS IN HIGHER EDUCATION INSTITUTIONS, UNITED STATES, BY FAMILY INCOME AND TYPE OF INSTITUTION
1976

Family Income Level	Public (Average Tuition Fees $ 526)	Private (Average Tuition Fees $2,365)
Under $5,000	7	2
$ 5,000 - $ 9,999	11	9
$ 10,000 - $ 14,999	17	15
$ 15,000 - $ 19,999	17	16
$ 20,000 - $ 24,999	16	15
$ 25,000 - and over	23	31
Not reported	8	12
Total	100	100

Source: C.E. Finn, Scholars, Dollars and Bureaucrats, The Brookings Institution, Washington, 1978, pp. 49 and 56.

A relationship between students' choice of institution and socio-economic background has been demonstrated in countries where no fees are charged. In most countries students from the higher income groups are considerably over-represented in medicine, which usually has the highest cost per student, and this is true regardless of whether fees are charged or not. A study in Sweden demonstrated that students from high income families are more likely to choose longer university courses, and children of manual workers are more

---

11. M.S. McPherson, "The Demand for Higher Education" in D.W. Breneman and C.E. Finn, Public Policy and Private Higher Education, The Brookings Institution, Washington, 1978, p. 183.

likely to choose shorter, non-university courses (12). Clearly, one factor at work here is the length of course, and the higher indirect costs of study (including earnings foregone) even though tuition is free.

There are various ways in which students' choice of institution may be influenced by their socio-economic background, and it is not necessarily through the direct costs of study. Courses with higher than average costs per student, such as medicine or engineering, frequently have the most stringent entry requirements, in terms of examination results, or grade scores, or operate a strict numerus clausus; they also tend to offer the highest returns to the individual, in terms of life-time earnings and social prestige. In any country, such courses are more likely to attract students from higher social groups, regardless of whether fees are charged. The OECD study of individual demand in post-secondary education concludes: "In general, in all the countries covered in this report... the stronger the academic selection at entry to a particular institution of higher learning, the more socially selective that institution appears as well(13)". This is a result of many factors, including the degree of social bias in secondary schools, the career motivation of students, the admission policies of the institutions as well as financial considerations.

In the United States and to some extent in Japan, where high and low fee institutions exist side by side, it is often the case that universities or colleges which charge the highest fees are also those with the most stringent entry requirements. On the other hand, short-cycle courses, with much more liberal admission policies (such as public two-year colleges in the United States), have the lowest fees. Thus, the financial and academic requirements for entry tend to reinforce each other, as hurdles to entry and as determinants of the "price" of education.

If, however, tuition is provided free, as in most European countries, then admission policies can still influence the financial cost of higher education, even if only indirectly. If a strict numerus clausus is applied, based on examination results, this may encourage pupils to re-sit examinations in the hope of gaining higher marks at a second attempt. This may mean that they prolong their secondary schooling in the hope of improving their examination results, that they enter some other type of institution in order to "mark time" while waiting to re-sit an examination, or that they seek private tuition. Whichever policy they adopt, additional indirect costs will be incurred, in the form of earnings foregone as well as direct costs, in the form of fees for private coaching. In either case, this increases the cost, or price, of higher education to the individual.

There are, therefore, many ways in which the admissions policies of institutions influence the price of higher education for the individual student, whether or not fees are charged. Even if governments

---

12. M. Woodhall, Student Loans: A Review of Experience in Scandinavia and Elsewhere, G. Harrap, London, 1970, p. 136.
13. Individual Demand for Education, op. cit.

do not determine the price of higher education directly - by means of regulating fee levels - they determine it indirectly, by decisions about the supply of places, which influence admissions policies, and by decisions about student aid, which determine the indirect costs of higher education for the individual.

2. FINANCING INDIRECT COSTS: STUDENT AID

Even if students are also to finance the costs of tuition, either because schooling or higher education is free, or because they receive grants or loans to cover fees, there may still be financial barriers to access in the form of earnings foregone while studying. In all OECD countries student aid policies provide some form of subsidy for students' living expenses, in the form of grants, loans or a combination of the two, often combined with tax concessions and subsidies for food, accommodation or travel (14). In most countries, one of the main objectives of student aid is to ensure that poor students are not prevented from entering or continuing higher education, by inability to finance their living expenses. Student aid programmes aim to weaken the influence of financial factors on access to higher education, but it is increasingly recognised that financial barriers at the point of entry to higher education may be less important in determining who has access than financial aid and admissions policy. If selection for higher or further education is on the basis of school-leaving certificates, then earnings foregone at the upper secondary level may be a far more effective financial barrier for working class pupils than fees in higher education. Yet most countries still devote far more to financial aid to students in universities or other higher education institutions than to upper secondary pupils.

Several countries now recognise that even though their policies on secondary school selection and admission are designed to extend educational opportunities, this is not sufficient to secure equality of opportunity when there are strong financial incentives persuading pupils from low-income families to leave school at the minimum age. The importance of earnings foregone as an indirect cost of completing secondary schooling has long been recognised. Recent high rates of unemployment of young school leavers, together with increased rates of social security payments for young people, means that young people may now be discouraged from completing their secondary schooling by high rates of unemployment benefit or training allowances for unemployed school leavers. The need for more financial aid for upper secondary school pupils is now increasingly recognised. For example a recent study in the United Kingdom showed that the average cost of maintaining a child at school beyond the school-leaving age is much higher than the cost of maintaining a university student, since financial aid for secondary school pupils is negligible, compared

---

14. For a more detailed description of student aid policies in ten OECD countries, see: M. Woodhall, Review of Student Support Schemes in Selected OECD Countries, OECD, Paris, 1973.

with grants for students in higher education. Furthermore, because subsidies at the secondary level are given mainly in the form of tax relief to parents, which varies with level of income, it actually costs low-income families more than those with high incomes to support a child in school. The author's conclusion was that: "For low and medium-income families there is a high-cost hurdle from ages 15-17, before university, with much lower costs to the families, can be reached. Relative to net income, the cost of keeping a child in education is highest for a low-income family with a child at school (15)".

Since it is difficult if not impossible in most countries to qualify for post-secondary education without staying on at school to gain qualifications, this means that the financial hardship associated with completing secondary school education is a real barrier to higher education for many young people.

Many countries now recognise that serious anomalies exist between the levels of different types of support for young people, and efforts are being made to co-ordinate much more closely the levels of financial aid for students in higher education and pupils in upper secondary schooling and training allowances and unemployment benefits for unemployed school leavers.

This means that more attention may be paid to another type of anomaly, that is the different criteria determining eligibility for different types of financial aid. The criteria for awarding student aid are often quite different from those governing admissions policies. This means that poorer students have to satisfy two sets of criteria to gain admission to higher education, whereas those with higher levels of family income only need to satisfy the formal entry requirements. For example, in Ireland, there have been recent complaints about the fact that the entry requirement for some university courses is two honours grades in the school-leaving certificate, but no grant is payable to students unless they have a minimum of four honours grades. This means that poorer students have to face a higher academic hurdle than those who can afford to pay their own fees and living expenses.

Countries differ markedly in their criteria for financial aid, and in the degree of selectivity. In Scandinavia and the United Kingdom, a very high proportion of students receive some award. In the United Kingdom over 90 per cent of all home students receive an award from public funds although the level of assistance depends on parental income. In Norway and Sweden the proportion of students receiving grants or loans is over 70 per cent, and eligibility depends only on the student's own level of income; parental income is ignored in determining the amount of aid students receive. In these countries, students' ability to finance their maintenance costs is less important in determining access to higher education than in Japan, for example, where only 10 per cent of undergraduates receive financial aid from government funds.

---

15. D. Piachaud, "The Economics of Educational Opportunity". Higher Education, Vol. IV, May 1975, p. 207.

There are considerable differences in the criteria for awarding aid, and in the terms on which it is offered. In Japan and in France, grants or loans are awarded to students on the basis of ability, as well as financial need, whereas in the United States, Scandinavia or Australia, most awards are made on the basis of financial rather than academic criteria, once students have satisfied the basic standards required for admission. Loans at subsidised rates of interest are a predominant form of aid in Canada, the United States and Scandinavia and interest-free loans combined with grants are provided in Germany, whereas in Japan all aid is in the form of interest-free loans. Australia and the United Kingdom are the only Member countries to provide all aid in the form of grants, although the possibility of introducing student loans has been recently discussed in both countries.

Variations in the level or terms of student aid therefore provide governments with a mechanism for influencing student demand. One way for governments to attract students to particular types of higher education, or particular subjects, is by influencing admission standards, either directly or by controlling the supply of places. An alternative policy is to influence demand indirectly, through variations in student aid policy or other financial measures. There are a few cases where more favourable grants or loans are offered to students taking particular types of course, but on the whole the use of this type of financial incentive is not common.

How governments can vary the terms of student aid in order to influence students' subject or career choice, has been shown by the attempts in the United States and other countries to recruit teachers by means of "loan forgiveness" schemes, and the use, in France, of "pre-salary" payments for students intending to enter teaching or the public service. Such schemes are now waning in popularity, mainly due to the declining demand for teachers. Most of the loan forgiveness schemes in the United States (under which a portion of loan would be "written off" for each year's service as a teacher) have now been abolished, as has a similar scheme in the Netherlands, and a system of "bonded scholarships" in Australia. In France, the "pre-salaries" or "pre-employment contracts" are diminishing in importance. They accounted for 20 per cent of all government aid to students in 1960, but only 12 per cent in 1974. However, this form of aid has interesting links with admission policies. The purpose of the payments is to recruit manpower for certain occupations in the public sector, rather than to increase social equality. Only students with the highest grades are awarded pre-salaries. Thus, these payments are intended to reward ability rather than promote equality of opportunity.

The general trend in OECD countries, however, is towards more egalitarian systems of student aid, which treat students equally, regardless of the subject they study, or the occupation they hope to enter. Differences in the amount students receive are related to differences in the direct costs of courses, and to differences in their own (or their parents') financial resources. In Norway and Sweden, the amount students receive is dependent entirely on their own economic circumstances, whereas in the United Kingdom, student grants are subject to a means test based on parental income, and in Canada and the United States, grants and loans are awarded on the basis of financial need. This general policy is very different from one which seeks to attract students to particular subjects or branches of higher education, by means of more favourable grants or loans, or which rewards the most academically successful students with higher than average assistance. There are not as yet, many instances of governments choosing to vary the level, or the terms, of student aid, in order to achieve admissions policy objectives, although it has been discussed in a number of countries, particularly with respect to mature students. For example, in the United Kingdom the previous government discussed the possibility of changing the higher education enrolment pattern in the 1990s by attracting more mature students: "It is unlikely that any of the developments envisaged could happen without a major lead from Government. This might mean new financial incentives to encourage take-up by people in employment (whether this was in the form of paid educational leave for continuing education or more generous grants for mature students on full-time courses at degree or equivalent levels) and perhaps also some compensation for employers (16)".

An interesting attempt to analyse the implications of this on university admissions and failure rates in France (17) shows that an important difference between the two types of subsidy is that the award or continuation of grants, loans or pre-employment contracts is dependent on students' academic performance, whereas food subsidies and tax relief for students' families are enjoyed by all students, and housing subsidies only by those who live in student accommodation. In addition, the various types of subsidy have different effects on how students allocate their time between study, leisure or part-time employment, which in turn help to determine the likelihood of passing or failing final examinations. Thus, the way in which the government chooses to allocate its student aid budget may have important implications for the proportion of students who pass their final examinations. This is another example of how student aid policy can have important indirect effects on admission and selection policies, by influencing the success or failure rate at the end of higher education. Once again, we see that governments can regulate or manipulate the price of education by a variety of means, both direct and indirect, and this raises the important question of whether the objectives of student aid and financing policies are consistent with other policy objectives, particularly those relating to admissions and the supply of places.

---

16. Department of Education and Science, Higher Education into the 1990s. London, 1978, p. 9.
17. B. Lemenicier, "Direct and Indirect effects of In-Cash versus In-Kind Payments on the Labelling of Individuals: the French higher education case"; CREDOC. Paris, 1976. This is an English summary of part of a more detailed study in French: Lemenicier, Lévy-Garboua, Millot and Orivel, L'aide aux étudiants en France: faits et critique, CNRS, Paris, 1975.

3. GOVERNMENT POLICY OBJECTIVES ON ADMISSIONS AND THE FINANCING OF HIGHER EDUCATION

Government policies on higher education embody a variety of social, political and economic objectives, including both efficiency and equity. Educational policies too, are concerned with a wide variety of objectives: providing sufficient places to satisfy demand for skilled manpower, ensuring quality and diversity of institutions, promoting equality of opportunity and other broad social objectives. Choices between different selection and admission procedures, and different methods of financing higher education must take into account all these objectives, and the priority given to economic, social or educational objectives necessarily varies between Member countries.

In Sweden changes in admissions policy to attract mature students to higher education have been accompanied by more generous financial aid for adults, but in general there are few instances of clear co-ordination between the two types of government policy, and it is usually difficult to discern any obvious correlation between student aid and admissions policies. In fact there frequently appear to be inconsistencies between the criteria used for awarding student aid and selecting students for higher education.

In some cases, if selection takes place relatively late, and a large number of secondary school pupils gain leaving certificates, student aid is awarded mainly on the basis of academic criteria. For example, in Japan where the proportion of school leavers gaining a leaving certificate is high, university selection is based on specially administered tests and student loans are also awarded on a competitive basis. In Scandinavian countries, on the other hand, matriculation is traditionally taken by a smaller proportion of secondary school pupils, and success at this stage virtually entitles pupils to a place in higher education (except for the highly competitive "closed" faculties, such as medicine). Student aid, in these countries, however, is awarded on the basis of need, rather than academic attainment; grants combined with loans are available to all students, simply on the basis of their own level of income.

Several countries, however, have both selective and non-selective institutions, and in some cases different types of student aid may be based on different selection criteria. For example, in the United Kingdom a distinction is drawn between "mandatory awards" for students taking first degree or similar courses, and "discretionary awards" for students taking certain lower level courses, or who wish to get a second qualification. Where such distinctions exist, they may have repercussions for admission policies, since it may be in the interests of institutions to "upgrade" courses by raising entry standards in the hope of qualifying for a superior grant status. Alternatively, students may have to satisfy more stringent requirements in the case of "discretionary" awards than "mandatory" grants.

In the case of student grants or loans, aid is provided directly in the form of cash, or in some cases, interest subsidies for graduates who are repaying their loans. Governments also provide indirect subsidies in the form of cheap food, accommodation or travel facilities for students. In some countries, this aid may be substantial; for instance, in Germany, Norway and Sweden such indirect aid represents between 13 and 20 per cent of direct aid, though in Australia and Japan the proportion is only 5 or 7 per cent. The proportion of expenditure devoted to food and accommodation subsidies and tax relief for students' families, is much higher in France than in other countries.

The term "admissions policy" may involve either keeping students out, or attracting more students, depending on the institution; it may mean influencing student preferences or responding to student choice. Similarly governments, when developing admissions policies may be concerned with controlling excess demand, or with stimulating demand from new groups.

In view of this wide range of objectives, it is hardly surprising that admissions policies and financing mechanisms often do not seem well co-ordinated. Several examples of this lack of co-ordination have already been noted, such as the inconsistency in some countries between entry requirements and student aid criteria. Several countries have recently changed admission procedures in order to encourage participation of adults by relaxing entry requirements, or other means. Student aid rules, however, are often framed to suit the traditional student, entering straight from school. Levels of aid, terms of repayment of loans and even age limits for eligibility, may be inappropriate for adult students. In most countries, changes in student aid have lagged behind changes in admission policies for adults. Similarly, the common trend in Europe in the past few years to reduce selectivity in secondary education has not been matched by increases in financial aid to secondary school pupils, to prevent drop-out of low-income students. The result is that indirect financial barriers may still be very important at the secondary stage, partly nullifying attempts to "democratise" post-secondary education. Changes in admissions policies have also been introduced in some countries to break down barriers between different types of institution, yet at the same time student aid often differentiates between these institutions in such a way as to reinforce the barriers.

Other examples exist of conflicts between financial or student aid policies and the stated objectives of other government policies. It has been suggested that in France, although a policy of "equal access" to higher education has been proclaimed, "highly selective secondary schooling and student aid policies in fact limit access more than in other countries. Although in the words of the persons responsible for French higher education the aim is mass education, the facts show an orientation towards elitism (18)".

---

18. F. Orivel, "Facts and Words": The Ambiguities of the French Higher Education System". Paper presented at the Third International Conference on Higher Education at the University of Lancaster, September 1975.

All these examples of lack of consistency in financial and selection policies reflect the fact that the policies are designed to satisfy the often conflicting objectives of efficiency and equity. For example, selection procedures for numerus clausus faculties may, on grounds of efficiency, aim to select the most able candidates, regardless of income, whereas on grounds of equity student aid is often geared to low-income students, regardless of ability (provided that some minimum level of qualification is reached by all recipients). Changes in admission policies are advocated in some countries, in order to increase diversification of institutions and "open access" to higher education, on the grounds that this would lead to a more equitable distribution of opportunities. At the same time, it is sometimes argued that it would be more efficient to administer student aid more selectively (19), and that loan schemes should seek to reduce default rates by choosing loan recipients more selectively (20).

Even if admission and finance policies attempt to satisfy the same objectives, there is often disagreement about what the objectives mean. For example, does equity require that access be made more equal, or that the distribution of costs be more closely related to benefits? Should policies be more concerned with the distribution of education between different social groups or with the distribution of costs and benefits between those who gain directly from higher education and those who do not?

Finally, there is the question of how governments resolve the dichotomy between making student aid programmes more generous in order to alleviate the financial burden and encourage participation, and reducing levels of expenditure in order to meet economic policy goals. This is now a major issue in a number of countries.

There are many signs that governments are becoming more aware that financing policies and admissions policies must be viewed as a whole. This means that the interaction of different government policies and mechanisms are likely to be more carefully analysed in future, to ascertain whether they are in fact consistent. If direct and indirect methods of influencing and regulating student demand come to be seen as complementary mechanisms, more attention will have to be paid to the incentive or disincentive effects of different methods of financing and of different methods of students selection. Questions such as whether government subsidies should be given to students or to institutions, whether students should receive grants or loans, whether fee and fee differentials should be abolished or increased, are all concerned with the price of education. Similarly, decisions about selection procedures, the use of quotas in determining

---

19. For example, see the argument of R. Hartman, Credit for College: Public Policy for Student Loans. McGraw Hill, New York, 1971, that student loan subsidies are inefficiently distributed at present.

20. The problem of identifying students most likely to become defaulters is discussed in E.C. West, Student Loans: A Reappraisal, Ontario Economic Council Working Paper, Toronto, April 1975.

admissions or pass rates in final examinations, also influence the price of education for the individual.

Governments can influence the price of education by a wide variety of means - direct and indirect. Decisions about the supply of places, and the allocation of resources between different levels of education, the choice between different methods of finance and student aid or between different methods of selection, all help to determine the price of education for the individual student. The effects of all these decisions need, therefore, to be analysed together, to see how they interact to determine demand for higher education. As one recent American study concluded: "Policy makers must consider the inadvertent as well as the intended consequences of policy changes affecting higher education (21)".

---

21. S. Nelson, "Financial Trends and Issues" in D. Breneman and C. Finn, op. cit. p. 105.

STATISTICAL ANNEX*

Evolution of total enrolments in higher education and the corresponding age groups (1)

As shown in Table A-1 for most of the countries examined the high increase observed between 1965 and 1970 in total university enrolments slowed down quite sharply during the ensuing five-year period. Only four countries (Germany, Denmark, Spain and Yugoslavia) recorded an annual growth of 7.5 per cent or more during the early 1970s. With some exceptions, the slowdown has continued since 1975 and growth rates have even become negative in certain countries (e.g. Canada, Denmark). It should be noted that in countries where a first degree can be taken outside universities (CAE (2) in Australia, other institutions in Denmark and the United States, "Grandes Ecoles" in France) a similar trend is observed, although it is not always as pronounced.

In the few countries for which data are available, it will be seen that the number of post-graduate students also rose rapidly until around 1975, often more quickly than first degree enrolments. However, from that year on there was a slowdown in growth or even, as in the case of full-time students in the United Kingdom, a fall in numbers.

For non-university-type higher education the period of rapid growth also seems to have ended. Throughout the 1970s it still continued to expand at a more rapid pace than university education in certain countries, notably the United States, France and Greece, but this was far from being the case everywhere, especially in more recent years.

To what extent was this slowdown due to a shrinkage in the relevant age group? Table A-2 gives annual growth rates for the 20-24 age group which, although only indicative, are nonetheless a valid basis for comparing national trends. It is seen that growth

---

* This analysis was prepared by Monique Solliliage of the Secretariat.

1. Only the following countries are covered in this survey: Australia, Austria, Canada, Denmark, Finland, France, Germany, Greece, Italy, Japan, Netherlands, Spain, Sweden, United Kingdom, United States and Yugoslavia.
2. Colleges of Advanced Education.

rates for this age group are usually lower than those for student numbers, but not sufficiently so as to account for the levelling-off in expansion. In certain countries such as Canada and Australia a reverse phenomenon has started to take place: the 20-24 age group is growing at a quicker pace than the number of students.

Table A-2 also shows that, with some exceptions - in particular Japan - the 20-24 age group will diminish in size in the late 1980s and has already begun to do so in some countries. This decline will continue for a fairly long time judging by the forecasts for the 15-19 age group, whose growth rate during the period 1985-1990 is negative everywhere, except in Japan and to a smaller extent Sweden.

Proportion of students taking a postgraduate university degree

As already noted, the fall in growth rates observed since the early 1970s has affected all categories of students, whether taking a first degree or engaging in postgraduate studies, although it was not felt in the same way or at the same time. Table A-3 shows that the proportion of postgraduate students in total university enrolments varies from country to country. In Australia and Canada (full-time students) this proportion is still expanding very slightly, whereas in France, the United Kingdom (for full-time students) and Sweden it is shrinking. Almost all part-time students in the United Kingdom and a rather larger proportion of part-time than of full-time students in Canada are pursuing postgraduate studies.

Proportion of part-time students

Table A-4 shows the proportion of part-time students for five countries only. In all cases part-time students amount to 30 per cent or more of the total number of students (except for those taking a first degree in the United Kingdom) and is tending to rise, except in the Netherlands. It is higher for postgraduate students and for institutions other than universities.

University and non-university type higher education

It is clear from Table A-5 that there are great differences between countries as regards the distribution of students between these two types of higher education. In France, about 17 per cent of all students are in non-university education, whereas this proportion is more than a third in Canada and Denmark and more than 50 per cent in the Netherlands. In England and Wales it is falling quite sharply for part-time students, but in 1977 more than two thirds of part-time students were enrolled in the non-university sector. Similarly, while non-university students account for some 15 per cent of all full-time students taking a first degree in England and Wales, the figure is 30 per cent in France and 43 per cent in Canada.

New entrants to university and to non-university type higher education

The number of new entrants is more sensitive to fluctuations in supply and demand for higher education than is the number of total enrolments. Annual growth rates in university education during the period 1965-1970 were high and generally higher than for total students; on the contrary, from 1970 to 1975, most countries for which figures are available (Table A-6) witnessed a slowdown in growth, many of them with lower growth rates than for total enrolment. As a rule, this downward trend dipped more sharply after 1975, indicating a likely fall in the number of university students over the next few years.

Due to lack of data it is not possible to discern a clear trend for new entrants to non-university type education. However, since 1975 to the latest available year, the number of new entrants in this sector increased more quickly - or fell less rapidly - than in university-type education in Spain, France, Germany, and Japan, while the opposite situation prevailed in Australia and Yugoslavia.

Distribution by sex of new entrants

It is interesting to point out that the slowdown in overall growth has been accompanied in every country by an increase in the proportion of girls among new entrants to universities (Table A-7). This phenomenon was particularly marked between 1965 and 1975, especially in Spain and the Netherlands, where female participation had been lowest; it also occurred elsewhere and is continuing in the majority of countries, although at a slower pace. Around 1979, women accounted for 40 per cent or more of all new university entrants in most of the countries examined.

The situation is somewhat different in non-university education, depending in particular on whether or not this level includes training of paramedical personnel and primary and pre-primary teachers, who are mainly women. As a general rule, where female participation at this level was initially relatively small (as in Germany), it has tended to rise, but where it was large - more than half the total enrolments - it has either continued to increase though at a slower rate (Australia, Canada and the United States, for example), or has slackened slightly (Denmark).

New entrants by fields of study

Since male and female students tend to favour different disciplines, Table A-8 shows the distribution of new entrants by field of study and by sex. Category 1, including the arts, social sciences and education, accounts for more than half of the total number of new university entrants in all countries except the United Kingdom. But while between 45 and 55 per cent of all male students were enrolled in these disciplines in the latest available year (the exceptions being, on the one hand, Denmark and Sweden with over 60 per cent and the United Kingdom with 31 per cent on the other), the proportion was over two-thirds for females in most countries and over 75 per cent in Australia, the Netherlands, Sweden and Yugoslavia (the United Kingdom again constituting an exception with about 50 per cent).

Since around 1975 the proportion of new entrants in the arts and social sciences has slightly declined in a few countries - Austria, Germany, and Italy (females). Other countries such as the Netherlands, Spain, and Yugoslavia (females) witnessed the opposite trend.

The percentage of students entering science and technology varied between 30 and 40 per cent for male students and was only 15 per cent or less for female students (except in the United Kingdom, with 50 per cent and 20 per cent respectively). If only technological subjects are considered differences by sex are still greater since female participation is almost non-existent.

According to the scanty data brought together in Table A-9, roughly the same characteristics are found in non-university education as in the universities: predominance of female students in the tertiary sector, predominance of male students in subjects of a technological nature.

Age distribution of new entrants

As seen in Tables A-10 and A-11 age of entry into higher education varies considerably according to countries. In Australia, some two-thirds of all 18-year-old students are already in higher education, while this proportion is about 50 per cent in Canada, and practically nil in Germany, Denmark and Sweden. At 19, the differences are less marked but still substantial: in Australia, Canada and the United Kingdom (for full-time education) most students are in higher education, whereas they are still in secondary school in Germany, Denmark and Sweden. It should be noted that in some countries enrolment rates for these two age groups have declined since around 1975.

Owing to these differences in the internal organisation of education systems, the proportion of new entrants to university education aged 18 or under (see Table A-12) varies from 40 per cent or more in Australia (full time students), the United Kingdom, Austria, Spain, Greece and France to being practically non-existent in Germany and Finland. In every instance, girls go to university relatively earlier than boys.

Table A-12 shows the rising proportion of older students (over 25) entering university-type education in most countries. In Finland and Spain (and probably Denmark and the Netherlands if the trends observed up to 1975 have continued), this proportion is 15 per cent or more, which is far from negligible. In Sweden, where the government has taken steps to facilitate access to higher education for adults, especially those aged 25 or over and with at least 4 years' work experience, some 50 per cent of all students in 1976 were over 25, nearly half of whom had taken advantage of the 25/4 rule. Except for Sweden and Australia, more "older" students are male than female.

The age of entry and the proportion of students over 25 are particularly high in further education in the United Kingdom and in part-time education in Australia.

Table A-13 shows for the four countries for which figures are available that the situation in non-university education is less clearcut. Compared with the universities, the proportion of young new entrants - 18 and under - is smaller in France and Greece, but slightly higher in Australia and Germany, while those aged 25 or over are fewer in France, Greece and Australia (for part-time study) but higher in Germany and Australia (for full-time study).

There may be two reasons for the changing age of entry into higher education: first, secondary school leavers with the traditional qualifications for entry to higher education and, secondly, new groups are now being admitted to higher education. The scanty information given in Tables A-14 and A-15 throws some light on this problem, in spite of the small number of countries concerned.

Interval between leaving secondary school and entering higher education

Table A-14 shows that the proportion of secondary school leavers entering higher education immediately after obtaining their school-leaving certificate is very high in Australia (for full-time education), France and the Netherlands, but only slightly over 50 per cent for high school graduates in the United States, where it has shrunk considerably since 1965. The drop also observed in Australia is not really sufficient on its own to explain the higher average of university entry mentioned in the last section. The opposite trend is found in France where the increase in the proportion of secondary school leavers proceeding directly to higher education may explain the rising percentage of new students aged 18 or under.

School or other background of new entrants into higher education

From the figures given in Table A-15 it is not possible to conclude - at least for those countries which are listed - that higher education as a whole has thrown open its doors to new categories of students. Indeed, except in Sweden and Denmark (mainly for the non-university level "Teknika") the great majority of new entrants consists of young people who have successfully completed their general secondary education. In fact, except in Italy, even technical secondary school-leavers are only marginally represented. Even in France, which introduced an examination for candidates with no baccalauréat and provided greater facilities of access, the percentage of new entrants without traditional qualifications was no more than 3.5 in 1975, fell to 1.2 in 1977 for the university sector (including IUTs)(3) and continued to hover around 2.5, for the IUTs alone. Among all the countries Sweden has the highest percentage of new entrants with a non-traditional background. Priority students and those covered by the 25/4 rule accounted in

---

3. Instituts universitaires de technologie.

1976 for over 30 per cent of the total number of university new entrants, while the proportion of "Gymnasium" graduates fell from 86 per cent in 1968 to 54 per cent in 1976. However, the trend appears to have reversed slightly since 1976, with a relative rise in traditional students and a decline in other categories.

Rates of transfer from secondary to higher education

Since in most countries secondary school-leavers still form the majority of new entrants in higher education it seemed interesting to show (Table A-16) rates of transfer from secondary to higher education for the few countries where data are available. In most European countries where secondary education is quite selective, i.e. only a small segment of an age group qualifies for access to higher education, rates of transfer are very high compared to, say, Canada and the United States, where secondary education is comprehensive. Moreover, judging by experience in France, entry into the university or non-university sector depends very much on the type of certificate obtained. In this country, holders of a technician's baccalauréat are not only much less likely to go on to higher studies than their peers with general baccalauréat but, when they do so, tend to enter the non-university sector. Similarly, in the United Kingdom, far more pupils with high grades go to university (66 per cent males, 55 per cent females) than to further education (15 per cent males, 23 per cent females), whereas the reverse is the case for less successful pupils.

In France, transfer rates both for holders of a general baccalauréat and a technician's baccalauréat are rising, whereas they are falling in Canada, Denmark (up to 1975), the Netherlands and the United Kingdom.

To conclude, the proportion of secondary school-leavers proceeding directly to higher education appears to be declining in certain countries at least, while the proportion of those delaying their entry is rising. However, these two trends are not counterbalancing and since in the majority of countries higher education has not opened its doors to new groups to any significant extent, the number of new entrants and students is falling in relative terms - in both the university and non-university sectors. Should the above trends continue, this relative decline has every chance of becoming an absolute decline when combined with the dwindling size of the age groups typically entering higher education.

Table A-1

ANNUAL GROWTH RATE OF UNIVERSITY (U) ENROLMENTS
ACCORDING TO DEGREE STUDIED AND NON-UNIVERSITY (NU)
ENROLMENTS IN HIGHER EDUCATION

Percentages

	1965-70	1970-75	1975-76	1976-77	1977-78	1978-79
GERMANY FT						
U	6.4	10.6	3.6	3.8	3.4	3.6
NU	3.3	10.2	8.2	5.3	4.5	5.6
AUSTRALIA FT + PT						
U 1st degree	6.0	4.2	3.7	2.2	1.3	0.2
Master		9.9	5.1	5.7	3.1	4.5
Doctorate		2.7	6.0	3.8	5.5	1.7
Not studying for a degree	4.5	4.6	2.6	6.8	- 4.8	- 2.5
CAE 1st degree			22.5	23.3	17.7	12.2
Master			41.3	21.2	25.8	30.1
Postgraduate degrees			4.7	18.5	18.9	16.2
Diploma and associate diploma			2.6	- 9.1	- 3.9	- 7.2
AUSTRIA						
U	1.9	9.4	8.7	7.8	8.4	8.5
CANADA FT						
U 1st degree	8.1	3.7	1.6	- 0.7	- 2.0	0.9
Postgraduate degrees		3.8	1.8	0.2	1.2	0.5
PT						
U 1st degree	16.8	2.2	3.2	12.1	2.0	6.7
Postgraduate degrees			2.6	3.2	3.5	3.4
NU	19.1	5.9	2.5	6.4	2.6	1.5
DENMARK						
Universities	9.0	7.8	4.9	- 1.5	- 2.1	- 5.6
Other institutions	5.4	6.4	7.1	5.8	1.6	0
NU	7.0	6.3	-16.5	- 3.4	- 5.3	0.3
SPAIN						
U	11.1	13.1	5.5	14.9	- 5.8	
NU	11.5	4.5	13.9	11.9	- 1.7	
UNITED STATES						
4-year institutions FT	6.4	1.8	- 0.5	1.9	- 0.6	1.9
4-year institutions PT	6.1	4.5	- 2.8	1.5	0.9	1.4
2-year institutions FT	18.6	8.9	- 5.4	- 0.4	- 5.7	1.9
2-year institutions PT	25.0	15.9	0.5	7.6	3.4	6.3

FT = full-time
PT = part-time

Table A-1 (contd)

Percentages

	1965-70	1970-75	1975-76	1976-77	1977-78	1978-79
FRANCE						
U 1st and 2nd cycles	9.4	1.5	1.5	2.2	2.0	4.3(2)
3rd cycle	10.3	18.3	0.6	- 0.3	1.4	- 0.6(2)
Grandes Ecoles(1)	4.1	16.4	- 6.3	2.7		
NU	7.4	7.0	0.4	9.6	0.4	
GREECE						
U	5.9	5.7	- 0.4	1.7		
NU	6.9	9.5	26.9	-18.0		
ITALY						
U	11.0	6.5	4.9			
JAPAN						
U 1st degree	8.5	4.2	3.0	2.6	1.3	- 0.8
Master	10.5	5.1	1.7	1.9	- 1.9	- 2.2
Doctorate	2.4	2.4	5.4	4.5	4.3	4.7
Junior College NU	12.3	6.1	3.1	2.5	1.6	- 1.7
NETHERLANDS						
U	9.8	0.3	5.9	6.3	4.3	6.7
NU FT		5.7	10.4	4.7	4.7	2.0
NU PT		- 0.1	3.4	3.1	- 0.5	1.7
UNITED KINGDOM FT						
U 1st degree (3)	2.5(4)	2.5(5)	4.6	4.5	3.1	2.5
Postgraduate (3)	5.7(4)	3.4(5)	0.6	- 2.7	0.8	- 3.0
Further education (6)	5.0(4)	2.5(5)	- 4.5	- 5.0	- 4.2	
PT						
U 1st degree (3)	- 5.3(4)	0.5(5)	- 0.1	9.4	- 2.4	7.2
Postgraduate (3)	15.7(4)	3.2(5)	4.5	4.2	3.7	5.9
Further education (6)	- 1.2(4)	3.7(5)	2.3	8.2	8.7	
SWEDEN						
U Total	12.6	- 1.7	3.5		5.7	- 1.5
of which Postgraduate	11.6	3.3	4.8		2.5	3.1
YUGOSLAVIA						
U	8.6	9.1	4.9	6.5		
NU	3.2	7.6	- 1.4	0.3		
U Regular students only	10.0	6.9	4.4	6.9	6.0	
NU	5.2	1.8	15.8	2.4	0.2	

1. As the number of schools taken into account may vary from year to year the data are not really comparable.
2. 1978-80.
3. Universities only.
4. 1968-71.
5. 1971-75.
6. Including evening classes.

FT = full-time;   PT = part-time

Source : National statistics.

Table A-2

ANNUAL GROWTH RATE OF THE 20-24 AGE GROUP

Percentages

	Observed					Forecast		15-19 age group
	1965-70	1970-75	1975-76	1976-77	1977-78	1978-80	1980-85	1985-90	1985-90
GERMANY	- 0.5	1.3	0.9	1.6	2.6	1.6	2.4	- 1.3	- 8.4
AUSTRALIA	5.1	1.5	0.4	1.2	1.6	0.6	0.7	0.5	- 0.1
AUSTRIA	- 0.6	0.6	1.4	3.9	2.1	1.2	2.7	- 2.3	- 3.8
CANADA	5.7	2.7	2.7	3.0	2.3	0.8	0.6	- 3.4	- 1.3
DENMARK	- 0.6	- 0.3	- 0.5	0.3	0.3	0	1.3	0	- 1.3
SPAIN	2.9	1.0	2.2	2.3	0.9	2.1	1.0	0.3	0.3
UNITED STATES	4.6	2.3	2.1	2.3	1.8	1.2	- 0.4	- 2.6	- 1.4
FINLAND	5.5	- 1.2	- 1.3	- 1.6	- 3.7	- 0.8	- 0.4	- 1.8	- 3.1
FRANCE	7.2	1.0	- 0.8	- 0.2	- 0.2	0.1	0.2	- 0.6	- 0.3
GREECE	1.6	0.1	2.1	1.1	2.0	1.7	0.4	1.0	- 1.6
JAPAN	3.3	- 3.2	- 4.7	- 4.3	- 2.2	- 1.3	0.7	1.9	2.2
ITALY	5.3 ←0.9→	- 0.1	1.3	1.3	- 2.0	1.8	0.3	- 1.1
NETHERLANDS	5.3	- 0.9	0.9	0.9	0.9	1.2	1.1	- 0.5	- 3.1
UNITED KINGDOM	3.8	- 2.4	0.8	1.3	1.3	2.0	2.3	- 0.7	- 2.7
SWEDEN	2.6	- 3.5	- 0.7	0.2	- 0.7	0	1.0	0.5	- 1.0
YUGOSLAVIA		3.2	0.9	--	--	1.0	- 1.6	- 0.5	- 0.3

Source: OECD data file.

Table A-3

STUDENT DISTRIBUTION ACCORDING TO LEVEL OF
DEGREE STUDIED (UNIVERSITY EDUCATION)

Percentages

	1965	1970	1975	1976	1977	1978	1979
AUSTRALIA							
U 1st degree	84.4	82.1	81.0	80.9	80.4	80.5	80.3
Master	⎫ 7.1	6.5	7.9	8.0	8.2	8.4	8.7
Doctorate	⎭	3.6	3.4	3.4	3.5	3.6	3.7
Not studying for a degree	8.5	7.8	7.7	7.7	7.9	7.5	7.3
CAE 1st degree			30.8		40.7	44.8	48.4
Master			0.2		0.4	0.5	0.6
Postgraduate degree			6.9		8.3	9.3	10.4
Diploma and associate			62.1		50.6	45.5	40.6
CANADA FT							
1st degree		89.3	89.2	89.2	89.1	88.8	88.8
Postgraduate		10.7	10.8	10.8	10.9	11.2	11.2
PT							
1st degree				85.5	86.5	86.3	86.7
Postgraduate				14.5	13.5	13.7	13.3
DENMARK							
Universities	76.3	78.6	81.9	81.6	80.5	79.9	79.00
Other institutions	23.7	21.4	18.1	18.4	19.5	20.1	21.00
UNITED STATES							
1st degree	85.1	83.6	82.5	81.3	81.8	81.9	81.5
Post graduate	14.9	16.4	17.5	18.7	18.2	18.1	18.5
							(1980)
FRANCE (1)							
1st and 2nd cycles	76.3	78.8	67.4	68.3	68.6		69.9
3rd cycle	9.7	10.5	16.6	16.7	16.3		15.1
Grandes Ecoles	14.0	10.8	16.0	15.0	15.1		15.0
JAPAN							
1st degree	95.5	95.6	95.3	95.0	95.0	95.0	95.0
Master	1.2	2.0	2.1	2.0	2.0	1.9	1.9
Doctorate	1.2	0.9	0.9	0.9	0.9	0.9	1.0
Other	2.0	1.5	1.7	2.1	2.1	2.2	2.1
UNITED KINGDOM (2)							
1st degree FT	82.3	81.0	81.1	81.7	82.8	83.1	83.9
Postgraduate FT	17.7	19.0	18.9	18.3	17.2	16.9	16.1
1st degree PT	36.9	15.7	14.4	13.9	14.6	13.9	14.3
Postgraduate PT	63.1	84.3	85.6	86.1	85.4	86.1	85.7
SWEDEN							
1st degree	89.3	89.8	86.8	86.6	89.4	89.7	89.3
Postgraduate	10.7	10.2	13.2	13.4	10.6	10.3	10.7

FT = full-time
PT = part-time

1. As the number of "grandes ecoles" taken into account may vary from year to year the data are not really comparable.
2. Universities only.

Source : National statistics

215

Table A-4

PART-TIME STUDENTS AS A PERCENTAGE OF TOTAL STUDENTS

Percentages

	1965	1970	1975	1976	1977	1978	1979
AUSTRALIA							
Universities		36.9	34.5	34.7	35.0	36.7	38.4
CAE			39.0	38.6	39.5	43.8	47.3
CANADA							
1st degree	25.9	34.0	32.4	32.7	35.4	36.4	37.7
Postgraduate			40.4	40.6	41.3	41.8	42.5
UNITED STATES							
4-year institutions	27.2	26.9	29.6	29.1	29.0	29.3	29.2
2-year institutions	41.1	47.5	55.3	56.8	58.7	60.9	61.9
NETHERLANDS							
NU		40.1	36.2	33.2	32.8	31.7	31.6
UNITED KINGDOM							
Universities, 1st degree	2.7(1)	1.9(2)	1.7	1.6	1.7	1.6	1.7
Universities, Postgraduate	30.4(1)	30.4(2)	30.7	32.1	33.2	33.8	35.8
Further education (advanced)	37.7(1)	33.6(2)	34.7	36.2	39.3	42.3	

1. 1968.   2. 1971

Source : National statistics

Table A-5

NON-UNIVERSITY (NU) HIGHER EDUCATION ENROLMENTS
AS A PERCENTAGE OF TOTAL HIGHER EDUCATION
ENROLMENTS (T) AND OF THE
NUMBER OF STUDENTS 1st DEGREE (D)

Percentages

	1965	1970	1975	1976	1977	1978	1979
GERMANY							
NU/T	19.8	17.5	17.7	17.9	18.9	18.3	18.5
AUSTRALIA							
NU/T			28.1	27.1	23.8	22.0	20.0
NU/D			48.2	45.7	38.5	34.6	30.9
CANADA							
NU/T FT		34.9	37.4	37.6	39.2	40.8	40.7
NU/D FT		37.5	40.1	40.3	42.0	43.1	43.3
DENMARK							
NU/T	36.3	32.0	40.5	35.0	34.3	33.4	34.5
SPAIN							
NU/T	34.2	34.6	26.3	27.9	27.3	28.2	
UNITED STATES							
NU/T FT	12.6	19.9	25.8	24.9	24.5	23.5	23.5
NU/T PT	21.3	38.0	50.7	51.5	53.0	53.6	54.7
FRANCE							
NU/T	16.6	15.5	16.3	16.4	17.4	--	
NU/D	26.1	23.4	28.9	28.6	30.7	30.2	
GREECE							
NU/T	15.4	16.1	18.7	22.6	19.1		
NETHERLANDS							
NU/T FT+PT		54.4	56.7	57.6	55.7	56.8	55.7
NU/T FT		41.7	45.5	47.6	47.2	47.3	46.2
UNITED KINGDOM (England and Wales)							
NU/T FT	11.1	11.9	10.6		11.9		
NU/D FT	14.0	15.5	13.7		15.6		
NU/T PT	83.6	73.6	73.4		67.1		
YUGOSLAVIA							
NU/T(1)	25.9	22.6	17.9	19.5	18.8	17.9	
NU/T(2)	58.9	57.1	50.9	46.5	44.9	41.1	

FT = full-time   PT = part-time

1. Regular students
2. Non regular students

Source : National statistics

Table A-6

ANNUAL GROWTH RATE OF THE NUMBER OF NEW ENTRANTS TO
UNIVERSITY (U) AND NON-UNIVERSITY (NU)
HIGHER EDUCATION

Percentages

	1965-70	1970-75	1975-76	1976-77	1977-78	1978-79	1979-80
GERMANY (1)							
U	8.3	5.3	-1.0	-0.5	6.3	-0.3	8.2
NU	6.9	7.5	6.2	-4.3	-1.6	12.1	14.7
AUSTRALIA							
University level		20.5(2)		5.5(3)	8.7	3.8	
CAE (Diploma/Associate diploma)				-11.6(3)	2.5	-10.4	
AUSTRIA							
University			1.0(4)		10.5(5)	13.3	
CANADA							
U		3.6(6)	2.8				
NU		5.6(6)	0.8				
DENMARK							
U	7.5	5.3	-7.2	-10.6	-1.6	-0.7	3.9
NU			1.0		-0.7(7)	-5.0(7)	
SPAIN							
U	16.6(8)	8.8(8)	1.1	6.5			
NU			8.8	14.5			
UNITED STATES							
U	1.5	0.3	-3.1	1.4	0.1	2.9	0.2
NU	10.3	8.3	-9.6	3.1	-0.8	6.5	4.4
FINLAND							
U	-0.6	5.2	0.0	-4.8	-5.0	5.3	
NU	3.6	3.1					
FRANCE							
U		6.9(9)	-2.2	0.3	1.7		
NU (IUT and higher technicians)		10.2(6)	1.9	10.4	4.1		
ITALY (10)							
University	13.0	4.5	-0.1	-2.9	5.4	-2.2	-0.7
JAPAN							
U	5.9	4.9	-0.8	1.9	-0.6	-4.3	
NU	9.5	6.7	-0.1	4.9	-1.1	-2.3	
NETHERLANDS							
University (10)	7.9		5.2	8.5	-0.5		
UNITED KINGDOM							
Universities	3.3(11)	3.0	3.1	4.7	2.2		
SWEDEN							
University		-0.3	8.1				
YUGOSLAVIA (10)							
(All students)							
U	8.6(12)	7.8(13)	0.3	5.1	8.1		
NU	2.0(12)	8.9(13)	-3.6	-1.4	-3.0		

1. Excluding foreign students in 1965.
2. 1973-75. University only.
3. 1975-77.
4. 1972-74.
5. 1974-78.
6. 1971-75.
7. Excluding pre-primary teacher training.
8. Excluding university colleges.
9. 1965-75.
10. First year students and for the Netherlands Dutch students only as from 1975.
11. 1968-70.
12. 1965-69.
13. 1969-75.

<u>Source</u> : National statistics.

Table A-7

PROPORTION OF WOMEN AMONG NEW ENTRANTS TO UNIVERSITY (U) AND NON-UNIVERSITY (NU) HIGHER EDUCATION

Percentages

	1965	1970	1975	1976	1977	1978	1979
GERMANY							
U	32.4	37.8	41.1	38.5	42.8	42.9	41.6
NU		15.0	24.0	24.5	28.1	30.8	32.2
AUSTRALIA FT and PT							
Universities		38.7(1)	40.9	41.4	42.2	43.4	44.8
CAE (Bachelor)		24.7(2)	26.8		36.6	38.7	43.0
CAE (diploma, associate diploma)			58.5		61.3	63.2	63.7
AUSTRIA		(1972)	(1974)				
U		37.8	44.0			47.0	46.2
CANADA							
U		43.0	46.0	46.1			
NU		50.5	57.5	57.7			
DENMARK	(1966)						
U	28.5	31.5	36.4	39.4	38.8	39.4	40.5
NU				58.4	49.8(3)	49.0(3)	47.1(3)
SPAIN							
U	24.2	28.1	37.7	39.0	39.9		
NU			35.4	38.6	40.1		
UNITED STATES							
U	43.7	45.9	48.6	49.6	50.5	50.8	51.2
NU	39.6	42.2	46.1	50.8	52.9	53.7	54.5
FINLAND							
U	50.8	47.1	51.6	51.6	51.5	51.1	50.8
NU	56.3	62.0	65.8				
ITALY							
U		36.5	40.6	41.5	42.7		
GREECE							
U	34.7	31.4	39.2	39.6			
NU			36.4	34.8			
NETHERLANDS							
U	19.0	21.6	30.4	31.2	32.1	33.3	
UNITED KINGDOM	(1968)						
Universities	29.8	31.9	35.2	35.6	36.2	37.7	39.5
SWEDEN							
U		41.4	46.9	47.9			
YUGOSLAVIA		(1969)					
U	35.9	38.5	40.0	39.0	38.4	38.4	
NU	35.6	42.5	38.3	37.7	37.4	38.7	

FT = full-time
PT = part-time

1. 1973.
2. 1971.
3. Excluding pre-primary teacher training

Source : National statistics

Table A-8

DISTRIBUTION OF NEW ENTRANTS TO HIGHER EDUCATION
BY FIELD OF STUDY

Percentages

	1965 M	1965 F	1970 M	1970 F	1975 M	1975 F	1976 M	1976 F	1977 M	1977 F	1978 M	1978 F
GERMANY			1973									
Arts, social sciences			55.9		46.1	61.8	44.7	63.3	44.4	61.0	45.4	61.4
Science			22.4		22.8	18.8	20.7	17.9	19.8	18.7	19.8	18.3
Technology			9.8		19.4	2.4	23.1	2.6	22.5	2.9	20.2	2.4
Medicine			4.2		4.7	3.6	4.9	5.1	6.6	5.6	7.1	6.0
Other			7.7		6.9	13.4	6.5	11.1	6.7	11.7	7.5	11.8
AUSTRALIA (1)			1973									
Arts, social sciences, education			50.8	73.7	56.4	76.7	55.8	75.7	55.3	76.4	55.5	75.1
Science			20.5	15.8	19.6	13.6	19.8	14.6	20.4	14.1	20.3	15.2
Technology			14.5	0.5	12.2	0.5	11.8	0.4	11.7	0.4	12.1	0.9
Medicine			7.9	6.9	5.9	6.1	6.3	5.7	6.6	5.7	6.6	5.3
Other			6.8	3.2	5.9	3.1	6.3	3.6	5.9	3.4	5.3	3.5
AUSTRIA			1972		1974							
Arts, social sciences, education			55.4	76.5	52.9	72.5					47.3	65.2
Science			..	..	..	..					8.3	9.7
Technology			25.0	5.9	27.5	5.0					22.2	3.2
Medicine			14.3	17.6	15.7	20.0					15.3	19.4
Other			5.4	–	3.9	2.5					6.9	2.5
DENMARK (2)	1966											
Arts, social sciences, education	39.3	68.4	41.6	64.2	59.1	74.4			62.5	73.2		
Science	13.0	9.0	13.3	7.4	13.7	5.6			9.5	5.1		
Technology	19.7	1.5	16.9	2.8	9.9	1.1			16.9	3.0		
Medicine	18.5	18.9	14.5	18.1	11.0	15.6			4.7	12.7		
Other	9.5	2.3	13.6	7.5	6.3	3.3			6.5	6.0		
SPAIN (University type) (3)												
Arts, social sciences, education	34.8	54.5	35.8	58.0	42.2	52.8	46.4	54.8	49.2	57.2		
Science	28.5	24.7	19.8	20.8	14.8	15.1	14.0	13.1	13.9	13.3		
Technology	12.3	0.6	25.1	3.0	20.3	2.6	17.2	2.5	17.6	3.0		
Medicine	24.0	19.9	18.3	17.4	21.1	28.9	21.0	29.1	17.5	25.7		
Other	0.4	0.3	1.0	0.8	1.6	0.6	1.4	0.5	1.8	0.8		
FINLAND												
Arts, social sciences, education					49.8	71.6			47.0	71.7	49.3	73.4
Science					18.4	15.4			44.3	18.5	43.1	17.3
Technology					26.3	6.9						
Medicine					5.5	6.1			6.2	8.4	5.5	8.0
Other									2.5	1.4	2.1	1.3

1. Universities only.
2. According to the classification by institution up to 1976 and by level of study for 1977.
3. Universities, higher technical schools and university colleges, excluding the latter in 1965 and 1970.

Table A-8 (contd)

Percentages

	1965 M F	1970 M F	1975 M F	1976 M F	1977 M F	1978 M F
FRANCE (Universities and engineering schools)						
Arts, social sciences			60.6	60.0	59.3	59.3
Science			13.8	14.7	15.5	15.9
Technology			4.7	4.2	4.5	4.5
Medicine			17.1	17.3	16.0	15.0
Other			3.8	3.9	4.6	5.3
ITALY (4)						
Arts, social sciences	61.7	45.5 74.5	44.2 64.3	45.1 62.8		
Science	14.1	15.0 13.5	12.1 17.2	11.6 17.2		
Technology	13.3	21.1 2.8	21.5 4.0	21.1 4.4		
Medicine	7.0	14.3 6.8	15.6 11.1	14.7 11.3		
Other	3.9	4.1 2.4	6.6 3.6	7.5 4.4		
NETHERLANDS (4)						
Arts, social sciences	46.3 69.2	51.0 70.1	50.7 77.0	51.9 77.4	52.2 78.3	52.4 79.3
Science	14.0 10.6	13.1 9.8	14.9 7.7	14.5 7.6	14.8 7.4	13.7 6.9
Technology	22.0 2.1	21.9 2.9	18.5 1.8	18.7 1.6	19.7 1.9	20.0 2.3
Medicine	14.2 15.3	10.5 13.4	10.4 9.1	9.4 9.1	8.1 8.5	8.5 7.6
Other	3.4 2.9	3.5 3.8	5.5 4.4	5.4 4.4	5.1 3.8	5.4 3.9
UNITED KINGDOM (Universities)	68/69					
Arts, social sciences, education	29.2 52.3	28.5 47.9	31.9 49.7	31.2 49.5	31.0 49.8	31.0 50.6
Science	30.0 24.6	28.7 22.4	26.0 19.9	26.0 19.7	26.1 20.0	26.8 19.8
Technology	23.1 0.9	23.1 1.3	21.5 1.7	22.4 2.0	22.9 2.3	22.5 2.4
Medicine	8.5 8.1	8.8 9.2	9.2 9.9	8.9 9.9	8.6 10.1	8.5 9.7
Other	9.2 14.0	10.8 19.2	11.6 18.8	11.4 18.8	11.5 17.7	11.2 17.5
SWEDEN						
Arts, social sciences, education	59.6 82.8	67.2 84.7	65.1 84.5	66.4 84.6		
Science	21.1 10.3	17.4 7.1	13.8 6.4	12.8 6.4		
Technology	13.5 0.9	11.5 1.3	15.4 1.9	15.3 2.3		
Medicine	3.9 5.2	2.6 5.2	4.0 5.5	3.9 5.0		
Other	1.8 0.8	1.0 0.9	1.2 1.0	1.1 1.0		
YUGOSLAVIA (4)		1969				
Arts, social sciences, education	42.1 58.2	49.3 64.1	53.6 71.4	52.4 71.8	50.1 75.2	
Science	7.4 9.9	5.4 8.6	5.5 6.6	5.5 6.3	5.2 6.1	
Technology	35.2 15.1	34.0 12.5	30.0 9.5	31.7 9.5	33.2 9.5	
Medicine	6.0 11.5	3.9 8.3	3.5 7.8	3.2 7.8	3.4 7.6	
Other	9.4 5.3	11.2 6.4	7.5 4.7	7.3 4.5	8.2 4.6	

4. First-year students.

Source : National statistics

Table A-9

DISTRIBUTION OF NEW ENTRANTS TO NON-UNIVERSITY
HIGHER EDUCATION BY FIELD OF STUDY

Percentages

	1965 M	1965 F	1970 M	1970 F	1975 M	1975 F	1976 M	1976 F	1977 M	1977 F	1978 M	1978 F
GERMANY												
Arts, social sciences			40.4		27.9	64.7	29.3	64.6	29.5	66.8	30.4	69.3
Science			1.9		2.4	1.9	2.6	2.1	2.1	1.8	2.6	2.1
Technology			51.1		63.7	18.1	62.3	17.7	61.5	16.8	60.3	14.3
Other			6.5		6.0	15.3	5.9	15.5	7.0	14.6	6.7	14.2
AUSTRALIA (1)												
Arts, social sciences, education					68.1	83.2			64.5	80.5	57.3	78.4
Science					-	-			-	-	-	-
Technology					9.6	0.7			11.7	1.4	16.4	3.0
Medicine					3.9	6.3			4.7	8.4	4.6	7.9
Other					18.4	9.8			19.1	9.7	21.7	10.7
DENMARK												
Arts, social sciences, education					76.3	54.7	59.7	51.4	29.0	67.9		
Technology					8.6	0.1	23.6	0.2	31.0	1.4		
Medicine					12.0	44.4	10.7	47.7	4.8	28.8		
Other					3.0	0.8	6.0	0.7	35.2	1.8		
FINLAND												
Arts, social sciences, education	28.4		29.2		26.9							
Technology	27.1		27.7		30.3							
Medicine	41.7		39.0		39.4							
Other	2.7		4.0		3.5							
SPAIN (University schools)												
Arts, social sciences, education					39.3	93.7	40.6	94.0	42.8	93.4		
Technology					60.7	6.3	59.4	6.0	57.2	6.6		
FRANCE												
Primary and secondary sectors			53.9		47.7		40.3		41.1		41.8	
Tertiary sector			46.1		52.3		44.3		45.2		48.2	
Education			-		-		15.4		13.6		9.9	
YUGOSLAVIA (2)			1969									
Arts, social sciences, education	70.3	89.5	63.7	85.8	63.0	83.4	65.2	83.0	67.2	82.7		
Science	-	-	-	-	-	-	-	-	-	-		
Technology	25.9	5.0	31.8	7.8	34.5	9.3	31.9	8.5	29.8	8.0		
Medicine	1.3	5.0	1.0	5.6	1.1	6.7	0.9	7.6	0.9	8.4		
Other	2.5	0.5	3.6	0.9	1.4	0.6	2.0	0.9	2.1	0.9		

1. Diploma and Associate Diploma in the CAE.
2. First-year students, regular or not.

Source : National statistics

Table A-10

ENROLMENT RATES AT 18 BY TYPE OF EDUCATION

Percentages

	1965	1970	1975	1976	1977	1978	1979
GERMANY							
Secondary, 1st cycle	0.4	0.4	0.7		0.5	0.6	0.5
Secondary, 2nd cycle (1)							
- general	9.0	10.9	15.4		15.3	15.7	17.6
- technical/vocational FT	4.4	7.3	8.9		9.1	9.4	9.8
- " " PT	25.0	28.2	34.3		37.3	39.2	42.0
Higher							
- University	0.0	0.9	0.7		0.7	0.7	..
- Non-university	0.1	0.3	0.4		0.3	0.2	..
Total (2)	38.8	48.0	60.4		63.2	65.8	
	(13.8)	(19.8)	(26.1)		(25.9)	(26.6)	
AUSTRALIA (3)							
Secondary, 1st cycle	0.2	-	-				
Secondary, 2nd cycle	4.9	7.6	6.7				6.6
Higher							
- Universities	..	7.2	7.5				6.6
- CAE	..	1.9	6.8				6.3
Total		16.7	21.0				19.5
AUSTRIA							
Secondary							
- general and teacher training			8.9	9.6	6.8		
- technical/vocational FT and PT			28.4	28.8	34.1		
Higher			..	4.3	4.1		
Total				42.7	45.0		
CANADA		(1971)					(1980)
Secondary		27.3	23.7		20.9		20.3
Post-secondary		16.5	19.3		19.4		18.6
Total		43.8	43.0		40.3		38.9
DENMARK							
Basic school					1.0		
Secondary, 2nd cycle							
- general					22.8		
- technical/vocational					30.1		
Higher							
- short					0.3		
- medium					0.1		
- long					0.4		
Total					55.3(4)		
SPAIN							
Secondary, general and teacher training	5.1	7.8	9.9	11.5	10.5	12.2	
Technical/vocational	2.2	4.9	5.8	6.4	7.3	6.9	
Other secondary	0.6	1.5	1.8	1.9	1.4	1.3	
Higher	3.0	5.2	11.2	13.2	14.3	12.2	
Total	10.9	19.4	28.7	33.1	33.5	32.6	
FRANCE							
Secondary, 1st cycle	0.5	0.1	0.1	0.1	0.0	0.0	0.0
Short vocational	3.5	5.1	5.8	5.8	5.9	6.2	6.7
Secondary, 2nd cycle	16.9	17.8	17.7	18.0	18.1	18.6	19.3
Higher technicians	0.6	0.6	0.8	1.0	1.2	1.2	1.2
Universities (5)	4.9	..	9.1	9.4	..	..	..
Total	26.4		33.5	34.3			

FT = full-time   PT = part-time

1. Including some pupils in part-time education.
2. The first figure refers to total full-time and part-time education and the figure between brackets to full-time education only.
3. Excluding apprenticeship and the TAFE.
4. Including some 200 pupils not distributed by level.
5. Including the preparatory classes for the Grandes Ecoles.

Table A-10 (contd)

Percentages

	1965	1970	1975	1976	1977	1978	1979
GREECE							
Secondary, general		13.0	14.2				
Secondary, technical/vocational		8.5	11.3				
Non-university		2.4	2.1				
University		5.2	7.3				
Total		29.1	34.9				
ITALY	(1966)						
Secondary, general and teacher training	7.7		32.9				
Technical and vocational	12.4						
NETHERLANDS		M F	M F	M F	M F	M F	M F
1st cycle secondary							
- general		2.4 1.4	2.6 1.7	3.1 2.1	3.2 2.1	3.1 2.2	3.2 2.5
- vocational		3.0 0.3	3.9 0.5	5.9 1.2	5.9 1.4	5.6 1.5	5.3 1.6
2nd cycle secondary							
- general		13.5 6.6	16.2 10.2	17.4 11.7	17.6 12.2	17.5 12.9	17.2 13.3
- vocational/technical		10.9 6.2	13.2 7.3	15.1 9.0	15.7 11.3	15.9 12.9	16.7 13.7
Higher							
- university		4.3 1.4	3.5 1.7	.. ..	.. ..	3.9 2.0	.. ..
- non-university		4.9 4.9	5.7 5.4	5.9 6.1	5.8 6.4	5.8 6.2	5.5 5.7
Part-time education		23.1 5.8	16.6 10.4	13.9 5.0	14.7 5.5	13.9 5.8	
Total (2)		62.1 26.7	61.7 37.1			65.6 43.5	
		(39.0)(20.9)	(45.1)(26.7)			(51.7)(37.7)	
UNITED KINGDOM FT							
Secondary		6.4	6.2	6.6	6.4		
Further education, non-advanced (6)		3.8	5.1	5.6	5.7		
Higher		7.4	7.0	6.8	6.7		
Advanced courses PT (6)				0.5	0.6		
Non-advanced PT		25.4	26.0	24.6	23.3		
Total		43.0	44.4	44.1	42.7		
		(17.6)	(18.4)	(19.0)	(18.8)		
SWEDEN		(1969)					
Secondary		39.9	34.4			35.0	
Higher		0.2	0.2			0.8	
Total		40.7	34.6			35.8	
YUGOSLAVIA							
- Skilled worker training	15.0		18.4				
- Other technical/vocational schools	12.6		17.0				
- Secondary, general/teacher training	13.0		14.1				
- Higher	..		..				

6. Including evening classes.

Source: National statistics.

Table A-11

ENROLMENT RATES AT 19 BY TYPE OF EDUCATION

Percentages

	1965	1970	1975	1976	1977	1978	1979
GERMANY							
Secondary, 1st cycle	0.0	0.2	0.1		0.2	0.2	
Secondary, 2nd cycle (1)							
- general	6.2	5.0	7.4		7.0	6.6	
- technical/vocational FT	3.4	6.1	7.4		8.2	8.2	
- technical/vocational PT	9.4	9.4	13.7		16.9	18.4	
Higher							
- university	0.7	3.6	4.2		3.7	3.5	
- non-university FT	0.5	1.1					
- non-university PT	0.1	0.1	0.9		0.9	0.8	
Total (2)	20.2	25.5	33.7		36.9	37.7	
	(10.8)	(16.1)	(20.0)		(20.0)	(19.3)	
AUSTRALIA (3)		(1971)					
Secondary, 2nd cycle		1.1	1.4				1.4
Higher							
- university		6.5	7.2				6.8
- CAE		1.9	6.4				6.5
Total		9.5	15.0				14.7
AUSTRIA							
Secondary							
- general and teacher training			2.1	2.3	..		
- technical/vocational FT and PT			10.3	10.8	..		
Higher			..	7.9	7.5		
Total				21.0			
CANADA		(1971)					(1980)
Secondary		7.5	5.7		4.0		3.6
Post-secondary		22.4	24.2		24.3		23.0
Total		29.9	29.9		28.3		26.6
DENMARK							
Basic school					0.3		
Secondary, 2nd cycle							
- general					12.8		
- technical/vocational					28.6		
Higher							
- short					0.2		
- medium					0.7		
- long					3.1		
Total					47.7(4)		
SPAIN							
Secondary, general	3.6	4.9	4.8	5.8	6.0	5.3	
Technical and vocational	2.6	4.3	3.9	4.2	4.4	4.2	
Other secondary	0.4	1.1	1.7	1.6	1.4	1.3	
Higher	3.2	6.7	12.2	14.4	14.4	15.1	
Total	9.8	17.0	22.6	26.1	26.2	25.9	
FRANCE							
Vocational, short	1.5	1.7	1.5	1.5	1.6	1.6	
Secondary, 2nd cycle	8.3	7.9	6.8	6.1	6.3	6.4	
Higher technicians	1.4	1.3	1.4	1.7	1.9	1.9	
Universities (5)	7.1	..	12.2	12.9	..	..	
Total	18.3		21.9	22.2			
GREECE		(1972)					
Secondary, general		4.8	5.3				
Secondary, technical/vocational		8.1	13.2				
Non-university		2.6	4.0				
University		6.9	10.9				
Total		22.4	33.4				

FT = full-time   PT = part-time

1. Including some pupils in part-time education.
2. The first figure refers to total full-time and part-time education and the figure between brackets to full-time education only.
3. Excluding apprenticeship and the TAFE.
4. Including some 500 pupils not distributed by level.
5. Including the preparatory classes for the Grandes Ecoles.

Table A-11 (contd)

Percentages

	1965	1970	1975	1976	1977	1978	1979
ITALY							
Secondary, general and teacher training	3.7						
Technical and vocational	7.8						
NETHERLANDS		M F	M F	M F	M F	M F	M F
Secondary, 1st cycle							
- general		0.3 0.1	0.3 0.1	0.4 0.2	0.4 0.3	0.4 0.3	0.3 0.2
- vocational		0.9 0.1	0.8 0.1	1.3 0.2	1.3 0.3	1.2 0.3	1.1 0.4
Secondary, 2nd cycle							
- general		5.9 1.6	7.2 2.6	7.1 3.2	7.3 3.2	7.2 3.2	7.2 3.6
- vocational/technical		8.5 3.5	10.4 3.8	12.4 4.6	12.8 5.2	13.6 6.4	13.8 6.8
Higher							
- University		6.8 2.3	6.0 2.7	.. ..	.. ..	7.0 3.5	.. ..
- Non-university		7.9 5.8	9.5 7.4	10.0 8.6	10.0 8.7	9.5 9.0	9.3 8.7
Part-time education		15.8 4.8	12.6 5.0	11.5 4.9	11.7 5.0	13.2 5.3	
Total (2)		46.1 18.2	46.2 21.8			52.0 27.9	
		(30.3)(13.4)	(34.2)(16.8)			(38.8)(22.6)	
UNITED KINGDOM FT							
Secondary		0.5	0.5	0.5	0.6		
Further education, non-advanced (6)		2.0	2.8	2.9	2.9		
Higher		11.7	11.8	11.7	11.2		
Advanced courses PT (6)		19.9	21.2	1.1	1.2		
Non-advanced PT				19.0	19.8		
Total (2)		34.2	36.3	35.2	35.7		
		(14.3)	(15.1)	(15.1)	(14.7)		
SWEDEN		(1972)					
Secondary		18.2	9.0			10.9	
Higher		1.2(7)	5.0			4.5	
Total		24.0	17.6			15.3	
YUGOSLAVIA							
Skilled worker training	9.0		6.8				
Other technical/vocational schools	11.4		11.8				
Secondary, general/teacher training	10.8		9.1				
Higher	..		..				

6. Including evening classes.
7. Excluding universities.

Source : National statistics

Table A-12

AGE DISTRIBUTION OF NEW ENTRANTS TO UNIVERSITY HIGHER EDUCATION

Percentages

	1965		1970		1975		1976		1977		1978	
	M	F	M	F	M	F	M	F	M	F	M	F
GERMANY	Tot. (1)		Tot.		Tot.							
17 and under	-	-	-	-	0.1	0.1			0.2	0.3	0.1	0.2
18	0.2	0.2	9.6	12.6	5.1	7.3			4.2	8.0	4.2	8.4
19	10.5	18.2	30.3	43.5	25.0	40.2			16.5	37.9	16.7	38.3
20-24	81.9	75.7	51.3	38.5	54.8	41.0			71.0	46.2	71.5	46.1
25 and over	7.4	5.7	8.7	5.5	14.9	11.3			8.1	7.6	7.4	7.5
AUSTRALIA(2) FT			1971									
17 and under			41.9	52.8	44.9	48.8	43.7	49.2	42.5	45.4	34.2	38.2
18			38.4	36.8	36.5	33.8	37.0	32.1	35.8	33.6	30.7	30.4
19			8.9	4.5	8.2	6.3	8.6	5.9	9.4	7.4	11.4	8.8
20-24			8.5	3.7	6.9	4.3	6.7	5.1	8.1	6.2	15.9	12.0
25 and over			2.4	2.1	3.5	6.8	4.0	7.6	4.2	7.3	7.7	10.6
AUSTRALIA PT			1971									
17 and under			13.7	9.0	13.0	8.0	8.9	5.0	11.8	4.6	4.3	1.5
18			20.3	11.2	17.3	8.5	15.7	5.5	15.6	5.4	6.2	2.5
19			6.3	7.3	6.0	3.7	6.3	3.8	4.6	3.5	3.6	2.1
20-24			27.5	31.2	19.1	19.6	17.6	18.2	17.5	17.4	25.3	24.6
25 and over			32.1	41.2	44.5	60.3	51.5	67.5	50.6	69.1	60.6	69.2
AUSTRIA	1970		1972		1975							
17 and under	-	-	-	-	-	-						
18	19.9	41.6	29.3	46.4	32.8	48.9					29.5	44.1
19	22.4	32.2	25.9	28.9	25.2	29.2					31.4	29.7
20-24	52.0	21.0	38.7	20.2	35.4	17.2					32.9	20.7
25 and over	5.7	5.1	6.1	4.5	6.6	4.8					6.1	5.5
DENMARK												
under 21			48.8		44.5							
21 - 26			43.9		42.0							
27 and over			7.2		13.5							
SPAIN												
17 and under			13.9	15.3	28.2	21.7	34.2	39.5	34.6	37.5		
18			20.7	19.8	21.4	24.1	22.8	23.6	22.3	22.3		
19			16.5	17.2	14.8	15.0	14.2	12.4	12.2	10.7		
20-24			34.1	33.3	23.6	27.4	18.6	16.8	14.0	13.0		
25 and over			14.8	14.5	12.1	11.8	10.2	7.8	16.9	16.5		
FINLAND												
17 and under					-	-	-	-	-	-		
18					1.8	2.0	1.8	2.0	1.6	2.6	1.8	2.2
19					30.1	32.3	29.0	34.1	30.1	33.2	29.0	35.1
20-24					53.5	51.2	53.0	50.5	53.1	49.3	52.6	48.3
25 and over					14.6	14.5	16.1	13.3	15.1	14.8	16.5	14.3

1. Excluding foreign students.
2. Students starting a bachelor's degree at university.

FT = full-time   PT = part-time

Table A-12 (contd.)

Percentages

	1965		1970		1975		1976		1977		1978	
	M	F	M	F	M	F	M	F	M	F	M	F
FRANCE	(3)											
17 and under	6.2	8.3				7.7		8.2		7.9	5.4	8.9
18	18.2	23.1			26.8		31.2		32.6		26.2	37.5
19	22.9	24.5			22.9		25.0		25.1		26.6	24.6
20-24	40.5	37.3			27.2(4)		24.3(4)		23.9(4)		28.6(4)	19.0(4)
25 and over	12.3	6.7			15.4(5)		11.3(5)		10.5(5)		13.1(5)	9.9(5)
GREECE (3)												
18 and under	28.3	43.6	24.4	37.2	31.5	46.5	42.8	60.5				
19	20.9	27.8	23.0	30.8	18.4	21.5	18.5	20.2				
20-24	31.6(4)	25.1(4)	32.7	25.9	25.9	20.1	22.0	12.9				
25 and over	19.2(5)	3.5(5)	20.0	6.1	24.1	11.9	16.7	6.4				
ITALY			1964		1967		1973					
18 and under	0.3	4.4	10.6	26.9	9.5	22.6						
19	14.2	27.3	31.3	36.5	36.8	43.5						
20-24	72.4	44.4	48.1	31.5	38.7	26.5						
25 and over	13.0	9.5	10.0	5.1	15.0	7.4						
NETHERLANDS					1971		1974					
under 18			8.9	8.1	0.6	0.7						
18			25.2	28.8	31.1	35.5						
19			21.1	25.0	25.6	26.4						
20-24			31.8	26.2	29.7	23.5						
25 and over			13.0	11.9	13.0	13.9						
UNITED KINGDOM (universities)												
18 and under	44.6	55.9	42.2	54.0	39.9	47.6			40.3	45.9	40.6	45.9
19	34.3	30.1	32.1	28.0	30.9	29.5			30.9	30.3	30.6	29.7
20	8.4	5.7	9.7	7.1	10.5	8.7			10.7	9.3	10.6	9.1
21-24	8.4	4.4	10.8	6.6	12.3	8.0			11.8	8.2	11.9	8.4
25 and over	4.2	3.9	5.2	4.3	6.3	6.2			6.3	6.2	6.2	6.9
UNITED KINGDOM (further education - advanced)												
18 and under			17.6	27.1								
19			24.2	25.8								
20			14.7	11.2								
21-24			25.2	16.1								
25 and over			18.2	19.7								
SWEDEN (6)			1971									
25 and over			35.0	33.3	48.6	51.4	46.8	52.7				
of which, covered by the 25/5 rule			8.8	9.7	24.1	24.9	22.7	25.3				

3. First-year students.
4. 20-23
5. 24 and over.
6. New entrants in the Philosophy faculties.

Source: National statistics.

Table A-13

AGE DISTRIBUTION OF NEW ENTRANTS TO NON-UNIVERSITY HIGHER EDUCATION

Percentages

	1965 M F	1970 M F	1975 M F	1976 M F	1977 M F	1978 M F	1979 M F
GERMANY FT							
17 and under					0.5 0.6	0.0 0.1	0.0 0.0
18					4.4 8.2	3.8 8.1	2.8 4.7
19					7.3 22.5	7.5 23.6	7.1 25.5
20-24					74.6 59.1	76.2 59.6	76.8 60.3
25 and over					13.2 9.6	12.5 8.6	13.3 9.5
AUSTRALIA (1) FT							
17 and under			33.1 45.6		33.1 41.1	33.9 42.3	
18			31.3 31.2		32.6 32.1	31.7 32.9	
19			11.8 6.5		11.7 7.2	11.1 7.3	
20-24			12.6 5.9		12.7 7.7	13.7 7.5	
25 and over			11.1 10.8		9.9 10.0	11.1 10.0	
AUSTRALIA (1) PT							
17 and under			10.1 11.0		10.4 11.2	10.8 10.0	
18			13.8 14.6		11.8 12.4	10.7 11.2	
19			7.9 6.5		8.3 6.2	6.8 4.9	
20-24			26.5 18.9		26.0 19.2	24.7 20.5	
25 and over			41.7 49.0		43.6 51.1	47.1 53.3	
FRANCE (IUT)							(1980)
17 and under				4.0	3.7		2.7 5.5
18				31.7	33.1		29.9 44.5
19				35.3	35.3		36.7 33.3
20-23				26.8	25.8		28.9 15.6
24 and over				2.2	2.1		1.8 1.1
GREECE (2)							
18 and under			19.9 33.5	27.9 43.7			
19			33.3 38.3	29.5 32.7			
20-24			40.0 26.2	37.2 27.3			
25 and over			11.7 2.0	5.4 1.3			

FT = full-time
PT = part-time

1. New entrants to the CAE, whatever degree or diploma is being taken (university or not)
2. First-year enrolments.

Source : National statistics.

Table A-14

INTERVAL BETWEEN 2nd CYCLE SECONDARY SCHOOL GRADUATION
AND ENTRY INTO HIGHER EDUCATION

Percentages

	1965 M	1965 F	1970 M	1970 F	1975 M	1975 F	1976 M	1976 F	1977 M	1977 F	1978 M	1978 F
GERMANY												
Same year									46.4	81.0	46.1	78.1
1 year later									34.9	11.0	34.1	12.0
4 years or more									18.7	8.0	19.8	9.9
AUSTRALIA - University FT												
Following calendar year					92.2	92.6	85.9	85.5	83.6	82.8	82.2	81.0
1 year later					7.4	7.2	8.1	8.0	8.1	7.7
More than 1 year later					4.5	4.4	3.8	3.7	4.8	4.7	4.3	3.9
Other (1)					3.3	3.0	2.9	3.6	3.5	4.5	5.3	7.3
CAE - FT												
Following calendar year					82.7				79.4	86.2	78.8	85.4
1 year later					7.8				10.8	7.1	10.0	7.0
More than 1 year later					9.5				9.8	6.7	11.2	7.6
Other					-				-	-	-	-
Universities PT												
Following calendar year					46.3	33.0	31.7	27.1	33.8	27.0	30.7	17.2
1 year later							8.4	7.3	7.2	7.8	7.6	8.3
More than 1 year later					28.5	37.6	29.6	33.8	30.7	30.8	20.4	22.2
Other (1)					25.3	29.4	30.3	31.8	28.3	34.4	41.3	52.3
CAE PT												
Following calendar year					48.0				45.3	45.5	40.4	38.3
1 year later					13.0				14.3	11.0	13.0	14.6
More than 1 year later					39.0				40.4	43.5	46.6	47.1
Other (1)					-				-	-	-	-
UNITED STATES												
Same year			65.4		55.7		54.8		54.1			
1 to 3 years			17.5		22.2		22.1		20.9			
4 years and more			17.1		22.1		23.1		24.9			
FRANCE												
Total university + IUT												
Same year					74.3						79.0	
1 year later					11.8						5.8	
2 years or more					12.7						12.3	
Indefinite					1.2						2.9	
IUT												
Same year					86.6						92.3	
1 year later					10.3						4.9	
2 years or more					3.0						2.2	
Indefinite					0.1						0.6	
NETHERLANDS												
University - Transfer rate and interval according to secondary school-leaving certificate												
Gymnasia			(1971)		(1974)							
Same year	75.5	63.4	85.8	68.3	79.6	56.9						
1 year later	13.9	12.7	..	..	..	..						
4 years or more	2.4	2.0	..	..	..	..						
Total	91.8	78.1	..	..	..	..						
HBS (Atheneum in 1974)												
Same year	44.2	21.1	53.4	29.3	69.4	39.3						
1 year later	11.7	6.2	..	..	..	..						
4 years or more	4.0	3.6	..	..	..	..						
Total	59.9	30.9	..	..	..	..						

1. Including qualifications obtained through adult or "concessional" education which are only classified in the "other" category by all universities for 1978.

FT = full-time   PT = part-time

Source: National statistics

Table A-15

EDUCATIONAL BACKGROUND OF NEW ENTRANTS TO UNIVERSITY (U) AND NON-UNIVERSITY (NU) HIGHER EDUCATION

In percentages

	1965	1970	1975	1976	1977	1978
AUSTRIA						
- University						
General Secondary		84.6	83.7			77.4
Technical and vocational		15.4	16.3			22.6
DENMARK						
- Total U + NU						
Studentereksamen		77.1	68.6			
HF(1)		7.0	17.5			
Other		16.0	14.0			
- Faculties of Arts						
Studentereksamen		91.3	69.7			
HF		1.7	18.4			
Other		7.1	11.9			
- Faculties of Science						
Studentereksamen		92.6	77.4			
HF		0.7	11.6			
Other		6.6	11.0			
- Technical university						
Studentereksamen		87.4	85.7			
HF		-	1.7			
Other		12.6	12.6			
- Schools of economics and management						
Studentereksamen		68.5	76.8			
HF		-	3.8			
Other		31.5	19.5			
- NU teacher training colleges						
Studentereksamen		72.3	57.4			
HF		27.3	38.8			
		0.5	3.9			
- NU Teknika						
Studentereksamen		3.0	10.5			
HF		-	2.3			
Other		97.0	87.2			
SPAIN						
- Faculties						
- Pre-university - COU* (1)				85.4	86.8	73.6
- Technical education				6.1	4.7	12.3
- Students over 25				1.7	1.9	3.4
- Other				6.8	6.6	10.7
- Higher technical schools						
- Pre-university - COU* (1)				87.4	85.6	70.0
- Technical education				7.2	9.0	20.5
- Students over 25				0.4	0.4	0.9
- Other				5.0	5.0	8.6
- Architecture, technician-engineers						
- Pre-university - COU* (1)				70.7	74.5	63.8
- Technical education				6.6	6.2	11.4
- Students over 25				0.5	0.5	0.6
- Other				22.2	18.8	24.2
- Basic school teachers						
- Pre-university - COU* (1)				93.2	92.9	92.1
- Technical education				0.8	0.6	1.2
- Students over 25				0.5	0.7	0.8
- Other				5.5	5.8	5.9

* COU = University foundation course.

1. Preparatory examination for higher education intended mainly for people who have not completed secondary education and wish to resume their studies.

Table A-15 (contd.)

	1965	1970	1975	1976	1977	1978
FRANCE						(1980)
- Universities + IUTs			(2)			
- BAC A, B, C, D			80.4	81.6	77.6	76.5
- BAC E, F, G, H			8.3	15.2	15.6	16.7
- Equivalent examinations			7.8	1.4	5.6	5.3
- Special entrance examinations			2.3	1.2	0.9	1.2
- Social advancement programme			1.2	0.6	0.3	0.2
- IUTs only						
- BAC A, B, C, D			50.1	49.4	47.2	51.4
- BAC E, F, G, H			43.1	46.9	47.8	44.8
- Equivalent examinations			2.5	1.1	2.7	2.2
- Special entrance examinations			2.0	2.3	2.0	1.4
- Social advancement programme			0.4	0.3	0.3	0.2
ITALY						
- University, total						
- Secondary, general	44.2	37.4	45.0	45.3		
- Secondary, teacher training	18.1	19.4	12.2	12.0		
- Secondary, technical	34.8	40.2	37.9	35.3		
- Secondary, vocational	-	-	-	4.0		
- Other	2.9	3.0	4.9	3.4		
- Faculty of Arts						
- Secondary, general	35.1	27.2	36.4	35.1		
- Secondary, teacher training	55.1	58.6	39.5	38.2		
- Secondary, technical	7.0	12.6	19.1	20.2		
- Secondary, vocational	-	-	-	3.7		
- Other	2.8	1.6	4.9	2.7		
- Technology						
- Secondary, general	58.8	40.9	41.2	42.7		
- Secondary, teacher training	-	0.4	0.6	0.6		
- Secondary, technical	37.4	54.5	51.9	47.4		
- Secondary, vocational	-	-	-	3.8		
- Other	3.8	4.3	6.3	5.6		
- Economics						
- Secondary, general	14.3	19.3	26.4	30.2		
- Secondary, teacher training	-	3.0	4.4	3.9		
- Secondary, technical	82.6	76.4	64.4	58.4		
- Secondary, vocational	-	-	-	4.4		
- Other	3.1	1.2	4.9	3.0		
SWEDEN						
- University						
- Gymnasium (3 or 4 years)	86.3		56.8	54.0		
- Other secondary school-leaving certificates	0.7		4.4	5.7		
- Priority students	-		11.9	12.6		
- 25/5, 25/4 (3)	-		18.3	18.1		
- Adults with no secondary school-leaving certificate	-		-	-		
- Other	13.0		8.6	9.7		
- Total higher education						
- Gymnasium (3 or 4 years)					54.9	57.4
- Other secondary school-leaving certificates					6.7	9.4
- Priority students					6.4	5.5
- 25/5, 25/4					13.5	11.2
- Adults with no secondary school-leaving certificate					4.7	4.3
- Other					14.5	12.2

2. Excluding IUTs.
3. People of 25 and over who have five or four years' work experience.

Source: National statistics

Table A-16

RATES OF TRANSFER FROM SECONDARY EDUCATION
(BY TYPE) TO HIGHER EDUCATION

Percentages

	1965	1970	1975	1976	1977	1978	1979
CANADA							
High School Total		51.7	54.5	52.4	52.6	51.3	51.4
- University		25.0	24.1	23.2	21.9	22.6	23.2
- Non-University		26.7	30.4	29.2	30.7	28.7	28.2
DENMARK	(1966)						
Universities and Centres	59.3	54.6	53.8				

SPAIN
Ratio of pupils enrolled for a pre-university or COU year and those who have taken a sixth general baccalaureate year or a 7th technical baccalaureate year in the preceding year.

	1965	1970	1975	1976	1977	1978	1979
	51.7	50.2	82.5				
UNITED STATES	(1966)						
"High School" U + NU	52.5	61.5		58.1		58.8	
FRANCE		(1973)					
Preparatory classes for Grandes Ecoles							
- General baccalaureate		12.1	12.1			12.9	
- Technician's baccalaureate		0.3	0.2			0.8	
Universities							
- General baccalaureate		53.3	54.7			55.5	
- Technician's baccalaureate		13.5	15.0			16.5	
IUT							
- General baccalaureate		6.4	6.9			7.3	
- Technician's baccalaureate		14.0	13.3			14.7	
Higher technician							
- General baccalaureate		6.4	7.7			8.9	
- Technician's baccalaureate		18.1	18.6			19.0	
Total							
- General baccalaureate		78.2	81.4			84.6	
- Technician's baccalaureate		45.9	47.1			51.0	

JAPAN
New entrants to the universities and junior colleges as a percentage of 1st cycle secondary school-leavers three years previously

	M F	M F	M F	M F	M F	M F	M F
	22.4 11.3	29.3 17.7	43.0 32.4	43.3 33.6	41.9 33.3	43.1 33.5	41.4 33.

NETHERLANDS
First-year university students as a percentage of pre-university school-leavers
(1971)

	79.4 52.7	94.6 69.7	94.0 60.7	93.0 61.9	91.5 58.6	86.0 58.8	

UNITED KINGDOM
Destination of secondary school-leavers with the following passes:

	1970	1975		1977		
Universities						
3 or more A-levels	68.2 57.6	66.9 55.2		66.0 54.9		
2 A-levels	20.9 11.3	21.7 14.8		18.7 13.7		
1 A-level	1.7 0.7	0.7 1.2		1.4 0.7		
5 or more O-levels	0.2 0.1	0.1 0.1		0.2 0.0		
1 to 4 O-levels	0.0 0.0	0.0 0.0		0.0 0.0		
Further Education						
3 or more A-levels	15.4 28.1	13.6 24.4		15.4 22.7		
2 A-levels	41.4 61.3	38.0 45.9		40.4 44.4		
1 A-level	41.7 61.0	35.6 46.3		36.8 42.8		
5 or more O-levels	26.5 42.2	27.7 40.2		24.0 38.1		
1 to 4 O-levels	16.6 25.8	14.7 27.3		13.3 28.4		
Total universities and further education						
3 or more A-levels	83.6 85.7	80.5 79.6		81.4 77.6		
2 A-levels	62.3 72.6	59.7 60.7		59.1 58.1		
1 A-level	42.8 61.7	36.3 47.5		38.2 43.5		
5 or more O-levels	26.7 42.3	27.8 40.3		24.2 38.1		
1 to 4 O-levels	16.6 25.8	14.7 27.3		13.3 28.4		

<u>Source</u> : Drawn from national statistics

OECD SALES AGENTS
DÉPOSITAIRES DES PUBLICATIONS DE L'OCDE

ARGENTINA – ARGENTINE
Carlos Hirsch S.R.L., Florida 165, 4º Piso (Galería Guemes)
1333 BUENOS AIRES, Tel. 33.1787.2391 y 30.7122

AUSTRALIA – AUSTRALIE
Australia and New Zealand Book Company Pty, Ltd.,
10 Aquatic Drive, Frenchs Forest, N.S.W. 2086
P.O. Box 459, BROOKVALE, N.S.W. 2100

AUSTRIA – AUTRICHE
OECD Publications and Information Center
4 Simrockstrasse 5300 BONN. Tel. (0228) 21.60.45
Local Agent/Agent local :
Gerold and Co., Graben 31, WIEN 1. Tel. 52.22.35

BELGIUM – BELGIQUE
CCLS – LCLS
19, rue Plantin, 1070 BRUXELLES. Tel. 02.521.04.73

BRAZIL – BRÉSIL
Mestre Jou S.A., Rua Guaipa 518,
Caixa Postal 24090, 05089 SAO PAULO 10. Tel. 261.1920
Rua Senador Dantas 19 s/205-6, RIO DE JANEIRO GB.
Tel. 232.07.32

CANADA
Renouf Publishing Company Limited,
2182 St. Catherine Street West,
MONTRÉAL, Que. H3H 1M7. Tel. (514)937.3519
OTTAWA, Ont. K1P 5A6, 61 Sparks Street

DENMARK – DANEMARK
Munksgaard Export and Subscription Service
35, Nørre Søgade
DK 1370 KØBENHAVN K. Tel. +45.1.12.85.70

FINLAND – FINLANDE
Akateeminen Kirjakauppa
Keskuskatu 1, 00100 HELSINKI 10. Tel. 65.11.22

FRANCE
Bureau des Publications de l'OCDE,
2 rue André-Pascal, 75775 PARIS CEDEX 16. Tel. (1) 524.81.67
Principal correspondant :
13602 AIX-EN-PROVENCE : Librairie de l'Université.
Tel. 26.18.08

GERMANY – ALLEMAGNE
OECD Publications and Information Center
4 Simrockstrasse 5300 BONN Tel. (0228) 21.60.45

GREECE – GRÈCE
Librairie Kauffmann, 28 rue du Stade,
ATHÈNES 132. Tel. 322.21.60

HONG-KONG
Government Information Services,
Publications/Sales Section, Baskerville House,
2/F., 22 Ice House Street

ICELAND – ISLANDE
Snaebjörn Jönsson and Co., h.f.,
Hafnarstraeti 4 and 9, P.O.B. 1131, REYKJAVIK.
Tel. 13133/14281/11936

INDIA – INDE
Oxford Book and Stationery Co. :
NEW DELHI-1, Scindia House. Tel. 45896
CALCUTTA 700016, 17 Park Street. Tel. 240832

INDONESIA – INDONÉSIE
PDIN-LIPI, P.O. Box 3065/JKT., JAKARTA, Tel. 583467

IRELAND – IRLANDE
TDC Publishers – Library Suppliers
12 North Frederick Street, DUBLIN 1 Tel. 744835-749677

ITALY – ITALIE
Libreria Commissionaria Sansoni :
Via Lamarmora 45, 50121 FIRENZE. Tel. 579751/584468
Via Bartolini 29, 20155 MILANO. Tel. 365083
Sub-depositari :
Ugo Tassi
Via A. Farnese 28, 00192 ROMA. Tel. 310590
Editrice e Libreria Herder,
Piazza Montecitorio 120, 00186 ROMA. Tel. 6794628
Costantino Ercolano, Via Generale Orsini 46, 80132 NAPOLI. Tel. 405210
Libreria Hoepli, Via Hoepli 5, 20121 MILANO. Tel. 865446
Libreria Scientifica, Dott. Lucio de Biasio "Aeiou"
Via Meravigli 16, 20123 MILANO Tel. 807679
Libreria Zanichelli
Piazza Galvani 1/A, 40124 Bologna Tel. 237389
Libreria Lattes, Via Garibaldi 3, 10122 TORINO. Tel. 519274
La diffusione delle edizioni OCSE è inoltre assicurata dalle migliori librerie nelle città più importanti.

JAPAN – JAPON
OECD Publications and Information Center,
Landic Akasaka Bldg., 2-3-4 Akasaka,
Minato-ku, TOKYO 107 Tel. 586.2016

KOREA – CORÉE
Pan Korea Book Corporation,
P.O. Box nº 101 Kwangwhamun, SÉOUL. Tel. 72.7369

LEBANON – LIBAN
Documenta Scientifica/Redico,
Edison Building, Bliss Street, P.O. Box 5641, BEIRUT.
Tel. 354429 – 344425

MALAYSIA – MALAISIE
and/et SINGAPORE - SINGAPOUR
University of Malaya Co-operative Bookshop Ltd.
P.O. Box 1127, Jalan Pantai Baru
KUALA LUMPUR. Tel. 51425, 54058, 54361

THE NETHERLANDS – PAYS-BAS
Staatsuitgeverij
Verzendboekhandel Chr. Plantijnstraat 1
Postbus 20014
2500 EA S-GRAVENHAGE. Tel. nr. 070.789911
Voor bestellingen: Tel. 070.789208

NEW ZEALAND – NOUVELLE-ZÉLANDE
Publications Section,
Government Printing Office Bookshops:
AUCKLAND: Retail Bookshop: 25 Rutland Street,
Mail Orders: 85 Beach Road, Private Bag C.P.O.
HAMILTON: Retail Ward Street,
Mail Orders, P.O. Box 857
WELLINGTON: Retail: Mulgrave Street (Head Office),
Cubacade World Trade Centre
Mail Orders: Private Bag
CHRISTCHURCH: Retail: 159 Hereford Street,
Mail Orders: Private Bag
DUNEDIN: Retail: Princes Street
Mail Order: P.O. Box 1104

NORWAY – NORVÈGE
J.G. TANUM A/S Karl Johansgate 43
P.O. Box 1177 Sentrum OSLO 1. Tel. (02) 80.12.60

PAKISTAN
Mirza Book Agency, 65 Shahrah Quaid-E-Azam, LAHORE 3.
Tel. 66839

PHILIPPINES
National Book Store, Inc.
Library Services Division, P.O. Box 1934, MANILA.
Tel. Nos. 49.43.06 to 09, 40.53.45, 49.45.12

PORTUGAL
Livraria Portugal, Rua do Carmo 70-74,
1117 LISBOA CODEX. Tel. 360582/3

SPAIN – ESPAGNE
Mundi-Prensa Libros, S.A.
Castelló 37, Apartado 1223, MADRID-1. Tel. 275.46.55
Libreria Bosch, Ronda Universidad 11, BARCELONA 7.
Tel. 317.53.08, 317.53.58

SWEDEN – SUÈDE
AB CE Fritzes Kungl Hovbokhandel,
Box 16 356, S 103 27 STH, Regeringsgatan 12,
DS STOCKHOLM. Tel. 08/23.89.00

SWITZERLAND – SUISSE
OECD Publications and Information Center
4 Simrockstrasse 5300 BONN. Tel. (0228) 21.60.45
Local Agents/Agents locaux
Librairie Payot, 6 rue Grenus, 1211 GENÈVE 11. Tel. 022.31.89.50

TAIWAN – FORMOSE
Good Faith Worldwide Int'l Co., Ltd.
9th floor, No. 118, Sec. 2
Chung Hsiao E. Road
TAIPEI. Tel. 391.7396/391.7397

THAILAND – THAÏLANDE
Suksit Siam Co., Ltd., 1715 Rama IV Rd,
Samyan, BANGKOK 5. Tel. 2511630

TURKEY – TURQUIE
Kültur Yayinlari Is-Türk Ltd. Sti.
Atatürk Bulvari No : 77/B
KIZILAY/ANKARA. Tel. 17 02 66
Dolmabahce Cad. No : 29
BESIKTAS/ISTANBUL. Tel. 60 71 88

UNITED KINGDOM – ROYAUME-UNI
H.M. Stationery Office, P.O.B. 569,
LONDON SE1 9NH. Tel. 01.928.6977, Ext. 410 or
49 High Holborn, LONDON WC1V 6 HB (personal callers)
Branches at: EDINBURGH, BIRMINGHAM, BRISTOL,
MANCHESTER, BELFAST.

UNITED STATES OF AMERICA – ÉTATS-UNIS
OECD Publications and Information Center, Suite 1207,
1750 Pennsylvania Ave., N.W. WASHINGTON, D.C.20006 – 4582
Tel. (202) 724.1857

VENEZUELA
Libreria del Este, Avda. F. Miranda 52, Edificio Galipan,
CARACAS 106. Tel. 32.23.01/33.26.04/31.58.38

YUGOSLAVIA – YOUGOSLAVIE
Jugoslovenska Knjiga, Terazije 27, P.O.B. 36, BEOGRAD.
Tel. 621.992

Les commandes provenant de pays où l'OCDE n'a pas encore désigné de dépositaire peuvent être adressées à :
OCDE, Bureau des Publications, 2, rue André-Pascal, 75775 PARIS CEDEX 16.
Orders and inquiries from countries where sales agents have not yet been appointed may be sent to:
OECD, Publications Office, 2 rue André-Pascal, 75775 PARIS CEDEX 16.

66145-2-1983

OECD PUBLICATIONS, 2, rue André-Pascal, 75775 PARIS CEDEX 16 - No. 42333 1983
PRINTED IN FRANCE
(91 83 03 1) ISBN 92-64-12448-9